The Short Oxford History of France

Fra

The Short Oxford History of France

General Editor: William Doyle

AVAILABLE NOW

France in the Central Middle Ages
edited by Marcus Bull

France in the Later Middle Ages
edited by David Potter

Renaissance and Reformation France
edited by Mack P. Holt

Old Regime France
edited by William Doyle

Revolutionary France
edited by Malcolm Crook

IN PREPARATION, VOLUMES COVERING

Modern France 1880–2000

The Short Oxford History of France

General Editor: William Doyle

France in the Later Middle Ages 1200–1500

Edited by David Potter

OXFORD
UNIVERSITY PRESS

OXFORD
UNIVERSITY PRESS

Great Clarendon Street, Oxford OX2 6DP

Oxford University Press is a department of the University of Oxford.
It furthers the University's objective of excellence in research, scholarship,
and education by publishing worldwide in

Oxford New York

Auckland Bangkok Buenos Aires Cape Town Chennai
Dar es Salaam Delhi Hong Kong Istanbul Karachi Kolkata
Kuala Lumpur Madrid Melbourne Mexico City Mumbai Nairobi
São Paulo Shanghai Taipei Tokyo Toronto

Oxford is a registered trade mark of Oxford University Press
in the UK and in certain other countries

Published in the United States
by Oxford University Press Inc., New York

First published 2003

British Library Cataloguing in Publication Data

Data available

Library of Congress Cataloging in Publication Data

Data available

ISBN 0–19–925048–0 (pbk)
ISBN 0–19–925047–2 (hbk)

10 9 8 7 6 5 4 3 2 1

Typeset in Minion
by RefineCatch Limited, Bungay, Suffolk
Printed in Great Britain by
T.J. International Ltd., Padstow, Cornwall

General Editor's Preface

During the twentieth century French historians revolutionized the study of history itself, opening up countless new subjects, problems, and approaches to the past. Much of this imaginative energy was focused on the history of their own country—its economy, its society, its culture, its memories. In the country's later years this exciting atmosphere inspired increasing numbers of outsiders to work on French themes, so that, more than for any other country, writing the history of France has become an international enterprise.

This series seeks to reflect these developments. Each volume is coordinated by an editor widely recognized as a historian of France. Each editor in turn has brought together a group of contributors to present particular aspects of French history, identifying the major themes and features in the light of the most recent scholarship. All the teams are international, reflecting the fact that there are now probably more university historians of France outside the country than in it. Nor is the outside world neglected in the content of each volume, where French activity abroad receives special coverage. Apart from this, however, the team responsible for each volume has chosen its own priorities, presenting what it sees as the salient characteristics of its own period. Some have chosen to offer stimulating reinterpretations of established themes; others have preferred to explore long-neglected or entirely new topics which they believe now deserve emphasis. All the volumes have an introduction and conclusion by their editor, and include an outline chronology, plentiful maps, and a succinct guide to further reading in English.

Running from Clovis to Chirac, the seven volumes in the series offer a lively, concise, and authoritative guide to the history of a country and a culture which have been central to the whole development of Europe, and often widely influential in the world beyond.

William Doyle
University of Bristol

Contents

List of contributors

PIERRE CHARBONNIER, Emeritus Professor of History, was for many years Professor of Medieval History at the University of Clermont-Ferrand, where he lectured on France and England in the late Middle Ages. He is the author of *Guillaume de Murol, un petit seigneur auvergnat au début du XVe siècle* (1973) and of *Une autre France: la seigneurie rurale en Basse Auvergne du XIVe au XVIe siècle* (1980). He has participated in numerous conferences with contributions on the subject of his chapters in this book.

ANNE CURRY is Professor of History at the University of Reading. She is author of *The Hundred Years War* (1993; 2nd edn. 2003) and *The Battle of Agincourt: Sources and Interpretations* (2000), as well as many articles on the English occupation of Normandy in the fifteenth century. She is currently working on a study of the treaty of Troyes as well as continuing her researches into the personnel and organization of the English army in the reigns of Henry V and Henry VI.

JEAN DUNBABIN is fellow of St Anne's College, Oxford, and Reader in Medieval History at Oxford. Since 1999 she has been editor of the *English Historical Review*. She is author of *France in the Making, 843–1180* (1985; 2nd edn. 2000); *A Hound of God: Pierre de la Palud and the Fourteenth-Century Church* (1991); *Charles I of Anjou: Power, Kingship and State-Making in Thirteenth-Century Europe* (1998); and *Captivity and Imprisonment in Medieval Europe* (2002).

MICHAEL JONES, Professor Emeritus at the University of Nottingham, is a leading authority on medieval Brittany, on which he has published numerous studies, including *Ducal Brittany, 1364–1399* (1970); *Recueil des actes de Jean IV duc de Bretagne* (1980); *The Creation of Brittany: A Late Medieval State* (1988); and *Recueil des actes de Charles de Blois et Jeanne de Penthièvre* (1996).

DAVID POTTER is Reader in late medieval and Renaissance French history at the University of Kent. He has written *War and Government in the French Provinces: Picardy 1470–1560* (1993); *A History of France 1460–1560: The Emergence of a Nation State* (1995); *The French Wars of Religion* (1997); *Un homme de guerre au temps de la renaissance: la vie* *et les lettres d'Oudart du Biez* (2001); as well as numerous articles on the French nobility, politics, and diplomacy in the Renaissance period.

GARETH PROSSER wrote his London doctoral thesis on Norman political society before and during the period of the War of the Public Weal and has written on magnate clientage among the lesser nobility and mobility across the boundary between nobles and non-nobles.

GRAEME SMALL is a senior lecturer in medieval history at the University of Glasgow. He has written *George Chastelain and the Shaping of Valois Burgundy* (1997) as well as other publications on political and historical culture in France and the Low Countries in the later medieval period.

Note on monetary units

Coinage was a 'regalian right' appertaining to the king, though in this period coins were also minted by the counts of Flanders, the dukes of Brittany, the Plantagenet rulers of Gascony, most of the Pyrenean rulers (Foix, Albret, Armagnac, etc.) and those of Dauphiné (still reputed territory of the Holy Roman Empire). The king, though, was by far the most important issuer of coins.

As was the case in France until the end of the Ancien Régime, money was expressed in terms of money of account for the purpose of keeping accounts but obviously existed in reality as coins of various kinds whose intrinsic precious metal content to some extent dictated its equivalence in units of account. 'To some extent' is used advisedly, as the crown, besides its profits from minting and debasement, could alter the value of coins in money of account according to its short-term needs by 'crying' them up or down. There were two main moneys of account, the *livre tournois* (*lt.*) (which was ultimately to predominate) and the *livre parisis* (*lp.*) used in the Île-de-France and some areas to the north. 4 *lp.* equalled 5 *lt.* Each was divided, as was the pound sterling, into 240 units, thus in France 1 *lt.* = 20 *sols* (20 *st.*) and each *sol* 12 *deniers.* In the mid-fourteenth century the pound sterling was worth about 5 *lt.* Around 1400, 8 *lt.* equalled around £1 (by 1600 the *livre tournois* stood at only 2*s*., a ratio of 10:1). In daily transactions French coins were given values in terms not only of money of account but also of foreign coins.

The largest silver coin in the early fourteenth century was the *gros*, equal to 1 *st.* The silver *denier* stood at 1¼ *derniers tournois.* These small silver coins remained relatively stable until the instability caused by debasement in the first two decades of the fifteenth century. To combat this, Jacques Cœur oversaw a new silver mintage, that of the *gros du roi* of 1447, sometimes called the *gros de Jacques Cœur.* The gold coinage issued from the 1260s onwards was very unstable because of the fluctuations in the gold–silver ratio. Coins called *écu*, *royal*, *agnel*, *mouton*, etc. were intended at first to represent 1 *lt.* but rarely did so. After the Black Death debasement of the silver coinage made the relations between the two coinages more unstable. In that period money of account was difficult to use for accounting purposes. In 1360 a new gold coin, the *franc d'or*, was issued at 20 *st.*, as was the *franc à cheval* of 1423 (the 'franc', or 1 *livre* coin, became a silver piece only in 1575); they tended to be 'cried up' to 22 or 25 *st.* over time. The *écu* and other French gold coins were very broadly worth half the English noble minted from 1344.

Introduction

David Potter

General characteristics of the period

In the depiction of September for the *Très riches heures du duc de Berry*, the château of Saumur towers like a fairy-tale castle over peasants harvesting the vines in the fields below.[1] The castle is still there, restored in the 1930s by using the *Très riches heures* as a model, but through this image we travel into a very different world. Part of a sumptuous work commissioned by a powerful royal prince at a time when France was virtually at its lowest point of chaos and depression in the late Middle Ages, it is a profoundly ambiguous scene. Apparently all is still and the world is in order and harmony. Yet this was a period which saw a deep structural crisis which swept across French society, accompanied by war and destruction. The period covered by this book saw the last crusades led by a king of France, the destruction of the most serious heresy to face the Western Church in the Middle Ages, the foundation of the University of Paris, the building of the cathedral of Amiens, the music of the *ars nova* in the age of Guillaume de Machault and of Guillaume Dufay at the court of Burgundy, and the unique if brief public career of Jeanne d'Arc. The *Très riches heures* themselves are a witness to a sharper awareness of the physical world which is apparent, too, in the views of the cities and towns of Auvergne composed by Guillaume de Revel around 1450. How is it possible to encompass a world so vast and complex and a timescale so long in so short a book? The answer is to concentrate on a few related themes.

[1] Commissioned by the duke of Berry, brother to King Charles V, from the Limburg brothers in 1413 (Musée Condé, Chantilly).

At the start of this period the kingdom of France was at the apogee of its age as a feudal monarchy, its territory a *mouvance* in which the king's power was primarily limited to his own hereditary domain and power rested effectively in the hands of a military-noble hierarchy with a variety of powers. Politically, the period embraces the great advances made by the Capetian monarchy in the early thirteenth century and the affirmation of royal power against the principalities in the late fifteenth, but includes the construction of great territorial principalities in the fourteenth; hence the emphasis placed in this book on the relationship between the crown and the provinces. It cannot, though, be unequivocally claimed that the end of the fifteenth century marked 'the end of the Middle Ages'. The medievalist Bernard Guenée remarked that the institutions of the time of Francis I were rooted in the Middle Ages and only the Wars of Religion overturned institutions and ideas enough to give the feeling of a real break. By 1500, though, France was recognizably the monarchical state it was to remain until the end of the Ancien Régime; the nobility remained immensely powerful and their ethos continued to dominate society (see Chapter 8), but it was no longer possible to equal or seriously challenge the crown's authority, even in the depths of the Wars of Religion. Politics had become much more a matter of influence on the great institutions of state and the court. The frontiers of the kingdom were no longer just the bounds of the feudal *mouvance* but something akin to modern borders, if still not very clear on the ground. What had happened in the intervening three centuries? Paradoxically, they had been centuries of disaster, endemic warfare, civil conflict, and demographic catastrophe on a scale unparalleled for centuries. Yet this was the age in which a French identity and political framework was born. It was also a period of severe economic and social crisis around a turning point of 1348–50 which is explored here by Pierre Charbonnier (Chapters 2 and 5). This deeply marked both institutions and politics. The latter were shaped by the dynastic instability stemming from the exclusion of the direct descendants of Philip IV in the female line (Charles of Navarre and Edward III) and two related major paroxysms of internal political breakdown: the 1350s and the period 1400–30. There was one lesser but still destructive period of internal upheaval, 1465–77.

The idea of France in the later Middle Ages

There has to be a certain fluidity in how we think of France as a physical entity throughout this period. The name Francia began to embrace the whole kingdom around 1200, and from 1254 the king is formally in documents Rex Franciae, rather than Rex Francorum. For many the name would still have meant only the lands around Paris itself. Whether it was even possible for the rulers of the kingdom to have in mind a picture of the country in the fourteenth century has been much debated. For some, the kingdom still involved bundles of rights and, physically, itineraries for travelling from one town to another. Maps were still very rare, and there were many current myths about the number of parishes in the kingdom. The great survey of hearths of 1328 (the sole attempt at such a general survey before the seventeenth century) covered the royal domain only, and knowledge of it was confined to the financial administration. The formal boundary of the king's suzerainty was the frontier with the empire that in one form or another dated back to the treaty of Verdun in 843. This had included Flanders and Catalonia but excluded most of the territory east of the Rhône and Meuse. It still had meaning in that those within it were subjects or vassals of the king and recipients of royal commands, whereas those beyond were treated as allies and friends. Catalonia was long lost to France by the fourteenth century, but Flanders remained deeply enmeshed in the politics of the French kingdom even though its economy and political elite were increasingly independent. It was in the process of becoming the bedrock of a new power in the north, the Burgundian state. Only in 1349 were the Alpine territories of the dauphin of Vienne willed by their last ruler, Humbert II, to France on condition that the eldest son of the king be invested with the name and arms of the dauphin. Until 1461 the dauphin's rule there was quasi-independent. Provence remained a fief of the empire ruled by members of the French house of Anjou, and only became part of the royal domain in 1484. There, too, the king thereafter ruled as count of Provence. France in the fourteenth century had no more than 100 kilometres of Mediterranean coastline from Leucate to Aigues Mortes. Confined, then, in the east, the kingdom faced westwards to the sea, where the English Channel, far from dividing it from England, united two French-speaking political communities. In the west the Plantagenet king-dukes dominated Aquitaine, while Brittany, though formally part of the king's *mouvance*, was being consolidated as an autonomous state.

How was France actually imagined? Learned scholars discoursed on the etymology of the name France, deriving it from 'free' (that is, free from tribute or taxes), an idea increasingly at odds with permanent taxation, and then more often 'valiant' and 'loyal'. The natural instinct was to personify the country and give it attributes: noble, chivalric, pious and learned, and well governed. To this were added, from the fourteenth century, allegories of France as a verdant garden and, increasingly, as a fair princess, the perfect female counterpart to the chivalrous knight. In Alain Chartier's poem *Quadrilogue invectif* of 1422, Dame France, sadly contemplating the ruin of the kingdom, summons her 'three children', the People, the Knights, and the Clergy to unite in the defence of their country. The idea of dying for one's country (*Dulce et decorum est pro patria mori*) was revived but in the context of chivalrous warfare. For Geoffroy de Charny, bearer of the oriflamme, the war banner of France, writing in the 1350s, knights could wage war on their own account and were usually to be ransomed if captured. The insistence of Honoré Bovet at the end of the fourteenth century that only kings had the right to wage war is testimony to the way in which during the late Middle Ages kings who stood at the summit of the chivalric world sought to lay hold of it and control the doctrines of chivalry for purposes of their own service. Chivalric warfare was thus transformed into training to serve the king in war. The imagery of France became increasingly monarchical in tone, revolving around the idea of the primacy of royal service and of the legitimacy of royal power: to die in the service of the king is also to die in the service of the country. France emerged in the late Middle Ages, then, as a 'royal state'. Ultimately, the dynasty were successors to a long line going back to the Carolingians and through them to the Trojans, blessed by the aura of the first Christian king, Clovis, as well as that of the crusader St Louis. This was fostered by the *Grandes chroniques de France*, a history of kings begun by Primat of Saint-Denis in the mid-thirteenth century. In the form of this which appeared around 1380, under royal supervision, this was the great vernacular 'best-seller' of late medieval France, in print from 1477 (it was the first book printed at Paris) though rapidly out of fashion after about 1520.

The imagery of France in the late Middle Ages, as Colette Beaune has argued, was many-layered and malleable; different groups could find what they wanted in it. There was a France for kings, one for the nobleman, one for the scholar, and another for the cleric. As yet, there was none for the peasant since the late medieval idea of national identity in all countries tended to trickle down from above and his was an oral culture. Some have argued that not until the later stages of the Hundred Years War did a full consciousness of national identity permeate to the depths of French society. The popularity of the *Grandes chroniques* is clear enough testimony that the nobility had a powerful idea of national history by the fourteenth century. The struggle with the English in the fourteenth and fifteenth centuries accelerated the process by which even the mass of the population would be incorporated into some inchoate idea of loyalty to a greater whole. In this the parish clergy, generally loyalist, relayed a modicum of royal propaganda which was backed up by visual imagery of saints, who stood for some sense of loyalty to the king, St Michael and St Louis, for instance. The general hostility that confronted English kings in their military ventures in Normandy from the 1340s indicates that the loyalties of the leading figures of local society were pretty firmly bound into the kingdom by the start of the fourteenth century. Popular insurrections against English rule between 1434 and 1436 deepened such sentiments and, as Anne Curry shows in Chapter 4, French historians were, in retrospect, to see France 'discovering itself' as a nation in the course of the wars with the English.

Centre and regions

One of the themes of this book is regional diversity. Marc Bloch noted in 1932 that 'historians of France have hitherto failed to shed light on this astonishing diversity from region to region'. Fortunately, we are now much more attuned to the tensions between centre and periphery in the history of the French state. Everywhere in pre-modern times regions, provinces, and *pays* compel loyalties and possess cultural distinctiveness, and many of the themes of 'national' loyalty were replicated at local level. The different legal customs and the very significant language differences between north and south in France fostered deep regional loyalties based on nobles' desire to run their own affairs and the economic and intellectual dynamism of the towns. As it happens the whole tradition of French culture has been to stress the progress of monarchical centralization, but the very word 'centralize' only came into use in 1794 so we have to beware of anachronisms and avoid confusing different kinds of centralization. In France it seems incontrovertible that there was institutional and personal centralization in the fourteenth and fifteenth centuries, at least in the expansion of the royal domain and the ways *parlements* and other agencies operated. The effectiveness of this, though, is by no means certain and that it also involved geographical centralization around a capital city is certainly more debatable. Even if Charles VII and Louis XI absorbed much of France into their domain, they could not hope to govern uniformly so vast a territory, especially since even their officials in the *pays* which were taken over in the fifteenth century became the most ardent defenders of local tradition. A case in point is the creation of local *parlements* in the fifteenth century. Moreover, there is little reason to suppose that the kings had any clear policy of uniform imposition on the kingdom of the authority of the Parisian institutions, which themselves objected to local *parlements.* Paris in any case was often not to be trusted by the crown in the late Middle Ages, so if the provinces demanded their own institutions as the price of their loyalty, the monarchy, mainly concerned to maintain internal peace so as to prosecute war and diplomacy, had little reason to object.

It has sometimes been argued, for instance by Henri Sée, that the late Middle Ages was the last great era of urban independence and that it was in the reign of Louis XI that the move towards controlling the towns by 'absolute monarchy' took place. Sée pointed to Louis's frequent orders to the towns, curtailment of their privileges, and the close monitoring of their activity. This view now seems outdated, especially since Bernard Chevalier argued that the reduction of the towns to tutelage was not apparent until the seventeenth century and started in the reign of Henri IV. The concept of the *bonnes villes* was actually one that developed in the fourteenth century, and it did so in parallel with the growth of royal power and was not inimical to it. As is shown in Chapter 6, though Louis may have interfered in town affairs, his relationship with them was favourable and initiated an age of cooperation between crown and towns after the severe upheavals of the fourteenth century which had seen the partial suppression of Parisian municipal independence. There is no evident desire on the crown's part to limit urban autonomy, more of an alliance between the two. The crown no longer feared the towns militarily and, after Louis XI, perhaps had less need to communicate by letter with them; the towns did send fewer deputations to court, but this was not because routine administration was taking their place (they began again during the Wars of Religion). However, they were certainly divided internally, and it was this that arguably provided scope for further royal intervention and tutelage in the future.

The political horizon for most people in the feudal age hardly stretched beyond their *châtellenie*; Guenée in fact argued that later medieval France remained an assemblage of *châtellenies* which were gradually being amalgamated into *bailliages* and *sénéchaussées* for administrative purposes (drawing up customs, for instance, as was being done from 1454) but which ran parallel to other loyalties, ecclesiastical and regional. Thus this localized horizon was being significantly enlarged in the fourteenth and fifteenth centuries more or less to include the whole kingdom. Philippe Contamine has by contrast stressed that the history of this period shows that France was 'in no sense a mosaic, a simple juxtaposition of peoples and nations, lands and territories'. But this is not the whole picture. Though local lords were losing their powers to command, political authority was crystallizing in other units, the kingdom, the royal domain, apanages, and great fiefs. Kings continued to grant out portions of their domain as apanages for good reasons, not because they were obtusely unaware of the demands of a march to national unity. Younger sons had to be supported, and regional communities guaranteed a degree of autonomy. The concession of apanages for the sons of John II and Charles V may seem imprudent in retrospect, but the building of powerful entities from those apanages was a symptom not a cause of political crisis.

It was once all too easy to think that the French principalities of the late Middle Ages were a last gasp of feudalism about to be swept away by the triumphant state. However, the success of great fiefs and principalities in the first half of the fifteenth century, as Edouard Perroy pointed out, is explained by the fact that they, as much as the crown, benefited from regional diversity and encroaching on the powers of feudal lords. Brittany, Burgundy, Guyenne, Béarn, Rouergue, the Bourbonnais, etc.—most of which have now been studied in depth by modern historians—were no more feudal entities than the monarchy itself. Thus, though there was no great controversy over the doctrine that 'the king is emperor in his own kingdom', there was over the nature of that imperial jurisdiction. Great princes too could claim to rule by the grace of God (see Chapters 3 and 6).This was a view rejected by the king's lawyers in the Parlement: 'no others can have sovereignty but him' (1454). Against the argument that fief-holders were *in loco principis*, the royal advocate argued in 1486 that 'the king is *solus princeps*'.[2] The unity of the kingdom was seriously put to the test during the era of the 'kingdom of Bourges' and during the Burgundian crisis of the 1460s and 1470s. Yet in the final analysis, that unity remained intact perhaps because the principalities could not combine for any length of time against the monarchy.

In the fifteenth century the kingdom was still to some extent regarded as a family concern of the royal kindred. Moreover, the members of the Capetian house seldom saw themselves as confined exclusively in their interests to France. Indeed, as a lineage which at one time or another occupied the thrones of Portugal, Hungary, Naples, and Sicily (and in more recent times Poland and Spain), this could hardly be otherwise. French relations with Italy were shaped by the dream of the two Capetian houses of Anjou to establish their rule in southern Italy and with the Low Countries by the state-building of the Valois dukes of Burgundy. These ambitions always gave to the French higher nobility an extra-national dimension, and the ambitions of the house of Anjou in Italy were taken over by the crown at the end of the fifteenth century. Internally, the ultimate success of the crown in its struggle with the great fiefs did not immediately have any significant effect on the way the country was governed; this remained ramshackle and shot through with exceptions and anomalies; the local institutions at *bailliage* and *châtellenie* level were still remarkably lively as a focus for public life.

[2] B. Guenée, 'Les tendances actuelles de l'histoire politique du Moyen Âge français', *Actes du 100e Congrès national des sociétés savants* (Paris, 1975), i.56 n.

The 'royal state' and its limitations

The massive disorders of the late Middle Ages prevented an institutional or ideological framework for limited monarchy from developing despite or perhaps because of the seriousness of political and social upheavals. This in itself did not create an 'absolutism' in the sense later used by historians, but it left French political society perilously dependent on monarchy for order and coherence. The first great period of consolidation had come at the precarious summit of economic growth in the thirteenth century. The reign of Philip IV in particular saw prodigious advances in the scope and demands of the crown (as is shown in Chapter 1). Philip's reign has bulked large in modern studies of the development of the French state, a view that has been built on in solid monographs during the twentieth century. What has emerged from all this work is that the notion that legists, whether taken in the narrow sense of the king's councillors or in the wider sense of all lawyers who at some stage entered royal service, were by no means uniformly bourgeois. Indeed, the lawyers of the royal council itself were nearly always nobles. The common denominator certainly was the study of Roman law, and there seems little doubt that legal procedure in the late fifteenth century was significantly overhauled by it. The primacy of the higher nobility in decisions concerning the succession between 1316 and 1328 add to the impression of a monarchical order largely run by or through the nobility.

Centralization depends to some extent on rapidity of communications. In times of adversity such as the 1420s and 1430s local governing bodies could feel extraordinarily isolated from the 'centre'. Much still depended on rapidity of transport. It seems that the realignment of routes into a network centred on Paris took shape in the twelfth and thirteenth centuries, but journeys remained long and were made worse by the weather. Though the royal postal routes were not formally organized as a system until the reign of Louis XI, it is now clear that, from the early fourteenth century, the letters of the wealthy and powerful could move much faster, up to 150 kilometres a day, using networks of messengers. When urgency required it, for instance to alter the course of coinage, in the fourteenth century messengers could reach every frontier in five days, but this was the exception and a very expensive move.

These difficulties of travel are related to the necessity for devolution of power. It has often been asked why France did not develop an effective system for formally limiting the power of the crown through representative assemblies. Did France in this period become a *Ständestaat*, of the type very common in late medieval Europe, in which state-building went hand-in-hand with the growth of representative institutions? The circumstances of the early fourteenth century seemed likely to foster this (Chapter 3). The associations of barons in northern France formed in 1314 to oppose Philip IV's levies for war in Flanders forced the king to back down, and his death cut off any plans to reverse this. With the relative political weakness of Philip VI and John II (a symptom of which was the latter's quasi-judicial execution of the constable de Guînes in 1350), assemblies of estates for large areas of France were called in the 1350s and became a major battleground. Simeon Luce argued that a great opportunity was lost in the final defeat of the estates and reform movements of that period. The relationship between crown and estates has often been viewed as a very unequal one. France was indeed a 'royal state', though one in which the representatives in estates could sometimes regard the power of the king as 'limited'. Whether this should be regarded as the cardinal feature of the period is a moot point, though. The fact that Philip VI was chosen by a council of princes and barons lends credence to the idea that his power was in a sense limited, yet this election did not create his legitimacy in the view of his contemporaries.

Some have seen estates as more robust; James Russell Major advanced the thesis that Renaissance France of the fifteenth and sixteenth century was an essentially decentralized country because of the prime importance he attached to the provincial estates which flourished in that period. The reason was the essential weakness of central government vis-à-vis the localities. Like many historians of the Anglo-American tradition, he saw the failure of the Estates General to develop as a sign of monarchical weakness rather than strength; the other side of the coin was the vigour of local assemblies. This was immediately a controversial argument for French historians who had been used to the framework in which it was the creation of royal corps of officials and *parlements* that constituted the important political dynamic of that period. Peter Lewis was convinced of the weakness of representative assemblies in late medieval France. For him, though, the consequences were not straightforward. He pointed to the fact that both Philippe de Commynes and John Fortescue on either side of the Channel had argued that Parliament made the English king stronger, not weaker; he was able through it to tax his nobility. As the editor of the political writings of Jean Juvénal des Ursins, Lewis saw a royal lawyer turn his invective against the practice of raising taxes without the consent of the Estates General after 1439 (see Chapter 7).

We know that by the time Philippe de Commynes was embroiled in princely frondeur politics in the 1480s he attached some importance to consultation and the rights of subjects to consent to taxes; he was not simply an advocate of authoritarian rule. In an extended interpolation on the qualities of a prince inserted during the events of 1477, he pondered whether kings should take pleasure in being able to tax at will and asked, 'Would it not be more just towards both God and the world to raise money this way [through consent] than by violence and disorder?' Why was Commynes concerned with the estates at this time? The year 1484 was to see the last such meeting until 1560: 'some there were (but considerable neither for their quality nor virtue) who said then, and have often repeated it since, that it was diminution of the king's prerogative, and no less than treason against him to talk of assembling the Estates, for that diminishes the king's authority'.[3] Commynes was not necessarily being opportunistic or inconsistent in promoting the role of the estates after Louis XI's death, for part of his vision of politics was order and measure, avoidance of risk, and ill-considered action. He saw the assembly of estates (as, for instance, in England) as a guarantee against disorder. The problem was that the failure of an Estates General to emerge for the whole country until late and the infrequency of its summons were crippling handicaps, while the failure to develop a proper system of representation at national level until 1484 limited the usefulness of such assemblies. Besides, as is shown in Chapter 6, there were other channels of communication which were more useful for local communities.

[3] *Mémoires de Philippe de Commynes*, ed. J. Calmette, 3 vols. (Paris, 1964–5), ii. 218–19, 222; trans. A. R. Scoble as *The Memoirs of Philip de Commines*, 2 vols. (London, 1855–6), i. 386, 388.

Clearly, though, provincial estates remained a vital part of the public life in much of France in the late Middle Ages. However, the reason for their failure to pose a significant restraint on royal power has often been misunderstood. Of course, it was possible for kings to play off province against province in this way, but the real reason was that, as in later periods, the provincial estates did not fully represent the interests of the urban and rural taxpayers, though they were effective as 'points of contact' between the crown and the regions. An Estates General, on the other hand, was both ineffective fiscally and dangerous.

The expansion of the royal demesne

The expansion of France vis-à-vis both great feudatories and neighbouring lands to the east has usually been seen by French historians as a logical process conducted by kings who had clear long-term strategies of 'gathering in' all French-speaking lands. In fact, there was no clear concept of French-speaking territory. As we have seen, France throughout the late Middle Ages was a multilingual country, even though the French of the north dominated the court and central officialdom. However, acquisition of new domains in the south began to incorporate those territories into a French political community. The king of France was a powerful suzerain who could offer protection to the counts of the empire near his borders, who little by little from the late thirteenth century were entering ties of dependence (Bar, Valentinois, Savoy, Vienne, etc.), especially when they held lands within the kingdom as vassals. Within the kingdom the king was surrounded by great vassals, who were often closely related to him by blood ties but who wished to maximize their freedom of action. The greatest example is that of the Plantagenets, but there were many others. Here kings had to rely on whatever instruments of power and control came to hand and could pursue no consistent line of absorption or control.

The period opens with two major advances for the power of the monarchy. In 1204 Philip Augustus dealt a death-blow to the Angevin empire as created by Henry II by taking advantage of John's difficulties to overrun Normandy (see Chapter 1). This in effect tore the heart out of the Angevin dominions and left the Plantagenets to fight an increasingly difficult rearguard action for the rest of the century to maintain their foothold around Bordeaux and in Gascony. This long intermittent struggle was temporarily settled by the treaty of Paris of 1259, which conceded Gascony to the Plantagenets in homage and formalized their position as peers of France, a settlement replete with contradictions but which provided a modus vivendi until the 1320s (Chapter 4). In Languedoc the power of the leading princes, the counts of Toulouse, already under pressure from the kings of Aragon as well as the Plantagenets, was faced by the problem of the growing influence of what can more usefully be thought of as a rival religion rather than a Christian heresy, in the form of Catharism. Since the middle of the twelfth century this dualist theology had taken hold in response to severe disenchantment with the Catholic clergy, the conviction that sinners could not be true priests, and the age-old preoccupation with the problem of evil. By the 1160s the Cathars had their own organization of bishops, deacons, and 'bonshommes' outside the Catholic Church, and quite evidently posed a threat both to the Church and to the feudal order. This is why the king and nobility responded to Innocent III's call for a crusade in 1208 which not even the submission of Raymond VI of Toulouse (who was blamed for the spread of heresy in his dominions) in June 1209 could head off. The crusade, led by a leading baron of the Île-de-France, Simon de Montfort, ravaged Languedoc for several years and led to the collapse of the power of the counts of Toulouse. The latter fought furiously against this northern invasion, but the 1229 treaty of Paris signalled a royal victory: royal power was now established in parts of Languedoc and Raymond VII agreed to marry his daughter to Alphonse de Poitiers, Louis VIII's brother, with succession to go to the crown even if they had no children. As Jean Dunbabin points out (Chapter 1), had Alphonse de Poitiers fathered sons, a new dynastic agglomeration might have emerged, but by the middle of the thirteenth century royal power was irrevocably anchored in Languedoc. The absorption of territories into the domain was not consistent. Throughout the late Middle Ages kings granted out new apanages, some of which became powerful and threatening, as was the case with Burgundy. Then the extinction of lineages led to reabsorption and a new shuffling of the territorial cards. But the thirteenth century saw the monarchy transformed irrevocably into a power that embraced both northern and southern France.

The precarious royal succession

The Capetian dynasty went through a period of intense uncertainty in terms of succession law between 1316 and 1350. The idea of dynastic change to the house of Valois in 1328 is somewhat illusory since the crown remained in the hands of the 'third race' of French kings, the Capetians, who consciously claimed descent both from Hugues Capet and the Carolingian dynasty as well as, more recently, from St Louis. The assumption gradually took shape that only descendants of St Louis could claim a right to the throne, at the expense of other branches of the dynasty. It is, though, the case that the long centuries of uncomplicated succession from father to son were interrupted. The house of France in the early fourteenth century was rocked by scandal and intrigue. The early death of Louis X, followed rapidly by that of his posthumous son, John I, in 1316, raised the question of female succession, but doubts over the conduct of Louis's first wife placed a question over her daughter Jeanne, also heiress to the kingdom of Navarre. In the event, Louis's brother the count of Poitiers managed to obtain recognition as Philip V by the 'lords of France' in control of the government at the expense of Jeanne, whose rights to Navarre were also set aside. Similar doubts over the parentage of Philip V's three daughters on his death in 1322 could at least be raised, and when Charles IV died in 1328 his daughters were also ruled out (while a birth of an heir to the pregnant queen was awaited). By this stage there were too many conflicting claims through females. Claims for Edward III of England as the only male grandson of Philip IV through his mother, Isabelle, were undermined by doubts over the wisdom of recognizing a 'foreign' prince. When the queen gave birth to another daughter, the case for the cousin in the male line of the last direct Capetians, Philippe de Valois, was therefore compelling and sealed by the agreement to concede legitimate succession in Navarre to Jeanne de France and her husband, another Capetian prince, Philippe of Évreux. Out of all this gradually emerged one of the great constitutional myths of French history, the Salic law, which royal lawyers later claimed proved the immemorial system of male primogeniture in the succession to the throne, ensured dynastic continuity, and excluded all foreign succession. France thus ended up with a very distinctive and powerful dynastic instrument for state-building even though this is visible only in retrospect. Jeanne of Navarre's son Charles, king of Navarre, became a major disturbing force in the politics of mid-fourteenth-century France (see Chapter 3) and, though he never formally advanced his claim to the throne, it lurked beneath the surface. The principle was to be overturned briefly by the exclusion of the dauphin Charles, son of Charles VI, in the treaty of Troyes of 1420, but the circumstances were those of murder and civil war. The diversion of the succession to the Lancastrians was a party device and only provoked further civil war until waning of English military power allowed the general acceptance of Charles VII. The succession of the Orléans (1498) and Angoulême (1515) branches were relatively uncontroversial and reinforced the doctrine of the Salic law.

Added to this was the quasi-mystical aura of the monarchy arising from the continuation by the Capetians of the sacred rite of anointing (the *sacre*) as well as coronation at Reims, in an age when the real power of the monarchy was feeble. This set kings apart from other princes and gave them some of the characteristics of priest-kings. The rite incorporated the famous holy ampulla of Clovis, believed from early Capetian times if not before to have been brought from heaven. So, in the reign of Charles VI the theologian Gerson wrote that 'when Saint Remigius baptized the first king Clovis he anointed him with holy oil sent by miracle and consecrated him as a sign of royal power and as a sacerdotal and pontifical dignity.'[4] From the late thirteenth century the kings of France could claim descent from a saint, Louis IX, and the ritual of healing scrofula, well established by this time, was from Philip IV's reign consciously defined as hereditary in the kings of France. The 'miracle' of the fleurs-de-lis and the sacred origins of the royal war banner, the oriflamme, are consciously stressed from the 1260s. In the fourteenth century the monarchy added to this repertoire of ideas and images that of the Rex Christianissimus, Most Christian King, an epithet from the reign of Charles V annexed exclusively by the kings of France as their special title. The dynasty whose succession laws were honed in the period could be seen as the bearer of a messianic role to become emperors of the West, rulers of Jerusalem, and usher in the millennium.

[4] J. Krynen, *L'empire du roi: idées et croyances politiques en France, XIIIe–XV siècles* (Paris, 1993), 28.

Foreign war and civil war

After 1316, then, France was faced by an as yet unresolved crisis of political legitimacy caused by succession problems and a socio-economic crisis which became visible after the Black Death of 1348. The unresolved problem of the Plantagenet domains in Gascony (problems papered over by the treaty of Paris of 1259) generated from 1337 a sequence of conflicts between English and French monarchs that were to become indelibly labelled the Hundred Years War in the nineteenth century (see Chapter 4). These wars were not continuous, of course; the first phase was brought to an end by the unratified peace of Brétigny in 1360 (after two shattering defeats of the French military nobility at Crécy and Poitiers in 1347 and 1356), but they were renewed on French initiative in 1369, subsided into prolonged truces in the 1390s, and then renewed again on English initiative in 1415. It is easy to dismiss French military organization between the defeats of Crécy (1346) and Verneuil (1424) as hopelessly obtuse and conservative in its reliance on the individualistic charge of heavily armoured aristocratic cavalry. The emergence of a 'standing army' in 1439–45 thus seems a completely new development. While it is the case that the cavalry visibly expressed the idea of noble pre-eminence in French society, French commanders began to learn from their mistakes in the 1350s in trying to parry English military tactics and, despite spectacular defeats, began to put together the organization of a truly royal army well before the end of the fourteenth century, one moreover that was in effect if not in name paid for by permanent taxes.

The greatest periods of internal breakdown were, of course, closely bound up with the English invasions. At the start of 1417 the Chronicler of Saint-Denis, Michel Pintoin, wrote a lamentation on the 'Miserable State of the Realm of France' followed by another 'Tearful Song on a Desolate France', having already written of the battle of Agincourt: 'I do not believe that for fifty years France had experienced such a great disaster and one likely to have, in my opinion, more dire consequences.' In the same year, 1417, at the height of the civil wars between the Armagnacs and Burgundians, his friend the scholar and chancellery secretary Jean de Montreuil, then in his sixties, wrote a letter to Nicolas de Clamanges on the woes of his age ('Tempora nostra pessima sunt'), in which he outlined the misfortunes of his youth: Crécy, Poitiers, and the English conquests, the revolutions in Paris of Étienne Marcel and the 1358 peasant rebellion of the Jacques. In the midst of the worst civil war of the late Middle Ages this was indeed a catalogue of woe. It is even more poignant when we remember that Montreuil was slaughtered in the massacre of the Armagnac prisoners in June 1418.[5]

The reason for the final renewal of conflict between 1415 and 1453 cannot be divorced from the chaotic internal state of French politics between 1400 and 1430, after two generations of economic crisis. The fundamental facts which dominated the politics of late fourteenth- and early fifteenth-century France were, first, the minority (1380–8) and then the periodic paranoid schizophrenia of Charles VI (1392–1422), military disaster (in the Balkans at Nicopolis, 1396; in France at Agincourt, 1415), disputed rule and disputed succession (from 1420 onwards). Though he was technically in his majority at his thirteenth birthday, Charles VI's 'adult' rule began at the age of 20 (November 1388), when the council agreed that he was old enough and that the royal uncles—Philip the Bold, duke of Burgundy, and John, duke of Berry—could return to their estates. The power of the Marmousets, men long in the service of Charles V but now much more significant and including figures such as Bureau de La Rivière, Jean de La Grange, and, from the highest nobility, Enguerrand de Coucy, lasted from the exclusion of the royal uncles from power in 1388 to the king's illness in 1392, which saw the return of the uncles to authority. This period was one of relatively prudent financial administration and fairly abundant and regular revenues. The regime of the uncles was marked by occasional returns of the king to lucidity but not on a sustainable basis. Peace moves with England, the military disaster of Nicopolis, the establishment of a policy to end the Great Schism by withdrawing obedience from Benedict XIII and plans for adventurism in Italy were the dominant features.

The political crisis was perceived in starkly personal terms. The Burgundian–Armagnac struggle was generally thought to have stemmed from the feud created by John the Fearless, duke of

[5] J. de Montreuil, *Opera*, ed. N. Grévy, E. Ornato, and G. Ouy, 2 vols. (Turin, 1963–75), i. 327.

Burgundy's murder of Louis of Orléans in 1407. So, in the later fifteenth century Thomas Basin wrote: 'That was the origin and the beginning first of the civil wars then of foreign wars which overwhelmed not only the whole kingdom but many neighbouring countries with numberless ills and calamities.'[6] The echo went on down to the last decade of the fifteenth century, when the author of a treatise on how to govern (Robert de Balsac?) wrote of the ease by which the country could slip out of control: 'when Monsieur d'Orléans was killed at Paris there was such peace everywhere that you could carry gold in your hand from one end of the kingdom to another without being harmed. Within three weeks of his killing, not a man could travel without being robbed . . . a war could start through the death of one man, an outrage.'[7]

In fact, the rivalry of the royal princes, simmering from 1401, deteriorated after Philip the Bold's death in 1404 and succession by John the Fearless, and broke out openly in 1405. Attempts to settle it by talks were devastated above all by Burgundy's openly avowed assassination of Orléans in November 1407, then his aggressive policies in 1408–9. John the Fearless seemed to have triumphed in March 1408 when the king formally accepted his case for the murder. Only by staying in Paris, though, could he hope to control the situation, and this was not possible in view of his other commitments. Drawn away on campaign to Liège, on his return in November he found that, on the advice of the *grand maître* Jean de Montaigu, the court had withdrawn to Tours out of his reach. The rest of the royal kindred were unable to offer a solution to this division of power and ravaging of the country had already broken out. In March 1409 a formal reconciliation took place at Chartres Cathedral in which Charles VI obliquely pardoned Burgundy, though the Orléans princes did so most unwillingly. On the surface it was another Burgundian triumph, and in the autumn of 1409 came a Burgundian coup followed by the execution of Montaigu. However, the Burgundian regime failed largely because of the alliance of the Orléanists and the rest of the royal kindred. The League of Gien (April 1410) effectively founded the Armagnac party and a new struggle which saw the countryside

[6] Thomas Basin, *Histoire de Charles VII*, ed. and trans C. Samaran, 2 vols. (Paris, 1933–44), i. 21.

[7] P. Contamine, 'Un traité politique inédit de la fin du XVe siècle', *ABSHF 1983–84* (1986), 162.

around Paris devastated again. Charles VI briefly regained his sanity and tried to bring peace; there was a temporary one at Bicetre (November 1410) by which the princes agreed to return to their domains, but it lasted only the winter and in the spring both parties mobilized again with another quasi-siege of Paris broken by Burgundy in November. Charles VI, now with Burgundy, declared against the 'rebels', who in turn negotiated with the English for help in the form of the treaty of Bourges (May 1412). The summer culminated in the siege of Bourges led by the king in person and Burgundy; formidable artillery was trained on the walls and all seemed likely to come to a showdown. But neither the king nor the League were eager for a decisive battle and money was running out on both sides, not least because of the financial obligations contracted to the English allies of the Armagnacs; hence another reconciliation at Auxerre (August 1412).

Is the use of the term 'parties' anachronistic for this period? Françoise Autrand described these factions as akin to political parties with programmes and territorial roots but was careful to stress their fragility, particularly in resources. Both of them depended on the control of the royal financial administration and that is their dominating characteristic. Maurice Rey estimated that the dukes drew an average of 800,000 *lt.* per year from the royal finances throughout the reign of Charles VI. These funds allowed them to construct clienteles consisting of both gentilshommes and bourgeois who hoped to gain a myriad of minor offices and benefits from their patrons' political clout. Thus one of the salient characteristics of the factions was that the princely leaders sought to succeed by 'colonizing' the royal administration as far as possible (in that respect the Orléanists were more successful). To this were added two further dimensions. After the death of Orléans the Armagnac party which emerged from his clientele was cemented by formal oaths which made the grouping both a private alliance and something akin to a treaty.

Finally both 'factions' sought to appeal to public opinion by distributing political programmes in the form of letters to great institutions and pamphlets, songs, and pasquils for street distribution which stressed the good of the kingdom, the control of abuses, and 'reform'. This was even more apparent at times of great upheaval such as after the murder of John the Fearless in 1419, when both the Burgundian and Dauphinist leaderships issued batteries of letters to the towns of their obedience in order to gather and maintain support. The Dauphinists went to the length not only of deliberately falsifying the events of the murder but also of distorting the reactions of their enemies to it in order to create the impression on their own side that the new duke of Burgundy was happy with this version of events. This looks very like conscious news management. Attempts to brand Burgundy as a traitor by the revelation of the December 1419 Arras agreement, though, met with little response in Burgundian territory.

This long, tangled foreign and civil war eventually helped to generate national loyalty; transfers of allegiance generated trials for treason and the laws of treason refined the boundaries of loyalty. Battlefields gave rise to national symbols, seeing the white cross of France pitched against the red cross of St George and the red St Andrew's cross of Burgundy.

Recovery and consolidation

France reached it lowest point in the 1420s with the division of the kingdom and endemic civil war. Whether it was the unique intervention of the Maid of Orléans, Jeanne d'Arc, between 1429 and 1431 that rescued the tottering Valois dynasty is much debated, but ultimately the ability of the Plantagenets to dominate depended upon the continuation of Burgundian hostility to Charles VII. In fact Philip the Good was uncomfortable in the long run as ally of the Lancastrians and eventually came to terms in the treaty of Arras (1435). This sounded the death knell for the English in France. The consolidation of the monarchy under Charles VII and Louis XI can now therefore be placed in a more long-term context. It took place at a time of fragile recovery from this social, political, and economic disaster. In 1441 English and French armies shrank for lack of 'victuals and peasants' from which to live.[8] From the 1430s and 1440s the first signs of real economic recovery from the crisis began to emerge with population recovery in some areas and tentative commercial recovery. Much of this was linked to the end of the English wars in the north and west. From the abyss of the 1350s and 1410s France recovered under

[8] Basin, *Histoire de Charles VII*, i. 267.

energetic regimes led by intelligent kings and councillors. However, underlying all this was a process of state-building that had been long maturing. Augustin Thierry, in the nineteenth century, argued that, from the reign of St Louis, the state was appearing with a new face, that new institutions were developing. Of course, it has long been thought that the French monarchy played a pivotal role—provided a 'royal mechanism'—for the solution of the centrifugal structures of French political society. If the power of the king around 1200 did not look appreciably different from that of the Holy Roman Emperor in Germany, historians with hindsight are able to point to the powerful dynastic security and longevity of the Capetian dynasty as an explanation for the path towards royal state-building in the late Middle Ages. While many have emphasized the pivotal reign of Philip IV, others such as Claude Gauvard suggest that it was the reign of Charles VI 'which was the moment when the bureaucratic state was established in matters of justice and finance', and one moreover capable of surviving long periods of royal incapacity. All such insights have something to contribute, but the notion of a slow evolution rather than revolution in royal power as well as the social diversity of royal service needs to be emphasized. Philippe Contamine's work on military history, government, and the nobility stresses the slow evolution of the French state over two centuries. The outcome of much of the collaborative work done by J.-P. Genet on the origins of the modern state had emphasized the *longue durée* in that process, starting in the decades around 1300.

The ability of Charles VII and Louis XI, therefore, to surmount the formidable combinations of power launched against them becomes much more understandable. They had at their disposal a military and administrative machine which was much more than the creation of the 1430s, with an ideology of loyalty long in the making. Above all, perhaps, they had at their disposal a composite political elite made up of middle-ranking nobles and notable bourgeois who perceived their interest to rest in the maintenance of royal power (see Chapter 7). This was why Charles VII was able to deal with the Praguerie in 1440 and why Louis XI, almost submerged by the ferocious hatred of the League of the Public Weal in 1465, was able to create what some historians have called a reign of terror in the 1470s, moving against suspects individually, killing Armagnac (1473), executing Saint-Pol (1475) and Nemours (1477), and outwitting his Burgundian enemy in

1475–7. The accession of his young son Charles VIII in 1483, though accompanied by political upheavals, did not substantially change the composition of the ruling elite. Nor did the accession of a classic frondeur noble in the person of Louis XII in 1498.

1

The political world of France, *c.*1200–*c.*1336

Jean Dunbabin

The expansion of French power and the consolidation of a sense of identity in France could not easily have been predicted in 1200. By then Philip II had been ruling for fifteen years, but his great triumphs were all still to come. It would have needed prophetic insight to foresee that he would be victorious, not only over the counts of Flanders, since 1191 angry and vengeful; but also over King John of England, who held the duchy of Normandy, the counties of Anjou, Maine, and Touraine, and, through his mother, Eleanor, the duchy of Aquitaine (which included Gascony). Between them, Baldwin IX of Flanders and King John controlled the whole of the western side of modern France from Ghent to Bayonne, with the exception only of the duchy of Brittany, held by the young Arthur, John's nephew and Philip's ally. It is true that the formidable alliance between Flanders and England, forged by Richard I, John's predecessor, was weakening by 1199. Philip had succeeded in capturing Baldwin's brother Philip of Namur, which forced Baldwin to the negotiating table. The French king drove a hard bargain. In January 1200, by the treaty of Péronne, Baldwin IX agreed to abandon the English alliance, though in return for various contested towns. Signed as it was at the beginning of the new century, the treaty of Péronne symbolized the start of a new, more assertive, era for French power.

The royal demesne

The most startling feature of the reign of Philip II was the huge expansion of the royal demesne, that bundle of rights and lands which supplied the king with the money and men on whom his power depended. Philip inherited from his father Louis VII a demesne that had not substantially increased in size over the past century. It still comprised lands and rights concentrated in the areas surrounding and between the two towns of Paris and Orléans, the fertile lands of the Île-de-France. Philip's predecessors had, however, increased royal revenue very considerably from these lands by careful housekeeping, buying good estates, and finding reliable stewards (*prévots*) to oversee them. They had also extended their lordship (judicial and financial rights over people) by constant assertion and a certain amount of aggression. At the same time they had made tentative steps to annex some new places to the demesne, in particular the northern part of Berry and the Auvergne, neither of which was subjected to a powerful lay prince or lord. Louis VI and Louis VII saw the point of pushing their claims to superiority where they would not meet with much opposition.

From the start of his reign Philip had favoured a more aggressive policy of expansion. By his marriage to Isabelle of Hainault in 1186, he stood to gain the county of Artois (rich territory that had been disputed since the tenth century between the count of Flanders and the king of France) as an endowment for the couple's eldest son. In 1191 he secured it, though at the cost of alienating Isabelle's father, Baldwin V, count of Hainault, who succeeded as Baldwin VIII to the county of Flanders in the same year. At the same time Philip laid claim to Vermandois, which came completely into his hands in 1213 on the death of Countess Eleanor, but of which he enjoyed a share earlier, as a reward for defending Eleanor's claims. Relatively small though these gains may seem, they were significant in terms of the wealth they brought, and they made an impact on French public opinion. The monk Rigord, who was engaged in writing Philip's life for the collection of royal biographies kept at the monastery of Saint-Denis, said that Philip had, by 1193, earned the title Augustus because he had increased the size of his demesne.

What had been achieved before 1200, though, paled into insignificance against the gains soon to come. When Philip declared in 1202 that King John, in failing to respond to a summons to the French royal court, had forfeited those lands he held in fief from the French crown, a bitter war broke out. By 1204 Philip had gained what was certainly his chief, and may initially have been his only, objective, the duchy of Normandy. He had also, by alliance with the *sénéchal* of Anjou, made headway in the counties of Anjou, Maine, and Touraine. King John's alleged murder of Arthur, duke of Brittany, had brought the Bretons firmly over to the French side. By the end of 1206 the powerful Angevin empire had disintegrated to such an extent that nothing of it remained north of the Loire, while the death of Duchess Eleanor in April 1204 had meant that John's lordship south of the Loire was now seriously under threat. Philip's victory at the battle of Bouvines in 1214 over a combined army from England, Flanders, and the empire caused the French gains across western France to look permanent.

It was fortunate for Philip that he had already experimented with a new means of government before so much land fell into his hands. Before his departure on the Third Crusade in 1189, he had instituted *baillis*, officials nominated to preserve royal interests in the demesne and to ensure that all the king's *prévots* collected the revenues of the crown in the king's absence. This measure, intended to be temporary, subsequently provided the model for the government of the enlarged demesne. Initially the duties of the *baillis* (in the south often called *sénéchaux*) were fluid; but by the end of the reign of Louis IX they had become the chief local financial and legal agents of the crown operating within fixed areas to carry out their employer's wishes. Given their tasks, their unpopularity was predictable. When, on the point of departure for his first crusade, Louis IX in 1247–8 sent out *enquêteurs* (men who conducted enquiries) to hear complaints made against royal servants, the inhabitants of the royal demesne seized the opportunity to express their resentment. But recruitment to *bailliages* remained fairly easy because they offered their holders financial and social rewards.

By Philip's death in 1223 the royal demesne was the dominant principality in northern France. Royal revenues had swollen by 76 per cent as a result of the new income from Normandy, Maine, and Touraine. The king anticipated that the revenues of Anjou would soon come to him (in fact they did not until 1234). These, along with those from Vermandois and Artois, totally transformed Philip's position among his great lords. Instead of being only one planet in the firmament, he had become the sun around whom the others circulated. In fact his triumph appeared even greater than it was, since adverse family circumstances, including the deaths of two counts on crusade, had led to a decline of the house of Blois (the counties of Blois and Chartres were ceded to the crown in 1235), a series of regencies had made Champagne vulnerable, and utter defeat in 1214 had reduced Flanders to its nadir. At the same time the Albigensian crusade had broken up the county of Toulouse. Only Burgundy and Brittany remained relatively undisturbed by the tumultuous events that had devastated the other principalities.

The brief reign of Philip's son Louis VIII saw, if anything, larger gains for the demesne, this time south of the Loire. Now that the opposition had been cowed, the war to eliminate Angevin lordship continued, with huge gains in Poitou and La Rochelle between 1224 and 1226. By the treaty of Paris in 1259 signed between Louis IX and Henry III, these gains were made permanent, and Henry paid liege homage to the French king for his only surviving French territory, Gascony, still described as the duchy of Aquitaine. From then onwards there was constant friction over the terms of the treaty, over the implications of the homage paid to the French king, and over the precise borders of the duchy. Tension built up steadily. Yet there was also a desire on both sides to keep the peace. Only in 1293, 1324, and 1337 did war break out; on the first two occasions the campaigns were brief. Never before 1356 was French possession of the bulk of the former Angevin duchy of Aquitaine seriously threatened. Although the county of Poitou was granted by Louis VIII to his third son, Alphonse, his marriage was childless and Poitou became part of the royal demesne on Alphonse's death in 1271.

The reign of Louis VIII also saw the annexation of tracts of land in Languedoc which had been conquered by the French soldiers sent in by Pope Innocent III to wipe out Catharism. By 1226 Louis VIII was in control of much of the far south, including Béziers, Carcassonne, and Albi. Three years after his death, by the treaty of Paris of 1229, plans were laid whereby the great county of Toulouse should be inherited by his son Alphonse of Poitiers, who subsequently married Jeanne, daughter of Raymond VII of Toulouse. Had there been children of this marriage, Toulouse would not have fallen into the hands of the monarchy. But in 1271 it, like Poitou, became part of the royal demesne. The significance to the French crown of these lands acquired through a mixture of conquest and marriage was great. Not only did they bring additional wealth and military power, though at the cost of much effort; they also made the king of France a player in Mediterranean politics; as has been seen in the Introduction, they created the possibility that northerners and southerners might one day feel themselves to be citizens of the same political entity.

After 1271 the royal demesne was not far from being synonymous with the kingdom of France. With the exception of some small Pyrenean counties, the only principalities that lay within the kingdom but had not yet been absorbed into the demesne were Champagne, acquired in 1284 by the marriage of Philip IV to its heiress, the two duchies of Gascony and Burgundy, and the two counties of Flanders and Brittany. These four hung on as appendages around the edges of the demesne, their constitutional oddity forming almost the only common characteristic between them. The opposition of all four to the king of France at different times in the course of the Hundred Years War was repeatedly to humiliate the monarch. But all that was long in the future in 1271.

Louis VIII and to a lesser extent subsequent kings fragmented the royal demesne, temporarily at least, by making grants of lands to their younger sons, the apanages. The arrangement whereby Alphonse of Poitiers was endowed, first with Poitou and then with the county of Toulouse, has already been discussed; the return of these to the royal demesne by 1271 has also been noted. Most other apanages were much smaller than these. Exactly how and when it became the unbreakable rule that only direct heirs could inherit apanages is contentious; but Louis VIII had suggested this rule for two of those he proposed in his will. The consequence was that several apanages lasted only for one lifetime. Others also reverted to the demesne, though sometimes after a long period. For example, Louis IX granted his youngest brother, Charles of Anjou, the counties of Anjou and Maine in 1246. These remained in the hands of Charles's son Charles II of Naples and Sicily until 1291, when they were brought by marriage to Charles of Valois, younger brother of Philip IV. On Charles of Valois's death, they came to his son, by now Philip VI of France. The apanages of Artois and Clermont survived much longer. For the historian, apanages are not particularly important as independent fiefs because, despite the alienation of the demesne involved, most apanage holders behaved as faithful lieutenants to the kings. They were disinclined to follow in the footsteps of the sporadically rebellious counts of Flanders or dukes of Gascony. Only occasionally, as in the dispute over the succession to Artois of 1328–32, did an apanage feature largely in the history of the French kingdom, in this case in virtue of its unusual customary rules of inheritance.

After the large gains of the first three-quarters of the thirteenth century there was relatively little that later kings could do to expand the demesne. Nevertheless, they did what they could. Philip IV, in addition to an unsuccessful attempt to annex Gascony, took some land on the eastern frontier of France from imperial lordship. His aim was to control fully the west bank of the Rhône and both banks of the Saône. After he obtained the Vivarais in 1307, he sent his son and heir Louis to Lyon in 1310 to take over the city, long rent by quarrels between its archbishop and its citizens. Its ecclesiastical and commercial importance added lustre to the kingdom. The king also purchased the imperial county of Burgundy (although here the Capetian duke of Burgundy prevented its annexation to the royal demesne). While Philip was unsuccessful in his major ambitions in the county of Flanders, in 1312 he acquired Lille and Douai, two of its richest towns, from the count as war indemnity. His successors had some difficulty in holding on to this gain, but in the end the two towns did become French.

The reigns of Louis X, Charles IV, Philip V, and Philip VI provided few opportunities for successful annexation, taken up as they were with repeated conflicts in Flanders until 1328 and with the war of Saint-Sardos in Gascony in 1324–5. Nevertheless, the kingdom ruled by Philip VI before 1337 was huge compared with anything that Philip Augustus could have imagined in 1200.

As well as the temporal demesne, there was the ecclesiastical. By combining what they inherited from the Carolingians with their own extensive rights over abbeys, the Capetians had, since the reign of Hugh Capet, enjoyed lucrative and extensive rights in the Church. It has been calculated (by John Baldwin) that when Philip II came to the throne, there were about sixty-five regalian abbeys and at least twenty-five regalian bishoprics. In these the king could draw the revenues of the bishop or abbot during a vacancy, might or might not be able to influence the actual choice of candidate, and, in the case of bishoprics, could fill such prebends and benefices as belonged to the bishop between the death of one incumbent and the election of the next. The expansion of the secular demesne, the taking over of rights once held by the Angevins and other lords, along with the nomination of *baillis* and *sénéchaux* responsible for seeing that dues were actually collected in vacancies, potentially raised the revenues from these sources dramatically. The thirteenth century, though, saw frequent clashes about collection of regalia between royal officials and local clerics. Increasingly clearly articulated canon law procedures came up against royal claims. The revenue and rights that once had been fairly simple to collect or assert now became difficult. Therefore, later French kings tended to make less use of regalian rights and more of the new power to take tenths from clerical property to finance crusades, which by the end of the thirteenth century had brought substantial gains to the monarchy.

Money and might

Past experience had taught the Capetians how to exploit a small demesne to the full. If anything, they showed even greater ingenuity in the thirteenth century in extracting money and fighting men from the vast areas now under their control. The twofold result was that the French kings became the richest monarchs in western Europe and that royal armies, hitherto rarely successful in the field of battle, emerged as the most feared fighting force in western Europe.

In 1197 Philip II lost the royal archives while fleeing from Richard I at the battle of Fréteval. The records of his reign after 1197 are, however, voluminous, and show his determination to claim and collect all sources of revenue or manpower available to him, both in the old royal demesne (where his exactions were particularly heavy) and in the newly conquered or acquired areas (where he had to make some concessions, presumably to earn goodwill). His clerks made lists for him of all the ordinary sources of revenue he could expect to receive each year from the *prévots* who farmed his estates and those who collected his various tolls and regular exactions; by 1202–3 this information was presented in the form of an account, along with profits from justice and regalian rights over churches. John Baldwin has calculated that these forms of income added up to somewhere between 60,000 and 77,000 *lp.* per year. Reinforced, in a year of war, by a heavy tax for the commutation of various forms of military obligation that amounted to 26,000 *lp.* per year (and probably also by substantial sums for feudal incidents and confiscations), Philip's income permitted him to spend lavishly on effecting the defeat of King John, while still covering his ordinary expenses without strain. His financial surplus in peacetime aroused envy among all his contemporary European monarchs. Admittedly, this was not achieved without some grumbling on the part of his subjects, but his victories in the field sweetened the pill and brought new taxpayers into the system. As long as the demesne was expanding rapidly, discontent was muted.

Though an unremarkable general in the early years of his reign, Philip did learn military skills from his opponents. The French army began to use the crossbow, a more lethal weapon than anything thus far wielded by them. It employed engineers to mine below the foundations of castles it was besieging. Philip hired mercenaries, though in small numbers; the most famous of these was Cadoc, an important figure in the conquest of Normandy. The king built castles with strong defences. He also consulted the experts, the Templars and Hospitallers, whose dedication to the preservation of the Kingdom of Jerusalem provided them with invaluable experience of warfare. The tactical thinking of Brother Guérin, a Hospitaller and Philip's closest adviser in peace as well as war, was shown to good effect in the battle of Bouvines in 1214. Though the French army was smaller than that of its opponents, it fought under a united command and with greater cohesion. The decisiveness of its victory increased the standing of military men at the royal court. Philip's heir, the future Louis VIII, the only Capetian to show outstanding qualities as a military leader, learned his craft in an environment radically different from that in which his father had been brought up.

Even so, the sudden rise in French royal military fortunes was chiefly based on administrative improvements. Philip's ability to pay the wages of a relatively small number of knights and footsergeants for years at a time, so that they became the highly experienced kernel of his army, competent to take the most demanding positions in battle, was crucial to his success in the field. Almost as important was the support in terms of carting and provisioning which the peasants of the locality were obliged to provide to the troops. These, along with the heavy military obligations exacted from the towns and churches of the old royal demesne, transformed the potential of the hitherto undistinguished French army. Philip was therefore at last able to exploit the obvious Angevin weaknesses of lengthy frontiers, extended supply lines, and shaky finances. Without the support of his *baillis* and *sénéchaux* this would not have been possible.

By 1229 so much had been achieved by the sword that peace on the king's terms could prevail. With the exception of a few short campaigns, the most dangerous of which was in 1241–2, the king could now relax, secure in the knowledge that internal enemies had been overcome. Royal revenues were diverted from the building of defences to that of great churches. By 1247, however, Louis IX had determined on a military campaign of a different sort, a crusade of which he would be leader and to which France would be by far the major financial contributor. Militarily this and his second crusade in 1270 posed new problems. The royal treasury had to pay the expenses of the royal household, swollen to an unprecedented size. In order to recruit other soldiers, the king had to rely on a contract system, whereby he paid individual aristocrats or experienced men-at-arms to collect troops and bring them to the royal army. On some of these he conferred the privilege of eating with the royal household. Most soldiers expected to receive salaries from the substantial sums in crusader tax collected from both Churchmen and laymen across the kingdom (and from imperial territories that lay within the old ecclesiastical province of Gaul). Although Philip Augustus had called for crusader taxes for his expedition in 1189, he had been unsuccessful; popular opinion was against them. His grandson was far more fortunate; huge amounts were raised, especially from the French Church, which in the end provided about two-thirds of the sum required for the 1248 crusade. The burden was very great; but the objective ensured that Churchmen would keep their criticisms largely to themselves. The other major group to suffer, the Jews, were similarly silent because they knew they commanded little sympathy in the general population.

St Louis's crusades not only demanded new forms of recruitment and military financing, they also created the need for a navy. Determined to avoid the subservience to Venetian wishes that had characterized the Fourth Crusade, Louis ordered ships from shipbuilders across Europe, brought them together in his newly built Mediterranean port of Aigues Mortes, and set sail from there; while in 1248 the admiral of the fleet was a Genoese, by 1270 a French commander could be chosen. But if it seemed that France was on the point of becoming a naval power, that promise remained unfulfilled. For the most part, the country was for the foreseeable future to rely principally on warships provided by its allies. The failures of 1248 and 1270 had generated no enthusiasm for imitation.

The result of these campaigns and of the failed Spanish crusade of 1283 was that French royal officials came to expect the revenues of the Church to be at their disposal when required. Canon law, however, restricted the grant of such revenues to occasions specifically endorsed by the papacy. Consequently, when in 1296 Philip IV found himself at war both in Gascony and in Flanders, his demand for clerical tenths was met with strong opposition from Boniface VIII. Although the quarrel was, at this point, rapidly made up because the Pope desperately needed French assistance in Italy, the point of contention remained alive, and contributed to the more serious conflict of 1302–3. Boniface's immediate successors avoided conflict by their willingness to grant Church taxes to the king; but both John XXII and Benedict XII took a tougher line. In 1336 Benedict acted fast to prevent Philip VI from using the revenues collected for his projected crusade in his war against England.

While the revenues of the king of France in the reign of Philip Augustus had been large enough to finance war without strain, by the end of the thirteenth century this was no longer the case. Even in peace the costs of providing increasing numbers of salaried officials across what was now a very large demesne had become burdensome. In part, this was the result of an economic downturn that was not within the king's control. As will be seen in the next chapter, poor weather and bad harvests caused a contraction in the profits of agriculture and disruption to what industry there was. Taxation was more resented as conditions grew worse. In time of conflict it grew nearly insupportable, inflated as it was by the need to meet much higher costs of war: the large size of armies, the increase in equipment, the complex siege engines. Furthermore, most soldiers now expected to be paid, feudal military service being totally inadequate for the lengthy campaigns undertaken. However, Philip IV was slow to modify his aggressive instincts to suit the new conditions. Consequently, obstinate and enduring resistance from the Flemings, who inflicted on his army the terrible defeat at Courtrai in 1302, put the king's relations with his subjects under serious strain. His attempt to impose direct rule on Gascony against the wishes of the majority of its inhabitants had to be abandoned in 1303. In 1314 he faced substantial opposition from the Leagues.

Philip's reign saw experiments in the means of and justifications for taxation. From 1295 on he tried summoning assemblies to act as representative of the whole community in giving consent to taxes on personal property, a measure publicly justified on the grounds of the common good. This expedient, which would have led to a form of regular national taxation for war, met with strong opposition. By 1303 it was decided that negotiations should be conducted directly with local communities, and that the basis should be the commutation of military service. If less administratively satisfactory (a tax of this sort could only be collected when the army had been called out), this at least provoked far less outcry. The traditional tax for the marriage of a king's eldest daughter was collected assiduously in 1308, as was that for the knighting of the king's son in 1312. In addition to taxes, a devaluation of the coinage between 1296 and 1301 initially brought the royal treasury a large profit, but rapidly lost its earning power, and caused fierce anger among the aristocrats and Churchmen on whom the crown chiefly depended for support. The return to strong currency in 1306 was a politically essential move. Along with the ecclesiastical tenths granted by Popes Benedict XI and Clement V, the exploitation of the Jews until their expulsion in 1306, and the squeezing of the Lombard banking houses in 1309–10, Philip almost contrived to cover the expenses of war, but at the cost of growing unpopularity, which came near to rebellion just before his death in November 1314.

Therefore, although in the second and third decades of the fourteenth century the king of France still appeared to his neighbours as a mighty figure, with resources to match his ambitions, in practice prudence suggested that restraint in foreign policy was necessary. More than a year or two of war could put the whole country under serious strain. Neither the rout in Flanders in the reign of Louis X nor the inconclusive war of Saint-Sardos under Charles IV lasted long enough to expose the danger; but nor did they bring much glory to

French armies. Philip VI's calculated decision to annex Gascony in 1337 was based on the assumption that England's finances were in an even worse state than those of France. It was a gamble that took a very long time to pay off.

Law and lordship

The expansion of Capetian material resources coincided with a marked rise in legal power. To some extent, the two were directly linked. As the royal demesne rapidly increased in size, so the number of courts under the king's immediate or indirect control multiplied. Whether castellans or royal *prévots* presided over these courts, they called the king of France in aid to enforce their decisions. Represented by his *baillis* and *sénéchaux*, the king redistributed property or punished criminals as required by the verdicts reached (in accordance with local custom) in courts across his lands. He became a meaningful power throughout much of the kingdom; even on the Mediterranean shore men learned to think of his justice as ever present. Furthermore, his servants did not hesitate to extend his jurisdiction even where his customary rights were weak. The power that had been gained primarily by conquest was slowly increased by pressure. Some people gave in willingly to that pressure; Churchmen were frequently glad to hand over *justice de sang* (criminal jurisdiction that involved capital or corporal penalties) to the crown. Royal officials, though, could be unscrupulous in ignoring other men's claims. Either way, the thirteenth century saw the king and his officials emerging as by far the most important law enforcement agency in France.

As a result of its greater involvement in criminal matters, the crown sought to strengthen the hand of the prosecution in trials. The weakness of customary procedures had lain in the burden of responsibility placed on the victim or his family to prove the case against the defendant. In some cases customary law enjoined that the penalty appropriate for the crime should be exacted from an unsuccessful plaintiff after the verdict, a prospect which discouraged plaintiffs from turning to the courts; but as the king took on his own shoulders the duty of enforcing peace across his lands, the balance was tilted towards the victim. Influenced by Roman law, royal justices began to experiment with the inquisitorial process of trial, by which appointed officials conducted inquiries into crimes and presented cases against named individuals, thereby creating a form of public prosecution. When these officials found themselves frustrated by the absence of eyewitnesses to the crime, they pressed for the Roman law expedient of torture to extort confessions from guilty parties or even, in rare cases, testimony from those thought to be shielding them. This was conceded by Louis IX in his great ordinance of 1254. Although the inquisitorial process only slowly began to compete successfully with traditional modes of trial, by the middle of the fourteenth century defendants had lost many of their traditional protections.

Neither the expansion of the demesne nor the crown's new concern with the peace of the realm were sufficient to explain the rapid growth of the king's judicial competence. More important was the confidence of litigants, whether on or beyond the demesne, that the king was a reliable source of justice. Louis VI and Louis VII had attracted to their courts a variety of people who sought their arbitration or support in contested suits. They turned to the king as they might have turned to any other great man in whom they felt confidence. There was not yet anything unique about the royal court. It became unique suddenly at the beginning of the thirteenth century, when, in 1202, Hugh le Brun, lord of Lusignan in Poitou, appealed to Philip II against his own lord, King John of England, who had married Hugh's fiancée, Isabelle of Angoulême, and refused to hear Hugh's objections or demands for compensation. Philip upheld Hugh's plea, summoned John to his court, and, when John failed to appear, judged him contumacious and therefore justly to be deprived of all his fiefs held of the French crown. Philip's action was not fortified by custom and caused considerable uneasiness for the next fifty years, but it was reinforced by new military power that in the end prevailed. On the basis of the successful appeal of 1202, and of the crowds of people who subsequently turned to them for what appeared more disinterested judgment than they could obtain locally, the kings of France slowly built up a court of appeal for the whole kingdom. By 1254 this operated as the Parlement of Paris.

Appeals to the king were initially permitted only on two grounds: where justice had been denied—that is, as in 1202, where a lord had refused to hear a case—or where the verdict of the court did not follow from the evidence that had been presented. Although each appeal was heard in Paris, it proceeded in accordance with the customary law of the place in which the case had originally been heard. Gradually, though, the Parlement took powers to criticize as unjust particular local customs. In other words, though it could not create anything like uniformity of legal custom across France, because communities were deeply attached to their traditional ways of sorting out disputes, it nevertheless acquired a competence to iron out at least some discrepancies. Consequently appellants who regarded the injustice as proceeding from the inadequacies or failures of local laws could now hope for redress.

While in the early thirteenth century kings as individuals intervened in appellate jurisdiction, by the second half of the century the Parlement of Paris, which functioned in the king's name but which he only occasionally attended, had taken over the day-to-day working of what became a popular recourse. Historians with foresight can see here the potential in the system for Parlement rather than king to emerge as the sovereign power in France, but that possibility would have seemed nonsensical even by 1337. King and Parlement functioned together as the two sides of a coin. The king acquired the reputation of dispenser of justice, the Parlement stood in his shadow. The central legal, and hence political, question of the thirteenth and early fourteenth centuries was whether the Parlement could hear appeals against the jurisdiction of the four surviving princes, in particular that of the duke of Gascony (to be discussed more extensively in Chapter 4). While the French king was calmly confident of his rights over the whole kingdom, the duke of Gascony regarded interference in his legal affairs as a deliberate attempt to stir up trouble within the duchy. Appeals from Gascons to the crown became *casus belli* in 1293, in 1324, and again in 1337.

In addition to being a law enforcer and hearer of appeals, the king of France became a legislator. Before 1200 he did nothing that can be considered strictly legislative. The closest to a law was Louis VII's peace of 1155, by which he ordered that all men refrain from attacking ecclesiastics, merchants, peasants, and their beasts, under threat of punishment. This, however, was a measure intended only to last for ten years, but in one important respect it paved the way for future legislation: Louis gathered a large assembly, including two archbishops, the duke of Burgundy, and the counts of Flanders, Troyes, and Nevers. After he proclaimed the peace for the royal demesne before this assembly, he urged all lords present to enforce a similar peace in their own areas. When Philip II and Louis IX issued proclamations, often about the treatment of the Jews because they were under special royal protection, they too brought great men together to hear them, in the hopes that they would implement the same measures in their own lands. But as the demesne grew to involve the great bulk of the kingdom, and as royal ordinances became commoner on all sorts of matters, these carefully choreographed assemblies became less necessary. By the time of Louis IX's great reforming ordinance of 1254, designed to wipe out injustice from the kingdom, the king proclaimed it in his own name for the whole realm. From this time on the legislative power of the crown was uncontested and frequently put into action.

These developments led to another, more ideological one: the emergence of a doctrine of sovereignty. Royal servants trained in Roman law, looking at what had been achieved, began to equate the king of France with the emperor of Justinian's codex. They started to argue that the king was emperor in his own realm, that he recognized no temporal superior; even that all property or rights within the kingdom were derived from him. Yet despite this apparently supreme position in all branches of law—a vital ingredient in the royal self-image—the king of France met with a number of practical obstacles in the exercise of his claimed authority. The vast variation in local legal custom obliged him to use his enforcing powers primarily through such locals as he could recruit into his service. Over the *enquêteurs* he sent down to the provinces to check on what was happening he had rather little control once they left the Paris region. More importantly, the dukes of Gascony and Burgundy, with the counts of Flanders and Brittany, had political theories which did not accord with those of the crown. Moreover, the nobility within the extensive royal demesne regarded the maintenance of local privilege as one of the most important tasks a king should perform. As Beaumanoir, the famous late thirteenth-century customary lawyer, said, 'The king is sovereign in his kingdom, but each baron is sovereign in his barony.' The increasingly strident claims made for the monarchy by Philip IV's servants were opposed at a number of levels. His weaker successors had to hide their iron hands in velvet gloves.

Royal servants and counsellors

With the increase in bureaucracy and the better collection and storage of records, historians can chart the influence on political life of at least some royal servants and advisers. Something has already been said of the group of men Philip Augustus collected around him, and of his reliance on Templars and Hospitallers both for military and for financial advice. The Templars were the usual keepers of the royal treasure from before the departure of Louis VII on crusade in 1146 until Philip IV transferred it to the Louvre between 1292 and 1295. Given this, it was unsurprising to find Philip II using Brother Haimard as receiver of royal revenues. The order's banking skills were available to those who drew up the royal accounts, though what use they made of them cannot be determined. Brother Guérin of the Hospitallers was initially an energetic fiscal agent of the crown, but after about 1200 rather little is betrayed in the records of the identities of the men who devoted themselves to the enhancement of the royal income. That there were such men is not in doubt; the surviving accounts for 1202/3 and 1221 demonstrate their existence. Their job was to gather from the *baillis* and *sénéchaux* the full amounts owed to the crown, and perhaps also to use their imaginations in interpreting custom in their royal master's favour, but their activities were performed reasonably anonymously through most of Philip Augustus's reign, that of Louis VIII, and that of Louis IX.

In the reign of Philip III things changed. For the first time a royal financial agent aroused the anger of the king's relatives in Paris. Pierre de la Brosse, who had been given in 1268 as a counsellor to the young prince by his father, Louis IX, was for a long time held in high respect. He owed his influence to his competence in matching the income to the expenditure of the royal household. But whether because he attempted to cause trouble between Philip and his wife, as the chronicler Guillaume de Nangis asserted, or because he started to behave as though he came from the high aristocracy, as was commonly thought, or because the financial measures he suggested to the king hit in their pockets those who mattered at court, he was hanged as a common thief in 1278, to the considerable astonishment and, in some quarters, dismay of the people of the city. Philip III's attempts to shield him were brushed aside. It was an ominous moment for those who sought to rise socially by royal service. The danger in wielding too much influence over the monarch was now evident.

The more famous trial and execution in 1315, after Philip IV's death, of his minister Enguerran de Marigny followed the same pattern. In this case it is clear from the surviving records that Marigny's widespread unpopularity, brought about by his fundraising for Philip IV's Flemish wars, was exploited by Charles of Valois, uncle of the new king Louis X. Charles and his supporters deeply resented the influence Marigny had wielded over Philip, and also blamed him for the truce he had made with Flanders in 1314, which they thought had enriched him while denying them the chance to inflict a serious defeat on the recalcitrant Flemings. Louis X's resistance to their demand for the death penalty for his father's most distinguished minister was quickly overborne. Again, the execution caused shock, though little pity, among the Parisians. The careers of de la Brosse and Marigny revealed strikingly two features of a new order: that financial acumen could bring with it very great political power; and that power could excite dangerous jealousy at court. The lesson was reinforced by the fate of Géraud Gayte, master of the Chambre des Comptes (the royal accounts office) under Philip V, who was imprisoned on the death of his master and died in gaol. Yet others avoided arousing jealousy. For example, Nicolas Béhuchet, a citizen of Le Mans who served both Charles of Valois and his son the future Philip VI as a financial agent, was ennobled when his master became king; in 1331 he became royal treasurer, and combined fiscal with military roles for the rest of his life. Although he too was hanged in the end, it was by the king's enemy Edward III, not by pressure of aristocratic opinion. Financial agents were fewer in number among royal servants than lawyers.

To some extent, of course, all French nobles understood and had some experience in enforcing the customary law of their own areas. A layman like Pierre Flote, whom Pope Boniface VIII regarded as Philip IV's evil genius, could also demonstrate some knowledge of Roman law in compiling the evidence against Saisset, bishop of Pamiers, in 1301, a case that stirred up the great Church–state conflict already referred to. But from the reign of Louis VII onwards, clerks trained at the universities (particularly Orléans, but also Montpellier) in canon or Roman law began to find their place in the royal household. The most famous of these in the first half of our period was Gui Fulcois, the future pope Clement IV. Fulcois, renowned for his understanding of Roman law, had been an adviser both to Alphonse of Poitiers and to his brother Louis IX before, as a widower, he took orders and rose rapidly in papal service. His lay career provided a pattern for many others. As the Parlement of Paris grew in importance, so the number of royal counsellors trained in the law increased rapidly. Among those associated with policy-making in the reign of Philip IV were the distinguished law professor Pierre de Belleperche, and the two southerners Guillaume de Nogaret and Guillaume de Plaisians, who between them encouraged the king in pursuing many of the controversial policies of his reign, and took the front line in explaining them to a wider public. While their function as royal advocates did make them widely known, at least in Paris, they did not arouse the popular antipathy experienced by financial agents. Philip's successors continued his policy of employing lawyers in considerable numbers. They could hardly afford not to, given that the monarchy was envisaged first and foremost as the living embodiment of the law.

Weighing up just what such servants contributed to policy formation and what was left to the monarch is difficult. There has been a lengthy dispute as to whether Philip IV was in the driving seat during his reign, or whether he left the hard work to his ministers and concentrated on his family and aristocratic pursuits. On balance, it seems more likely that Philip controlled the broad outlines of policy while expecting his ministers to find the best ways of implementing his desires. But men of the calibre of Flote, Nogaret, or Marigny, serving an ambitious but rather lazy king, were almost bound to nudge policy along a path congenial to them while theoretically only carrying out orders. So historians will never know how far Nogaret's actions at Anagni in September 1303, when he joined up with Sciarra Colonna in an attack on Boniface VIII, were in accordance with Philip's desires, let alone his instructions. As was so frequently the case in the medieval world, Philip's servants had to act on their own initiative when faced with unexpected circumstances in places too remote for rapid reference back to their master.

Whatever the influence from below, it would be wrong to think of any medieval king as making policy without taking advice from what he regarded as the correct quarters: the members of the royal family, some bishops, and from the later thirteenth century onward, his confessors. Because close relatives and confessors had regular access to the king's ear and could relay their opinions informally without leaving any record, their influence is often minimized. Yet the military advice of his brother Robert of Artois was probably important in Louis IX's planning for his first crusade, as were the ambitions of Charles of Valois to Philip IV's view of international relations. The Capetians always enjoyed a reputation for good internal family relationships; if they had ignored the views of those closest to them, it is unlikely that harmony could have been maintained. Equally, though the content of confessors' advice was always secret, on questions relating to the Church its impact will have been great.

By contrast, from the reign of Louis VII onward, French kings were remarkably cut off from the opinions and views of those of the greater aristocrats, whether princes, counts, or lords, to whom they were not closely related. In this respect they were very different from the kings of Aragon, Castile, or England. In general, the French aristocrats' interests were concentrated in the locality from which they derived their titles. While many in the thirteenth century spent some time every year in Paris, this did not give them the entrée into the royal palaces. The age-old obligation to provide suit of court had died in the course of the twelfth century. Professional lawyers now represented great men in the royal courts. No channel yet existed for regular consultation between king and lords. Fighting in the king's army might create a personal bond, as might accompanying him on crusade, but such bonds were purely temporary. The absence of contact with the monarch was paralleled by a similar lack of cohesion between nobles of different areas. Consequently, discontent among lords usually took the form of a local rebellion, for example that of the duke of Brittany against the regency government of Blanche of Castile. It required unprecedented anger to bring about the Leagues of 1314–15, when the nobles of Champagne, Burgundy, and the north-east, driven to fury by Philip IV's unwillingness to cancel the war tax he had started to collect before he made peace with the Flemings, on top of his other exactions, banded together in leagues to demand reform. Their idea of reform was principally less royal interference in the localities, more deference to the local privileges built up over the centuries. Philip IV's successors, enjoying a weaker position than he, could not be deaf to the cries of opposition that came from the provinces. However, the rapid disintegration of the Leagues demonstrated that such confederations went against the grain of normal peacetime politics in France.

The principal overt aim of all the Leaguers was to insist that the king's servants comport themselves in accordance with what the Leaguers believed to have been the good customs of St Louis's reign. It was perhaps natural that aristocrats should have railed against the lesser men who served the crown and acquired both standing and fortune thereby. While contemptuous of the skills that brought the royal servants their jobs, and certainly not willing to take over administration themselves, lords resented the power and regular access to the king that a minority enjoyed. To conservative aristocratic eyes, the royal dependence on clerks and lawyers represented a sad decline from the standards of the past, which they probably reconstructed with the help of *chansons de geste*, and therefore imagined as characterized by the shared companionship in arms of the king and his lords.

Royal servants carried out the king's orders; the most prominent of them were also his advisers. Whereas, in the thirteenth century, the king's counsellors were simply the men he chose to consult on specific issues, by the fourteenth century a royal council was beginning to appear. This very amorphous body acquired a rather firmer shape under Philip IV's successors, especially after the death of Louis X. In the absence of primogenital heirs to the throne (for the first time since 987), Philip V, Charles IV, and Philip VI relied for their successions on the support of various members of the royal family and high aristocracy, who continued to be influential when their candidate had been elevated to the throne. In Philip V's case his coronation was preceded by a period of regency, when he ruled with an appointed council; in the early years of his reign the same men surrounded him. Philip VI's accession (also preceded by a regency) was more controversial, and so his obligation to his supporters lasted longer. But along with those who could not be ignored, the king was free to nominate others, either from among his predecessors' counsellors or from his own household, to the circle of his advisers. Therefore, while the circumstances of 1316–17 or 1328–9 might suggest that the king could be pressured into actions of their choice by his counsellors, fairly rapidly it became clear that the council was the king's agent rather than being his bridle.

Ideology

As has been pointed out in the Introduction, the Capetian family had always burnished their reputation as committed defenders of the Church and, in secular affairs, of the common good. The earliest major opportunity a king had for image-making was at his coronation. Although the rites were in the hands of an ecclesiastic, almost always the archbishop of Reims, there was room for choreography from laymen. Where the succession was disputed—from 1316 onwards—the coronation ceremony could be constitutive. This explains why Philip V in 1316 rushed to have himself crowned on the death of the baby John I, not leaving time for an inquiry into the rights of John's older sister Jeanne, the daughter of the allegedly adulterous Margaret of Burgundy and Louis X. But this was unusual; neither Charles IV nor Philip VI was under similar pressure. As for the earlier kings of this period, they were so secure in their rights that Philip II could afford to abandon the previous custom of his family by postponing the coronation of his heir until after his death. His successors followed his example without qualms. They, like their subjects, regarded the Capetian family's ability always to produce a direct male heir as proof of God's special blessing. They were not prepared for the shock of 1316 (when the dead king's brother succeeded) or 1328 (when the dead king's cousin succeeded).

In the course of the thirteenth century the coronation ceremony acquired distinctively French characteristics. At the beginning of our period each king had a heavy crown specially crafted for the occasion, which he later deposited in the abbey of Saint-Denis. However, at some point in the later thirteenth century this custom must have ceased, to be replaced by the king choosing to wear an older crown from the abbey treasury, sometimes perhaps the so-called Crown of Charlemagne (which was certainly used in many subsequent coronations). Philip III, who was regarded by the monks of Saint-Denis as responsible for the remaking of the Crown of Charlemagne, was also the first known king to claim that the sword carried before him at Reims was *joyeuse*, the sword of Charlemagne. The *ordo* used for his coronation created a specific link with the first Merovingian king, Clovis, in that it highlighted the use of what was believed to be the holy ampulla; thus it reminded the watching crowd of the story (first told by the eleventh-century monk of Fleury Aimon) that Clovis had been anointed with oil brought down from heaven by a dove. Then there were the more obviously religious elements in the ceremony: from 1223 onwards the French king was hailed as Rex Christianissimus, and he, like his predecessors, heard the Laudes sung, with the famous refrain 'Christus vincit, Christus regnat, Christus imperat', which symbolized the union of the king on earth with his heavenly counterpart. On a more mundane level each king received both the assent of his people to his elevation and the homage of his lords on the occasion. The whole ceremony was crafted to emphasize the unbridgeable gulf between the king and the other inhabitants, no matter how elevated, of his realm.

Once enthroned, the king was essentially the distributor of justice to all, including the weak, the needy, and the poor. Supported by stories from the Old Testament, especially those relating to the judgment of Solomon, and increasingly also by maxims from Roman law, he was called on to arbitrate, to give judgment according to law, and also to dispense equity where a literal following of the law would lead to injustice. His function was to create peace and harmony throughout the realm. To attain this end, his discretion was unfettered, but, beyond this, he had a higher duty: to assist the Churchmen of his realm in bringing the people to God, by setting an example of personal devotion, by liberal endowment of the Church, and by punishing those who stood in the way of truth and purity. While other rulers also had these duties, the king of France revelled in the public performance of them and in patronizing works of art that showed either him or his models, the Old Testament monarchs, engaged in these tasks.

Louis IX's canonization in 1297 gave new sharpness of focus to what had been a fairly conventional, if deeply held, set of monarchical aspirations. His successors saw themselves as the descendants of one who had given everything, including his life, to the cause of the crusade, of a man whose love of justice was proverbial throughout Europe, of a king who had taken responsibility for the elimination of Catharism from the Languedoc, who had reformed royal coinage and royal administration, and who had showed generosity in order to achieve lasting peace with his neighbours. To imitate his grandfather was Philip IV's declared aim, especially in the last eight years of his life. Yet Louis's memory was also appropriated by Philip's critics. The barons who formed the Leagues of 1314–15 pointed to Louis's fiscal probity and converted him into a preserver of local privileges. By distancing Philip from his grandfather, the Leaguers issued a warning to Philip's sons Louis X, Philip V, and Charles IV. These kings strove to derive what benefit they could from the blood of the saint that ran in their bodies, without proclaiming their inheritance so ostentatiously as to provide ammunition for those who deplored what they saw as the moral decline of their own days.

St Louis famously touched those suffering from scrofula to heal them. In the thirteenth century a miraculous power that had earlier been exercised by certain holy kings came to be interpreted as a sign of regality rather than of outstanding personal merit. When taken as proof of the sanctity automatically conferred on a legitimate king by his anointing, it became a powerful weapon in the hands of apologists of monarchical power. Inevitably Philip IV passionately imitated his grandfather in this respect as in all others, publicizing his activities so effectively that people came even from Italy to benefit. The last Capetians were obliged to follow suit, lest their failure to touch be construed as a sign that they were not true kings. In the same mode of imitation they were obliged to plan crusades, although events always conspired to prevent them from actually undertaking them.

The evidence for what the Capetians wanted people to believe about their monarchy is relatively abundant and coherent. The question of how far these ideas were absorbed, particularly outside Paris, is much less straightforward. While French intellectuals—unlike their English contemporaries—held back from criticism, the burdens imposed by royal policies might lead the resentful to question the royal 'religion', as Bernard Saisset notoriously did in 1301. When discontent was palpable, as it was at the end of Philip IV's reign, or when a king's right to succeed was disputed, murmurings of dissent could be heard. On the other hand, when Edward III finally decided to dispute Philip VI's claim to the throne of France in 1340, it was as the true heir of St Louis that he presented himself to the French people. He clearly thought it was a winning formula.

Conclusion

French royal achievements between 1200 and 1336 were astounding in scope and variety. By comparison with its neighbours, the French kingdom had grown and prospered to a high degree. It enjoyed a sense of identity, and its monarch had a clear role in the welfare of the population as a whole. Yet the late thirteenth and early fourteenth centuries had not been as happy as the first two-thirds of the thirteenth. Economically, circumstances were less propitious in 1337 than they had been in 1270 (see the next chapter). Politically, there were signs of strain within the body politic; in particular, neither Flanders nor Gascony fitted easily into the framework conceived for them in Paris. At moments of crisis clear fault lines in the unity of the kingdom had emerged. Furthermore, its inhabitants had learned how to put up opposition to demands for taxation that they regarded as unfair. None of these problems were in themselves serious. All could probably have been overcome with care and patience. A sustained period of peace was the first essential. Unfortunately, in 1337 Philip VI decided to wage war on the duke of Gascony, Edward III, king of England. Under the pressure of prolonged and initially unsuccessful war, the problems quickly multiplied.

2

The economy and society of France in the later Middle Ages: on the eve of crisis

Pierre Charbonnier

The fourteenth and fifteenth centuries are dominated by the caesura of a great economic crisis, but, since the period is so long and complex, it is useful to examine it in two parts: first, the state of France and the prevailing economic structures on the eve of the crisis, some of which remained constant over the two centuries. The crisis itself and its impact on French society will be examined in Chapter 5.

General principles

Profit was not the only economic motive in the late Middle Ages. There was also a place for Christian teachings, for instance the

This text was written directly in English with the help of Mrs Suzy Masseret, English teacher in Clermont-Ferrand, and revised by David Potter.

obligation of charitable giving and the theoretical prohibition on usury. The social order and its equilibrium were thought to be of divine origin and thus sacrosanct. However, at the same time there was a growth of secularism; for example, time came eventually to be measured by municipal clocks rather than the ringing of Church bells. Interest was in effect permitted since its rate was actually fixed in 1336 at 21.66 per cent per annum. Of course, in reality it was often higher than this, the duke of Burgundy borrowing money at rates which ranged between 17.1 and 37.5 per cent. In fact there were many ways of sidestepping the laws of both Church and state by, for instance, including interest in the principal owed or the sophistry, common among businessmen, of using bills of exchange in which the rates of exchange were faked.

The aristocracy in particular indulged in profitless conspicuous consumption. Great nobles and Church dignitaries were naturally surrounded by a plethora of servants and indulged in excessive expenditure on silk and cloth of gold, furs, and jewels. In turn, rich men of low birth came to emulate them, while the monarchy, fearing a loss of tax revenues as a consequence of diverting income into other channels, as well as economic dislocation and social disorder, enacted sumptuary laws. These decreed that bourgeois should wear neither squirrel fur nor ermine, and forbade them to buy wax torches or allow their wives to ride in coaches. As for the nobles, dukes were not supposed to have more than four gowns made a year. Not surprisingly, these laws were seldom obeyed.

Such defiance of law was general. The role of kings and princes in regulating economic life was thus small and consisted only of enacting ineffective laws, such as Jean II's act after the outbreak of the Black Death (see Chapter 5, 'The Plague'). In addition, royal intervention could be positively harmful, as in the incessant changes made to the value of the coinage and growing taxation. There was no concept of state investment in infrastructure or enterprise and little provision against general shortages of staples such as grain. Only in the reign of Louis XI did the crown begin to embark on effective economic policies.

However, lack of state intervention did not mean that enterprise was completely free. In agriculture there were many collective constraints. In towns monopolies were common and inhabitants enjoyed privileges in comparison with foreign merchants, such as the exemption from the *leyde* (a tax on market transactions) and the right to claim part of market deals concluded by foreigners (such the right to buy 5 out of 10 quintals of corn bought by the latter).

As for society in general, since the state was relatively inactive, people tended to protect themselves in collective groups. The fights and disputes described in letters of remission[1] often involved two groups and not individuals. These groups might be of several origins: extended family, trade, place, village against village, and pursuit of girls, in which the so-called *compagnons*, who aimed to control sexual activity in their communities, were involved. Another kind of group was the confraternities which were multiplying at that time. Besides their devotion to their patron saints, they were involved in merry-making as well as caring for sick members of the group. When a member was prevented by sickness from working, the others would contribute money to offset loss of wages.

Attitudes to economic life included fear of scarcity even before the great economic crises of the late Middle Ages. As a result, material possessions were often preferred to specie as a hedge of security, and customs bore down on exports, which were sometimes thought to be impoverishing the realm. By the same token, in a world in which transport was difficult and expensive, every well-to-do man sought to live off his own produce. Peasants, in order to get at least one good crop out of two, sowed wheat and rye in the same field. In this way they hoped that at least they would produce enough for their staple, bread.

Consumption

Consumption, a subject often neglected by historians, will be discussed here first because it often governs production and trade. Except for the highest aristocracy, food was by far the most important form of expenditure. There are two main aspects of this. First, most food was self-produced. The only goods bought were expensive items such as spices, salt (mostly to preserve meat), sea fish, and wine in those areas that could not produce it. Secondly, food consumption

[1] A *lettre de rémission* was a pardon given by the king, usually to men accused of mainly violent crimes. The interest of *lettres de rémission* lies in their minute description of events and attitudes. Such details are frequently drawn on below to illustrate points.

varied widely both socially and regionally. In Auvergne the seigneur of Murol ate lamb and gave his vine-growers goat's meat to eat. Butter was used for cooking in upland regions, while in the northern plains nut oil was preferred and in the southern ones olive oil.

Bread was the staple food, 1 kilo a day being the norm. Other foods were thus referred to as *companage* ('what goes with bread'). Bread could be baked from wheat or rye or by a mixture of the two called *méteil*, as well as from barley and oats, depending on the consumer's rank and region. It was less expensive than wine, of which 2 litres of probably very light wine was the normal daily consumption. Meat was not the preserve of the well-to-do. A letter of remission mentions a humble traveller lodging with peasants on a weekday evening being given some bread and a piece of pork for his meal (the case emerged from a fight the following morning when he realized that his hosts had stolen his dog). Pork is often thought by historians to be the meat of the poor, but it also crops up in accounts of aristocrats. The main meats were beef, mutton, pork, and poultry. Game, on the other hand, was scarce.

A serious problem for diet was the numerous meatless days: every Friday and Saturday, Lent, and the eve of feast days, in all 150 days a year. During Lent even eggs and cheese were prohibited and fish remained the only permitted meat. So in inland regions fishponds were established wherever possible and both salted and smoked fish were eaten. However, pound for pound, fish was three times as expensive as other meats, and the seigneur of Murol's workers had, during Lent, to be content with peas (with their high-protein content) instead of fish.

The second most important expense was clothes. These displayed social rank. We learn from the sumptuary laws that dukes could have several gowns a year but a poor man's clothes were worn by several generations. Colour was a greater indicator of status than cloth, though of course silk and cotton were expensive. Bright colours such as red were more expensive than dull ones.

Agriculture

Agriculture was the key sector of the economy, with about nine men out of ten involved in it. As everyone wanted to eat their own produce, mixed farming was nearly universal except in the high mountains, where only grazing is possible. In rare cases, a single product intended for the market, such as wine in the Bordelais, was given preference, though in the context of polyculture. Indeed land cultivated for wine brought in four times as much money as corn, but peasants gave priority to bread and therefore grain production.

In view of the dietary preponderance of bread, ploughed land represented 80 to 90 per cent of cultivated soils. Meadows were scarce, and though they were set aside for hay for winter feeding, they provided insufficient nourishment, and sometimes cattle were so weak by early spring that they could not stand by themselves and needed help to get upright! During the summer animals had other fodder from harvested or uncultivated fields and woodlands.

Cultivation was so extensive that Philip VI was worried by a possible scarcity of wood, and enacted laws forbidding clearance and limiting the rights of peasants in woodland. Corn yields were not insignificant compared to those of 1950, i.e. before the introduction of chemical fertilizers. In 1950 the average was 16 quintals per hectare. This figure was reached at the beginning of the fourteenth century in the good alluvial soils of Artois, while the general yield was 10–12 quintals per hectare. So in a normal year corn was sufficient to provide bread for the whole population, but climatic disturbance, as in the excessive rains in 1316, brought starvation.

As animal manure was in short supply, some fields had to be left fallow. There were four regional fallow systems. Exceptionally, in Flanders the cultivation of leguminous plants for cattle and to improve the soil made it unnecessary to leave land to lie fallow. In the great northern plains fields were left unsown one year out of three: one year wheat, one year oats or barley, and one fallow. In the southern regions, with less fertile soils, corn, often rye, and fallow went in rotation. Finally, in the poorest regions and especially in the west the village lands were divided so that some was well manured and cultivated every year and the rest only cultivated from time to time. The quantity and use of animals were not the same as nowadays. Pack animals were numerous, and cattle were bred for labour rather than for milk or meat.

Wine-growing was very important. Vineyards were to be found much further north than today. Thus, Gilles li Muisit of Tournai (now in Belgium) wrote that in 1316, a very rainy year that was very bad for wine, he had to drink vinegary local wine because he was short of the good southern wines which he used to enjoy.

Even where woodlands belonged to lords, they were a rich resource for the community, whose traditional rights safeguarded access to berries, pasture for their animals, especially acorns for pigs, and, naturally, wood. They could take *bois mort* (dry wood), *mort bois* (scrub of little value such as elder), and even timber, but only for their own use. In fact there were many infringements and prevention of this was attempted by setting aside a share of woodlands for the rights of each village.

Social organization was very different from that in England. In France the basic structure was of little farms managed by tenants who were practically proprietors so long as they paid rent to their lords; they might hand their lands over to their heirs, alienate them, and even choose not cultivate them. Exceptionally, in the west farms were leased for a term, paying either a fixed sum as *fermage*, or a part of the crops as *metayage*. Demesnes directly managed had become uncommon. Those owned by lay lords were reduced to meadows and vineyards, for the lords' corn was supplied by rents. The ecclesiastical demesnes were increasingly hired out to rich peasants such as those of the abbey of Saint-Denis, or broken up to make a new settlement such as a *bastide* in Aquitaine. One innovation was the demesne created by a bourgeois with lands bought from tenants. Three men had interest in these lands: the lord, the bourgeois, and the peasant who cultivated the demesne. This was possible because rents were moderate.

Other economic activity

Development was limited by shortage of resources. Credit was expensive, as was transport, particularly by land. Water carriage was less onerous, but rivers were burdened with tolls, and the sea was dangerous because of storms and piracy. A barrel of wine worth 200 *sols* cost 120 *sols* to transport from Bordeaux to Bayonne (150 kilometres) by land, 80 to 100 *sols* to Toulouse (200 kilometres) by navigating up the Garonne, and only 20 *sols* to England by sea (about 2,000 kilometres), although then it might not arrive at all! Numerous watermills on rivers, brooks, or pond effluents provided energy for various forms of equipment but always light ones.

Industrial and commercial business was rarely large-scale, but more often on a craft scale. The craftsman made items and sold them himself. For elaborate articles such as cloth several craftsmen passed on a more and more finished product from one to another up to the finished piece. At the beginning of the thirteenth century craftsmen worked freely, but regulations were soon to be set down such as those drawn up for Paris by the *prévôt* Étienne Boileau in 1268 in the *Livre des métiers*. The *métiers* aimed to guarantee quality for customers and prevent fierce competition between craftsmen, but they also blocked any development. For example, some makers of breeches wanting to provide breeches with laces to be tied to the belt had to beg the king to allow what was against the regulation. The crown kept a close eye on craft organizations because of fears that they might become involved in riots.

Large-scale industry may be discussed in two different forms. The first was when many clothmakers worked together in the same place, provided with wool by capitalists, who managed the trade of the finished cloth. The centre for such industry was Flanders, though this was to be increasingly detached from the French kingdom. The second were enterprises using complex technology: mines, metallurgy, and glassworks may be included in such industries, but their production was minuscule compared to present figures, being valued at a few hundred kilos instead of some million tons.

Because of the great predominance of self-sufficiency and transport difficulties, large-scale trade was limited. However, it is convenient to take regional differences into account. Provinces such as Normandy, Île-de-France, the Bordelais, and Languedoc were more open to trade and money than others. But everywhere objects of trade had to have a high value (e.g. a pound of pepper was as expensive as a quintal of wheat) or be produced in a very few places (e.g. salt) or not be produced in a particular area (e.g. wine in the mountains). Notably, corn was not traded on a large scale in normal years, but if the crop was insufficient, corn was marketed in speculative ways, corn-owners holding onto it, waiting for higher prices, thus increasing the starvation of the poor. Among the main commercial flows some were national, such as those for wine or salt, and others international, such as the export of wine from Bordeaux to England, which was at a high level as it is today. Oriental products, spices, and valuable fabrics were imported through the Mediterranean, and an exchange of salt and wine for northern products, furs, and salted or smoked fish took place through the Atlantic ports between Nantes and La Rochelle. Finally, the textile industry involved trade in English wool to Flanders, and Flemish cloths exported everywhere, but especially to Italy to be refined.

The most famous trading centres of the thirteenth century were the fairs of Champagne, where Flemish cloths and Mediterranean trade products crossed. But they were declining at the beginning of the fourteenth century, and this made an impression on contemporaries. An Italian trader petitioning Philip VI claimed, for the king's profit, to be able to set up these fairs again. In fact it is unlikely that he would have been able to do so since the decline was due to the fact that Italian ships were now venturing to pass through the Straits of Gibraltar. However, fairs and markets still took a prominent part in trade by spreading foreign goods around and collecting local ones.

The more important flows of goods were under the control of those now called 'merchants', nearly all Italians. They had very large capital resources and agents in many places so they traded in all goods and banking, particularly lending large amounts of money to the king and to princes. They might get large returns, but they were under the threat of confiscation, which set the debt aside.

Population

During the whole of the thirteenth century the economic trend was one of growth, and so was the demographic trend. On the density of the population, historians have at their disposal an exceptional source: a general survey of population known as the *État des paroisses et des feux* of 1328. This document gives the figures of parishes and hearths for each *bailliage*, but it poses serious problems of interpretation, notably about which *pays* and people are included in it. The best interpretation of it is by Ferdinand Lot, who concluded that the population in the area surveyed was just over 16 million and within the present boundaries of France 21.5 million, with a density of 7.7 hearths per square kilometre and 5 people per hearth in the countryside and 4 in the towns. These figures seem high compared to the 26.5 million for the rural population in 1846 (France in 1328 was essentially rural), more especially as there might have been a decrease owing to the starvation of 1316, so some historians are critical of Lot's interpretation. However, local surveys confirm it. For example, in Dauphiné in 1339 there were 6 hearths per square kilometre, excluding towns, and it is a very mountainous region.

France in 1328 was about 85 per cent rural, and few towns had over 10,000 inhabitants. The population of Paris has given rise to controversy. In the *État* it is given as 61,000 hearths, which corresponds to more than 200,000 inhabitants, a huge figure compared to about 50,000 in London. So, some suggest that 61 is a scribal error for 21 (LXI against XXI). Paris, though, was truly exceptional. Rural densities were not all similar. Near Paris the density of the rich plains of Valois was 19 hearths per square kilometre, whereas that of the poor Hurepoix did not reach 9.

This heavy population corresponded to a high birth and death rate without any noticeable demographic crisis during the thirteenth century. As births exceeded deaths only a little, the population was growing slowly. Indeed the birth rate did not reach its possible maximum because there was some contraception, as is clear from the aftermath of the plague, when a smaller population produced more births than before the epidemic.

According to lists of tenants, the nuclear family (husband, wife, and their young children) was preponderant at the beginning of the fourteenth century; extended families with several married couples would multiply after the crisis. A feature of marriages was the difference in age between husband and wife. Women got married very young, often before 20. In a letter of remission of 1469 a 24-year-old woman accused of infanticide had a grudge against her parents, who had not married her off at the due time, so causing her to fall into sin. On the other hand, men had to wait to be able to earn a family's living. Frequently they married when over 30. This difference gave rise to sexually tense situations which will be discussed below in the context of social disorder.

Social classification

It is difficult to say whether French people were classed according to honour or according to wealth. The old ideology of the three orders had not fully vanished and Froissart adapted it to the prologue of his *Chroniques*: valiant men perform heroic deeds, people talk about them, and clerks write down the story. The meetings of the Three Estates at first sight seem to confirm this ideology, but actually in these assemblies the Third Estate consisted only of townsmen, the lords being presumed to represent their peasants. Thus, many authors drew a more complicated picture of their society by subdividing groups; examples of this are G. Du Bus, in his discussion of the principal vices of each group in the *Roman de Fauvel*, and Philippe de Mézières, in the *Songe du vieil pelerin*, ended up with twelve groups by dividing four categories of dignity, Church, nobility, bourgeoisie, and people, into three levels of wealth. Eustache Deschamps used the same number of categories in his *Lay des douze estats du monde*, though in a less rational way.

The Church was not at the height of its moral standing at the beginning of the fourteenth century. However, its members were numerous, including students, the staff of almshouses and hospitals for the poor, as well as many simply tonsured men who had not been ordained, enjoying tax exemptions and judicial privilege such as not to be tried by lay courts. Its wealth remained great although it was declining, but this wealth was actually damaging because posts in the Church were sought for their incomes and not for a religious calling. Power of appointment to the highest Church dignities belonged both to the king and to the Pope, now established in Avignon, so the French Church was deprived of any freedom. The parish clergy had a reputation for ignorance and, as its members were forbidden to marry, many of them lived with a concubine. Old monastic orders decayed slowly by lack of calling and decline of endowments. On the whole, the mendicant friars constituted the only sound and active part of the Church. Unfortunately, the great debate on the vow of poverty set some Franciscans against the papacy, which wanted the friars to agree to hold property. To deal with such disorders, many inside and outside the Church demanded reforms, but the Council of

Vienne in 1312 was satisfied with suppressing the order of the Templars.

The nobility will be studied in Chapter 8. Here it will only be considered in relation to an aspect closely linked to it, i.e. the seigneury, for a nobleman was usually a lord. In some regions such as Normandy and Languedoc rents went down because they had been fixed principally in terms of money. Elsewhere, such as in Auvergne, they stayed buoyant because the proportion of payments in kind was higher. It was the same for regions in which farms were held on short-term leases. So in terms of the strength of the seigneury, there are two Frances to be distinguished:[2] in one, seigneury no longer played an important part; in the other, it remained the main framework of rural society.

Tenants in money-rent regions were somewhat less burdened, but everywhere peasants suffered from lack of land because they were too numerous; the *campagnes* were overcrowded. There were two main cases: in the rich plains there was a sharp contrast between a few rich landowners and the mass of peasants running tiny farms and even some landless peasants working others' land, while in other regions, such as in the mountains of Auvergne, all lived in the same state of low to middling wealth.

Thus, many peasants had to borrow, particularly to tide over the lack of corn in spring, when the price of corn was high. Then, after harvest, to offset their debt, they had to sell corn, but at a low price since by now there was plenty. In this way their difficulties grew, and finally they had to sell cattle or a field. Often they kept the sold animal, but as *cheptel* (livestock) in a half-issue lease. This agreement was widely used, even for oxen which were without issue, but where their traction strength was taken into account and paid by the farmer.

Peasants could also be divided, in terms of status, into freemen and serfs. Serfs were not necessarily poorer. On the contrary, some happened to be the wealthiest in their village because they were descended from the lord's land agents. The distinction between freemen and serfs was made on the basis of payment of taxes such as the *taille à volonté*, i.e. at the sole discretion of the lord. But the lower

[2] Most historians have applied the first scheme to the whole France, laying stress on the crisis of the seigneury. Thus I entitled my study devoted to Auvergne *Une autre France: la seigneurie rurale en Basse Auverge du XIVe au XVIe siècle* (Clermont-Ferrand, 1980). In fact Auvergne is not the only region in the second scheme.

status was gradually disappearing, for many lords sold freedom to their serfs, as did Louis X on his own manors.

In most towns there were no serfs because they had a charter giving freedom and other advantages to inhabitants. Indeed, the thirteenth century had been a good time for towns, which were then generally self-governing. But the crown tried to insert its authority and to raise taxes from the so-called *bonnes villes* ('good towns', called good because they gave so much!).

The population in towns was stratified by wealth and also by access to the town government. At the bottom the unskilled labourers had a wretched existence, earning less than 1 *sol* a day and sometimes being without work. Above them, craftsmen were divided into three groups. The masters owned an *ouvroir* (workshop) for making and selling. They employed both apprentices, who often remained for a long time, and *valets*, i.e. men who after apprenticeship did not become masters for lack of fortune. Many employees dwelt in the master's house and gathered round him, especially in the scuffles recounted in the letters of remission. Indeed, craftsmen frequently clashed over precedence, for example for their position in processions during the numerous feasts celebrated during the rhythms of town life.

At the top of urban society a group of merchants and people who lived off their properties, rents, and the kind of lending described above seized on the city government through co-optation, for example existing magistrates would choose new ones, thus creating a self-selecting oligarchy. They profited by their power to set very low taxes for themselves and to spend town revenues on sumptuous goods which they enjoyed. The men of law tried to enter this group; they were proliferating, especially the notaries who, in southern France, were responsible for drawing up authentic title deeds.

Christian foreigners were not of equal status to Frenchmen. For instance, they could not hand their property down to their descendants since the king had the power to take it into his own hands. Among them the Italians were the most numerous and also the most affluent.

It remains to deal with those excluded from society. Among these were the Jews, who were formally ejected from the kingdom in 1306 and again in 1322. After this date the only important Jewish community in France lived in Provence and in the papal states such as Avignon, outside the French kingdom. Lepers, who had been confined to special hospitals, were becoming less common as a result of the decline of the disease. On the other hand, beggars were numerous, relying on the duty of Christian charity. Finally, some lived outside the law on robbery or tolerated by the law, such as the prostitutes, who were accepted, as will be explained below.

Public disorder

Public disturbance will be described in terms of the damage it caused, from the individual level to the national. Some disturbances were linked to social–sexual problems since, as already noted, bachelors married late. While unmarried, they not unnaturally aimed to have sex with women as often as possible. They could go to prostitutes in an *étuve* (a bathhouse where beds were more numerous than baths!); such businesses were tolerated in order to avoid violence, which nevertheless occurred. Rapes were not infrequent, especially those perpetrated by groups. Indeed young men who had no women of their own, called *compagnons*, formed groups to control sexual activity in their locality, especially of the women who were thought to be 'common' or 'public', that is those who indulged in sexual intercourse. In a letter of remission of 1475 a young noble dwelling in Champeix (Puy-de-Dôme) had sold such a woman, his former concubine, to the *curé* of a neighbouring village. But when the *curé* came to take her away, the *compagnons* of Champeix gathered to oppose it and there was a battle, in the course of which the *curé* was killed.

Another source of disorder was debt, and town charters contained many articles relating to it. For example, there were complex arrangements allowing creditors to be repaid without pressing debtors hard. Thus the creditors might distrain upon their debtors, but at least the latter did not have the clothes taken off their backs in the street. In the towns, especially in the north but also in the south, where charters had been obtained for a long period, riots broke out at the beginning of the fourteenth century when people who were excluded from power rebelled against the abuses discussed above. Rioters gained little from all this, but above all it was the king, in arrogating to himself decisions on the outcome of conflicts, who in effect increased his dominance of urban government.

However, although at the beginning of the fourteenth century major heresies had been rooted out, the most serious disorder was ostensibly caused by religion. Indeed it came from Christians themselves. In 1320 some, who felt indignant at the failure to mount the crusade proclaimed by the king after the fall of the last Christian stronghold in Palestine in 1291, decided to carry it out themselves and made their way on foot to the Mediterranean ports. These were called the *pastoureaux* because some of them were shepherds, and the movement achieved great success among poor people. The *prévôt* of Paris took some of them prisoner, but others freed them by force, injuring the *prévôt*, and after that the king dared not act against them. Along their way they assaulted the Jews, especially in Languedoc, where the seneschal fought against them. Strangely, the movement suddenly evaporated, to the astonishment of the chroniclers, without doing anything against the Muslims, since only a very few actually went overseas. The movement had other consequences, though, for it was rumoured that the Jews aimed to wreak vengeance on Christians with the help of lepers, who were to throw poison given by the Jews into wells. Consequently, in 1322 the king decided on the expulsion of the Jews, and many lepers were slaughtered.

3

The crown and the provinces in the fourteenth century

Michael Jones

Although the huge realm over which the later Capetians and early Valois kings ruled had fairly stable external borders—essentially those demarcated as long ago as the treaty of Verdun (843)—internally it was fragmented into a myriad of smaller political units (duchies, counties, viscounties, baronies, lordships). Some (Auvergne and Burgundy, for instance) had histories as long as the crown of France itself. Most can be traced back to administrative arrangements made in the Carolingian or immediately post-Carolingian periods. Certainly by the fourteenth century virtually all had long existed within the general feudal structure of Capetian France. They had formed their own particular legal or institutional ties with the monarchy, whether as simple fiefs or as part of much larger complexes, whose rulers equally owed homage and fealty to the king. *Pays* rather than 'province' (a word only coined in the fifteenth century in the sense used in this chapter) was how contemporaries most frequently described them, though *pays* itself could cover a very broad range from the merely parochial (like the pays de Coglès or pays de Guérande in Brittany) to vast areas that embraced half the kingdom (Languedoil, Languedoc); even today in modern France it defies easy definition but is still invested with huge sentimental as well as historical significance.

Here the main concern is with those *pays* or provinces that enjoyed a political identity at the national level during the fourteenth century. In a word, these are *pays* or fiefs that were either major constituents of the royal demesne, royal apanages, or principalities ruled by dynasties, who acknowledged (sometimes reluctantly) the crown's ultimate sovereignty. These were the pieces moved around on the chequerboard that constituted early Valois France by the accidents of succession, marriage settlements, or treaties. The treaty of Brétigny in 1360, for example, transferred whole provinces amounting to a third of the kingdom to Edward III of England. In this period most were developing a greater awareness of their own identity as well as creating specific institutions; defence of their privileges was a notable feature of the fourteenth century. The grant of royal charters to many provinces in 1315–17, chief among them Burgundy, Champagne, Languedoc, and Normandy, was early recognition of this. Once these were issued, though, it was necessary for the crown to continue dialogue with their holders in later generations as the case of Normandy most obviously shows. The disturbed conditions created by the Anglo-French war that broke out in 1337, in some senses a French civil war, provided many opportunities for ambitious provincial rulers to advance their own interests against those of the crown. France had apparently entered an 'age of principalities' in which the unity of the kingdom laboriously constructed by the Capetians was to be sorely tested.

In some duchies and counties (for example, Forez, where a Chambre des Comptes similar to the royal accounting office emerged by 1317) precocious administrative developments had already occurred by the eve of the Hundred Years War, transforming older seigneurial forms of government into more structured, bureaucratic institutions. The pace of change in some long-established great lordships (like the duchies of Brittany or Burgundy) was slower, but in the late thirteenth and early fourteenth century even these had seen significant advances mirroring changes in central government. In the case of Brittany, for instance, recognition of its duke as a peer of France in 1297 not only enhanced his personal status, but also reinforced the system of justice that had been developing within the duchy. This happened because the crown acknowledged that appeals from the duke's judgment could only be carried to the Parlement of Paris in two instances, denial of justice and false judgment, once the remedies offered in the duke's own courts (which allowed for local appeals) had been exhausted. As a result, until the outbreak of the Breton War of Succession in 1341, not only is there evidence for increased judicial activity by the duke's seneschals and other legal officers, and a codification of local practice around 1325 in the *Très ancien coutume de Bretagne*, but there was also considerable cooperation between the Parlement of Paris and the Breton courts, with appeals being returned to the duchy for breaching agreed procedures. Such developments served to consolidate local institutions and customs.

For most *pays*, however, it would be the stimulus of war that provided the dynamic for change as rulers and public authorities from the king downwards sought resources to fight and defend their lordships. This was as true for urban communities, notably the *bonnes villes*, towns scattered across the kingdom which enjoyed a particularly privileged but hard-to-define relationship under the crown's direct safeguard, as it was for territorial lordships. By 1337 few French towns, even major cities, had complex administrations but, with the need to defend themselves, most from the mid-fourteenth century began, with royal or princely encouragement, to appoint permanent officials and councils, and, as Philippe Contamine noted, in raising taxation for defence, 'the ramparts gave birth to municipal institutions and liberties'.

The administrative developments that occurred in these various polities, and how this altered relations with the crown, requires analysis. Some ways in which the king communicated with the provinces, whether those under his own direct control, or those ruled by princes, will also be matters of concern, as is the extent to which *pays* developed a sense of their own identity in this period. First, some changes affecting the royal demesne in the fourteenth century will be sketched, before passing to an analysis of the crown's relations with the princes, notably those who possessed newly created apanages as well as the holders of older fiefdoms.

Changing patterns of territorial lordship

At the accession of Philip VI in 1328 the royal demesne comprised two-thirds of a kingdom that by then territorially covered some 414,500 square kilometres. The famous investigation in that year to revise the number of households (*feux*) which the crown might tax (cf. Chapter 1) showed the kingdom divided into some twenty-seven separate circumscriptions, of which fourteen were directly under royal control. Where in 1302 there had been twenty-eight royal *bailliages* and seneschalcies, in 1328 there were thirty-six. These naturally covered the heartland of early Capetian power in the Île-de-France and neighbouring regions, as well as provinces which had fallen to them in the course of the twelfth and thirteenth centuries in northern and western France (cf. Chapter 2). The inquiry also demonstrated the dramatic extension of royal control into central and southern France (the Midi) that had followed the overthrow of the Plantagenets and the success of the Albigensian crusade in the thirteenth century. Poitou, the Limousin, Saintonge, Berry, Auvergne, Rouergue, Périgord, Quercy, the Agenais, Gascony, Bigorre, and Toulouse were under direct royal control. Thanks to this great expansion, the king's officials daily exercised their jurisdiction in the Rhône valley, along the Mediterranean coast, and even high into the Pyrenees, as seneschalcies like Beaucaire and Carcassonne were firmly established. Southern lords like the counts of Armagnac, Comminges, and Foix for the first time felt the authority of the crown bearing down on them. New power-sharing agreements (*pariages*) with some southern bishops (Cahors, Mende, Le Puy) also helped the crown infiltrate its servants and administrative techniques into regions previously largely closed to royal influence. Distant towns like Périgueux, as its rich archives reveal, began to communicate frequently with the king and to buy the support of influential royal councillors.

The first Valois kings only added modestly to these already extensive territories under royal control. Two acquisitions, Montpellier and the Dauphiné, were however especially significant, even though they were not immediately attached to the royal demesne. Both were acquired in 1349, though the groundwork had typically been long prepared. Philip IV had purchased the ecclesiastical overlordship of Montpellier from the bishop of Maguelonne in 1293, while Philip VI finally bought out its bankrupt lay lord, the king of Majorca, for 120,000 *livres.* Here royal influence had been growing since the mid-thirteenth century as ties between the burgeoning city of Montpellier (which contained perhaps as many as 40,000 inhabitants in 1300) and Capetian France strengthened. The city had already been asked to contribute extensively to royal needs in the early days of the Hundred

Years War before its annexation; it was to continue to do so even after Charles V delivered the barony of Montpellier to Charles II of Navarre in 1371 in exchange for lands in Normandy (cf. below, this chapter, 'The problem of Navarre'). Montpellier was one of the largest and most cosmopolitan cities in western Europe. It had an internationally renowned university, from which many law graduates quickly moved into royal service. With economic links throughout the Mediterranean, it was the acknowledged leader of the Midi towns trading at the Champagne fairs. As the Hundred Years War unfolded, it naturally played a dominant role in the urban politics of Languedoc and held a continuous dialogue with the crown as the city's register-chronicles of the *Grand* and *Petit Thalamus* and other records so clearly demonstrate.

The acquisition of the Dauphiné built on that of another equally important and strategically sited city Lyon in 1312 (above, Chapter 1, 'The royal demesne'). This had extended the royal presence in the Rhône valley beyond the traditional south-eastern frontiers of the kingdom. Philip VI's purchase of the Dauphiné from the ageing, chivalric, but heirless Humbert II of the Viennois, for 120,000 florins and a life pension of 10,000 florins (sale agreed in 1342, transfer effected in 1349) was a further step in consolidating royal influence towards the Alps and Italy. To avoid any embarrassment caused by the need to proffer homage for lands that lay within the empire, it was agreed to invest Charles, eldest son of the heir to the throne, with the Dauphiné. He also took the title of dauphin previously borne by Humbert. After his accession as Charles V (1364–80), his younger brother, Louis, claimed the Dauphiné on the grounds that he was heir apparent, but he was bought off with a life grant of the Touraine (later released), while as soon as he could, Charles V invested his own eldest son with the Dauphiné. This practice lasted until Louis XI united it with the royal demesne in 1461, though the heir to the throne continued to be styled dauphin.

Further consolidation of the royal demesne occurred as Charles V bought a number of smaller lordships like the county of Auxerre for 31,000 *livres* in 1371 and the county of Dreux in 1378, while the lordship of Mouzon in the empire was acquired from the archbishop of Reims by exchange in 1379, and the *châtellenie* of Limoges was attached to the demesne in 1371. During a visit to Paris in 1378 Emperor Charles IV recognized the future Charles VI (1380–1422) as imperial vicar for life in the 'kingdom of Arles', further evidence of the spread of royal influence beyond the boundaries of 843 into Provence and the imperial county of Burgundy. The counts of Savoy could usually be depended on as allies, and many Savoyards and Dauphinois fought in royal armies, while Philip VI, notably, attached many minor imperial lords from Alsace, Lorraine, and even the Rhineland to his service by monetary pensions (*fief-rentes*). Along the north-eastern border of the kingdom, too, there was growing royal influence in the many prince-bishoprics that marked the frontier with the empire. These (like Cambrai, Metz, Toul, and Verdun), usually took their political lead from Paris, though Charles V was obliged in 1369 to release back to the count of Flanders Lille, Douai, and Orchies, the cities 'transported' in 1312 when negotiating the marriage of his brother Philip to the count's daughter and sole heiress. They would only return to the crown in the late fifteenth century.

Detaching land once annexed to the royal demesne was, however, becoming rarer as a concept of 'inalienability' slowly developed: in 1319 Philip V had declared that alienations made since the reign of Louis IX were revocable, future grants were only to be made with the consent of his council, and Parlement and the Chambre des Comptes were not to register any they considered excessive. Both John II (1350–64) and Charles V promised at their coronations not to alienate. An ordinance of 1361 declared Burgundy, Normandy, Champagne, and Toulouse united to the demesne, though it was almost immediately breached when Burgundy was granted as an apanage (below, this chapter, 'Burgundy in the late fourteenth century'). Nevertheless, several acts issued in Charles VI's reign, including the famous reforming Cabochian ordinance of 1413, reaffirmed the principle of non-alienation, which by the fifteenth century had become the norm for lands acquired or repossessed by the crown.

The king and the princes

Outside the royal demesne, but often inextricably entangled with it territorially and administratively, were the royal apanages, lands granted to cadets to sustain their dignity as members of the royal family. The word 'apanage' is first used in 1316, though the practice (as seen above, Chapter 1, 'The royal demesne') was by then already at least a century old, since the Capetians, like other great aristocratic lineages, felt obliged to make suitable landed provision for its younger sons. Nor had it posed any obvious threat to the crown. The introduction from 1314 of the principle that succession in apanages should be limited to males only and closer definition of the legal arrangements whereby the king and his Parlement at Paris retained ultimate judicial control (*ressort*) in any apanage, as well as the right to hear 'royal cases' (*cas royaux*) in the first instance, seemed added guarantees that apanagists would remain under effective royal control. Moreover, accidents of succession continued to favour the king as failure of heirs brought land earlier alienated back to the crown. Philip VI's own accession, for example, reunited Anjou and Maine with the royal demesne, though in 1328 the apanages owing their existence to generosity by successive Capetians kings still included Artois, Alençon, Chartres, Évreux, La Marche, the Bourbonnais, Angoulême, and Mortain.

Some of these (like Artois, Angoulême, and Mortain) would shortly return to the crown, only to be granted out again in different combinations, a practice in which the Valois followed Capetian precedent. Under Philip VI this meant the constitution in 1344 of a short-lived apanage for his younger son, Philip, based on Orléans and Beaumont-le-Roger (this latter confiscated from Robert of Artois in 1332, and later given to Charles II of Navarre), which returned to the crown on Philip's death without male heirs in 1375. His elder brother, John, who had been invested with the dukedom of Normandy on his father's accession, 'so that he might learn better how to govern even greater things and the kingdom of France',[1] was later also given Anjou, Maine, and Touraine in 1332, and Poitou in 1344, so that he could share the burdens of state with his father. In practice, however, John was allowed surprisingly little freedom of action, since Philip VI kept a tight and nervous control over officials acting in his son's name. At one point he even entertained suspicions about his son's loyalty and threatened to disinherit him, unusual evidence of disunity in the royal family. It was only as Philip's political troubles mounted after defeat at Crécy that he relented and allowed John a decisive say

[1] Cited by J. Tricard, 'Jean, duc de Normandie et héritier en France, un double échec?', *AN* 29 (1979).

in Norman affairs where local discontent arising from earlier royal maladministration broke out in revolt in 1348–9.

Of the old apanages, it was Bourbon, erected into a duchy in 1327, which was to enjoy the most enduring success as it was transformed from a congeries of scattered lordships into an impressive principality. But it was a long process, and although under Louis II of Bourbon (1356–1410) important steps were taken towards creating central institutions, with his long-serving councillor Pierre de Noury taking the lead in reforms, it was only in the fifteenth century that dukes of Bourbon played a significant national role, their lordship remaining the poorest and least cohesive of the great principalities. Like the neighbouring apanage of Berry (below, this chapter, 'Apanages and principalities in the late fourteenth century'). Bourbon's central rather than peripheral geographical position within the kingdom seems to have been a disincentive to its ruler to pursue external policies that were overly ambitious. Louis II, for instance, was content to serve for much of his life as a deputy to more powerful figures like Louis I of Anjou or John, duke of Berry. He was also one of the most active royal military commanders of his day, his deeds receiving a generous chivalric gloss in Cabaret d'Orville's *Chronicle*.[2]

It was John II's generosity to his younger sons, Louis, John, and Philip that decisively altered the traditional territorial balance between the crown and the apanaged princes and created major problems for the monarchy for generations to come. This could not have been easily predicted at the time, but the lavish scale of John's endowments, and the ambitions of some apanagists to treat their lands as increasingly sovereign principalities and capitalize on the urgent need for strong local action in the face of the political, economic, and military challenges facing public authorities in the latter half of the fourteenth century, seriously weakened the crown. The practice, for instance, of allowing the apanagists to share a large percentage—typically at least a third—of royal taxation levied in their lands, once regular taxes began to be imposed from the late 1350s, literally impoverished the king, especially since the expansion of the royal demesne was not accompanied by a dramatic increase in the

[2] *Chronique du bon duc Loys de Bourbon* compiled in 1429 from the reminiscences of Jean de Châteaumorand, a knight who had followed Louis in most of his campaigns, including his crusading expedition to Tunis in 1390.

crown's ordinary revenues. John II's apanages thus set up powerful provincial rivals to the crown, reversing the trend towards a centralized monarchy for which the Capetians had striven so hard. The dangers were further compounded by comparable developments in those great fiefs (most obviously Flanders, Brittany, and Gascony, but also in some smaller southern principalities like Foix-Béarn) lying on the periphery of the kingdom. On the eve of the Hundred Years War, most already enjoyed a high degree of administrative independence from the crown, which the war only served to enhance.

As a result, whether they derived from great lordships which had already adapted to new conditions before 1337, or whether they were new royal creations, the territorial principalities that now emerged transformed the political order. Since Charles V and Charles VI continued the policy of John II, the feudal geography of the kingdom was completely changed. Alongside the royal demesne, essentially centring on two major blocks of land from Normandy to Champagne, and in the Languedoc, there grew up several great principalities, whose rulers were the natural councillors of the king but whose subjects also expected them to use their positions to advance local interests. This engendered much rivalry between competing princely clienteles at the centre for control of royal policy and a share in the crown's wealth or patronage. During Charles VI's reign the vacuum in royal power caused by the king's chronic insanity from 1392 onwards allowed princely rivalry full rein and eventually exposed the kingdom to mortal danger at the hands of a foreign enemy, Henry V of England (cf. Chapter 5).

Paradoxically, however, one of the more positive consequences of princely rivalry was the renewed attraction of Paris as a place of residence for the princes and their entourages in the later fourteenth century. After the turbulence of the brief revolutionary period when Étienne Marcel was *prévôt des marchands* (1355–8) and the surrounding countryside was devastated by rural revolt, a lawless soldiery, and foreign invasion which twice brought Edward III to within sight of its walls, Paris briefly recovered its eminence as the cultural centre of the kingdom at large. Charles V, in particular, engaged in major construction projects at the Louvre, the Hôtel Saint-Pol, and Vincennes. All other royal princes and many territorial ones possessed palatial residences or *hôtels* there, as did many great Churchmen and nobles, while their servants were regularly occupied in legal and other business connected with running their apanages and estates that often required permanent attendance in the capital. Paris thus revived as a major craft centre for the production of works of art of the highest quality and latest fashions for an expanding clientele at the royal court and in princely households, as well as an important financial centre where the impecunious could contract loans from rich Italian merchants servicing the court.

At the same time, with the development of local government and the introduction, as Françoise Autrand has pointed out, of 'the apparatus of the modern state into their own territories . . . with an efficient administration and a fair legal system . . . [the princes' own] capitals and courts brought new life to towns in these provinces'. Angers, Poitiers, Moulins, Riom, Clermont, Lille, and Dijon were among the first provincial cities to benefit in the late fourteenth century from the growth of princely courts in the new apanages. Like the king, princes attracted many lesser nobles and aspiring bourgeois eager to benefit from employment and the material and social rewards of service to their 'states' (cf. Chapter 6). Princely service, too, provided opportunities for emerging dynasties of professional administrators and civil servants similar to those at the centre, whose interests were closely allied to the continuation of princely and provincial rule. In the most advanced of these polities there were also efforts to enhance the prince's image as a ruler as dignified and as powerful as the king himself. Such developments would not, of course, reach their apogee until the fifteenth century, but their origins in the fourteenth century are evident.

Apanages and principalities in the late fourteenth century

The late Capetians had already begun emphasizing differences of status between princes of the royal blood and other feudal lords. Under the Valois the position of the royal family and 'princes of the fleur-de-lis' was further enhanced; the new apanages reinforced these differences. In 1356 John II invested his second son, Louis (d. 1384), with Anjou and Maine. This apanage, which Louis himself further purposefully expanded by judicious purchases and exchanges as well as by marriage settlements, would not return to the crown until Louis XI's time. Under Charles V, Louis acted mainly as a loyal if high-handed royal lieutenant in the Languedoc. There he waged a series of successful military campaigns, often in conjunction with Bertrand du Guesclin, constable of France (1370–80). Anjou's incessant demands for money, however, in a period of grave recession eventually provoked serious local revolts, orchestrated by a Montpellier now in sharp economic decline (1378–9). Louis was later adopted as her heir by a distant relative, the much-married but childless Angevin Queen Joanna of Naples (d. 1382), and his ambitions turned to Italy. He and his successors as dukes of Anjou and counts of Provence spent most of their energies pursuing extravagant dynastic claims, styling themselves 'kings of Sicily and Jerusalem'. They thus posed little threat to the main branch of the Valois around 1400, only appearing at court intermittently, though they continued to be a drain on royal finances like other apanagists, for example, taking all the proceeds from royal *aides* (indirect sales taxes) raised in their lands.

The second new apanage created in 1356 was for John II's third son, John (d. 1416), who received Poitou (exchanged for Berry and the Auvergne in 1360). After its reconquest from the English in 1372 the duke of Berry was once again invested with Poitou. His powers as an apanagist were supplemented by appointment as royal lieutenant in succession to Anjou in Languedoc from 1380. He held this position more or less continuously until his death in 1416, having been named lieutenant for life in Berry, Auvergne, Poitou, Languedoc, and Guyenne beyond the Dordogne in 1402. As René Lacour, the historian of his administration, stated with little exaggeration many years ago, Berry came to exercise in his vast lordship virtually 'all the powers of a sovereign'. The only serious restriction was his inability to alienate any royal demesne lands in his jurisdiction. Nor was he particularly scrupulous, his government often provoking considerable local discontent. In many ways Berry was probably closest to what kings of France might normally expect of an apanagist. He has recently been described by Autrand as 'an active supporter of the progress of the state, inclined more towards efficient administration rather than dialogue with his subjects'. It is worth considering how he governed in more detail since Berry provides a paradigm for other contemporary princely administrations.

In creating a central administration for his lands in a period of great economic uncertainty in the wake of the Black Death and the violence and unrest provoked by the almost incessant pressures of war, Berry and his councillors displayed little originality: *mutatis mutandis* they applied or adapted royal practices and institutions to the lands which formed his apanage. Other apanagists—Anjou, Bourbon, Burgundy, Orléans—would act similarly, as indeed did the rulers of the older principalities like Brittany and Foix that lay beyond the royal demesne. Berry's own household (with around 250 officers receiving regular wages) functioned on the same principles as the grander royal household whose departmental structure and personnel it largely copied. His financial offices likewise reflected recent developments at Paris in a period when taxation began to be levied regularly for the first time. He took his share of royal taxes levied in his lands. He even occasionally struck his own money at Bourges (despite royal ordinances seeking to impose the circulation of royal coinage only). He had a treasurer-general, a Chambre aux Deniers for household expenses, and, from 1379, a central Chambre des Comptes to audit accounts. The Chambre usually sat at Bourges, which developed as a 'capital' endowed with new buildings like the duke's two palaces and a Sainte-Chapelle, modelled on that in Paris. Similar Sainte-Chapelles at Poitiers and Riom were also established. Berry's reputation as a patron of architecture and connoisseur of the most costly illuminated manuscripts, of which he amassed a huge library, is most famously exemplified in the remarkable Book of Hours, the *Très riches heures*, which was painted for him by the Limbourg brothers towards the end of his life. This includes vivid and accurate depictions of the many castles and palaces which Berry built or refurbished throughout his extensive lands.

Returning to his administration: there was also a chancellor (usually an ecclesiastic) and council, made up of a mixture of nobles, Churchmen, household officers, and even some bourgeois. In the words of Lacour, this, like the royal council, 'occupied itself with everything . . . its competence and authority being universal'. Equally the duke concerned himself with the administration of justice (he had a *procureur-général*) and with local affairs, even sending out general reformers (*reformateurs-généraux*) like the crown to carry out thorough investigations into the behaviour of officers, as in the *bailliage* of the Montagnes d'Auvergne in 1365. Overseeing this judicial machine was the Grands Jours, an appeal court, which by agreement with the king, was staffed by royal councillors or advocates from the Paris Parlement, to which the ultimate right of appeal naturally lay, though it was seldom exercised. Similar arrangements for the administration of justice can be found in other apanages like the Grands Jours at Beaune. Though ultimately derived from the feudal court of the dukes of Burgundy, this court too was reformed with the aid of experts from the Parlement of Paris in 1370.

Luckily for the crown, Berry did not have a surviving male heir when he died in 1416. His apanage was broken up to endow his heiresses, so that it did not long enjoy the rule of an independent and, by then, largely sovereign prince. Indeed the crown itself became a major beneficiary since many who had served Berry passed into the employment of 'the king of Bourges', Charles VII (1422–61). But as long as it lasted Berry's apanage was in many respects a state within a state, a territorial base from which he could exercise considerable political influence, though it only occasionally caused ripples on a national scale (as in the early stages of the Armagnac and Burgundian feud when Berry favoured the cause of his son-in-law Bernard VII, count of Armagnac). The case of Burgundy, the third of John II's new apanages, was in this respect very different; its creation eventually threatened the crown itself.

Burgundy in the late fourteenth century

The last Capetian duke of Burgundy, Philippe de Rouvre, died in 1361, bringing to an end a dynasty that had ruled for over 300 years. His patrimonial lands should have gone to his widow, Marguerite, daughter of Louis de Male, count of Flanders, while Jean de Boulogne, count of the Auvergne, claimed his matrimonial inheritance. In practice John II, who, since the death of Duke Eudes IV in 1349, had exercised an increasing influence in Burgundy as guardian of the young Philippe through the many royal officials appointed to posts there, took possession by legal sleight of hand. But in deference to local feeling, rather than uniting the duchy with the royal demesne, on 6 September 1363 he vested it in his fourth son, Philip, and his heirs. This very generous act (since, unusually, females were not excluded from future succession) is normally explained as gratitude to Philip for standing by him on the field at Poitiers as a 14-year-old, and displaying the courage for which he earned the nickname 'the Bold'. It was reinforced by further favours: Philip was named First Peer of France, all royal rights there except fealty and homage were transferred to him, as were John II's claims on the succession to the county of Burgundy, with which Emperor Charles IV had already invested Philip. When Charles V succeeded, he quickly confirmed these arrangements. Like his elder brother Berry, Philip of Burgundy also enjoyed the powers of a royal lieutenant. Charles V extended these to cover the dioceses of Lyon, Mâcon, Autun, Chalon, and Langres, assuring Philip, says Richard Vaughan, 'of pre-eminence and authority in France' as ruler of 'one of the largest and richest fiefs of the crown' and sharing 'as royal lieutenant, in its sovereignty over a much wider area'. Initially Philip repaid the trust shown in him by loyal service, though he proved a mediocre military leader.

Philip's already powerful position was further enhanced in 1369 when, with the encouragement of his brother and the flagrant cooperation of Pope Urban V in issuing the necessary dispensation, he married the widow of his predecessor as duke, the great heiress Marguerite de Flandres, whose hand Edward III had also been seeking for his son Edmund of Cambridge. On the death of her father, Louis de Male, count of Flanders (succ. 1346), on 30 January 1384, Philip united under his rule Flanders, Artois, and other extensive lands and claims of his wife in north-eastern France, with his own block of territories centring on the duchy and county of Burgundy. Philip was now a figure of consequence on a wider stage; a loyal and hard-working member of the royal family under Charles V, it was inevitable that besides playing his part as a French prince, he would be drawn into affairs in the empire and beyond.

Flanders was a county that had enjoyed almost complete administrative autonomy for many generations but which was dominated by the great cloth-manufacturing cities of Bruges, Ghent, and Ypres. The economic dependence of Philip's subjects on English wool was a determining factor in his foreign policy as it had been in that of his predecessor. In the wake of the revolt led by Jacques van Arteveldt in the 1340s and the death of his own father at Crécy, Louis de Male had largely abandoned the traditional alliance between the counts of Flanders (fearful of their great cities) and kings of France to forge an alliance with Edward III. But his commitment was always lukewarm. For most of his reign he pursued an adroit foreign policy that cleverly avoided over-commitment to either the French or the English cause, a model that certainly influenced other princes like John IV of Brittany (below, this chapter, 'The duchy of Brittany and the crown') with whom he maintained close relations. Philip the Bold inherited this tradition; inexorably he was also drawn into the domestic affairs of neighbouring Low Countries principalities: a reorientation of 'Burgundian' interests that predominated in the fifteenth century.

There has been considerable debate about the extent to which Philip the Bold deliberately developed policies that were intended to create a 'Burgundian state'. Richard Vaughan argued most forcibly that this was the case from early in his rule. He saw the creation of central governmental institutions after 1384 (in which Philip was following a path already well trodden by other apanagists, as seen above) and an imaginative series of marriage alliances with French and Netherlandish neighbours as preparing the way for a much expanded and more coherent Burgundian principality. Others remain sceptical, seeing many of Philip's responses as contingent on changing political conditions, arguing that not only he but his son John the Fearless (1404–19) considered themselves first and foremost loyal princes of the 'fleur-de-lis', hence their desire to dominate at Paris.

Following the deaths of Charles V (1380) and Louis of Anjou (1384), Burgundy, usually in conjunction with Berry, certainly dictated royal foreign policy. They eventually negotiated a long-term truce with England, and sought a resolution by peaceful means of the schism that had divided the western Church since 1378; perhaps this was in part in order to pursue his ambitions in the Low Countries. For some years the royal uncles faced opposition from councillors of the late king like Bureau de la Rivière and Olivier de Clisson (constable of France 1380–92), a group bent on reform known as the Marmosets, who enjoyed pre-eminence at Paris between 1388 and 1392. From the early 1390s Philip was increasingly engaged in a long struggle with Charles VI's extremely ambitious and energetic younger brother, Louis, duke of Orléans, to control affairs during the king's periodic bouts of insanity. All the princes of the blood drew pensions and other financial rewards from the royal treasury in these years. By the time of Philip's death in 1404, Orléans had achieved broad comparability in terms of income with his Burgundian rival, though, lacking the urban wealth that Burgundy could tap in Flanders, he was more heavily dependent on royal favour for maintaining it. In 1407 John the Fearless, whose hostility to Orléans and Queen Isabella was becoming increasingly personal, claimed nearly 200,000 francs of arrears of royal pensions owing to himself and his late father. In the absence of Orléans the royal council agreed to pay off this sum. But this did not prevent John from pursuing a feud that by now included differences of opinion over French foreign policy. Finally, on 23 November 1407 John arranged his rival's assassination and paid a Parisian academic, Master Jean Petit, to write a justification of the murder on the specious grounds that in obtaining and exercising royal power alone, Orléans was guilty of tyranny. This opened a new and more dangerous phase in the struggle for influence at Paris that only ended with John the Fearless's own assassination in 1419 and Henry V's occupation of the city in 1420 (cf. Chapter 6).

The duchy of Brittany and the crown

To turn from a new apanage to an older principality, by the fourteenth century the dukes of Brittany had much experience of living in the shadow of more powerful neighbours while protecting their privileges. The geographical position of their duchy astride the main sea-lanes from the English Channel into the western Atlantic made their alliance or neutrality a matter of perennial concern to the kings of England, dukes of Guyenne. Since the Conquest of England, members of the ducal family, often the duke himself, usually held the great honour of Richmond, with its vast estates in no fewer than thirteen English counties. In 1334 the honour devolved to Duke John III (1312–41), a loyal supporter of the Capetians and Philip VI, to whom he even once tentatively proposed leaving his duchy, though his nobility energetically vetoed the suggestion. But when he died without direct heirs in 1341, this opened up a succession dispute between his half-brother Jean de Montfort and his niece Jeanne de Penthièvre. She was married to a nephew of Philip VI, Charles, younger son of the count of Blois. Given the strategic position of Brittany, the dispute quickly assumed major political importance when, after legal arguments from the two rivals, Philip VI on

7 September 1341 issued the *arrêt* of Conflans, allowing Charles to proffer homage for Brittany on behalf of his wife. This alienated Montfort, who turned for help to Edward III.

Edward had already tried to obtain the hand of Jeanne de Penthièvre for his brother John of Eltham in 1336, before her marriage to Blois. Now eager to open a new front in his war with France, he quickly offered Montfort armed aid to reverse what he and his supporters in Brittany considered a miscarriage of justice. Within weeks a civil war had broken out in the duchy that was to last until 1364, when Montfort's son, also Jean, with English troops under Sir John Chandos, defeated and killed Blois at the battle of Auray. The Breton civil war proved to be a watershed in the duchy's history.

Within their own respective spheres of influence, two rival administrations had adapted conservative and still largely seigneurial forms of government to the urgent needs of raising resources to fight the war. In the first treaty of Guérande (April 1365) the Montfort and Penthièvre factions came to terms under negotiators sent by Charles V, who accepted John IV (d. 1399) as duke. Once the duchy was reunited, John IV continued similar policies, shamelessly borrowing from precedents established by his rival Blois. As a result, under the Montfort dynasty (1364–1514) Brittany came to enjoy almost complete independence from the French crown, with its own autonomous institutions and an ideology justifying ducal powers—significantly termed 'regalities'. It formed the most complete and coherent of all late medieval French principalities.

The crown fought hard to exercise its residual sovereignty, but circumstances favoured the dukes, who enjoyed growing personal freedom of action. Characteristically in 1366, for instance, when asked to perform homage, John IV's chancellor introduced an element of ambiguity by stating that the duke would simply render homage 'as his ancestors had done'.[3] Despite protests by royal officials that this should be liege homage, he refused to acknowledge it; later dukes would even proffer homage standing, with a sword at their side. Fear of driving John IV back into the arms of Edward III led Charles V to act circumspectly on this and other occasions early in the duke's reign, though he failed to prevent a new alliance between the duke

[3] Dom H. Morice, *Mémoires pour servir de preuves à l'histoire ecclésiastique et civile de Bretagne*, 3 vols. (Paris, 1742–6), vol. i, col. 1610.

and England in 1372. He was right to tread warily because when he did try to confiscate the duchy for this 'treason', and annex it to the royal demesne in 1378, it provoked a violent reaction from the Breton nobility and leading townsmen, who sprang to the defence of the duchy's independence just as they had rejected union under Philip VI. They formed defensive leagues, and with the consent of Jeanne de Penthièvre summoned the recently exiled John IV back in a remarkable show of solidarity. The duke was thus not alone in promoting the notion of Brittany as 'my country and nation' (*mon pais et ma nation*), as his contemporary biographer and secretary Guillaume de Saint-André expressed it.

Once safely reinstalled on his throne, John IV displayed great political astuteness under Charles VI in exploiting these feelings to build up loyalty to his dynasty. He was helped by generally friendly relations with Berry and Burgundy. Their indulgence allowed him to pursue his own foreign policy with few restraints; alliances with Navarre and England were a further protection against royal encroachment on his prerogatives. More importantly, and building on what had already been achieved between 1365 and 1373, John and his advisers continued overhauling every aspect of his financial administration. From early in his reign he imposed general hearth taxes (*fouages*), and introduced customs duties and indirect sales taxes (*aides, billot*) on food, drink, and other items. He exploited fully his seigneurial rights over lay lords (occasionally sharing with them the proceeds of taxation to get their consent as the crown did) and sternly exacted regalian rights during episcopal vacancies. A commercial treaty with the Basque ports was negotiated and a convoy system introduced. He sold safe conducts (*brefs de mer*) to mariners in Bordeaux and La Rochelle as well as Breton ports, guaranteeing them safe passage around Brittany's hazardous coastline, and generally took advantage of a modest upturn in economic conditions in the last decades of the century. In the fifteenth century his successors would similarly exploit the 'neutrality' of Brittany during the continuing Anglo-French war.

As a result, John IV enjoyed towards the end of his reign an income comparable with those of the leading apanagists but without any help from the crown, which was no longer able to levy any taxes within the duchy. It also tried vainly to control the emission of Breton coinage which from the days of Charles de Blois included gold as well as silver.

The administration of these finances, despite the presence of several Englishmen, including Thomas Melbourne, treasurer and receiver-general (1365–73), remained very similar to those used by the crown. There was thus a Breton Chambre des Comptes and, as in the kingdom at large, the circumscriptions for tax purposes were initially based on earlier ecclesiastical administrative arrangements, with the nine Breton dioceses forming the main divisions.

Alongside the Chambre des Comptes, the Breton chancery also underwent major change, expanding both in terms of personnel and in the range of business it transacted. Here too the duke began to exercise new regalian rights such as the power to ennoble, issue pardons and safeguards, create fairs and markets, or appoint notaries. John IV also naturally discouraged appeals to the Parlement of Paris, which became extremely rare. Unfortunate royal officials sent to exercise their jurisdiction in the duchy suffered violence and humiliation, even being forced notoriously to eat their mandates. An appellate jurisdiction was provided within the duchy, culminating in appeal to the Breton Parlement or, as it was increasingly called, the estates, which were held almost annually throughout the fifteenth century. If important army reforms had to wait until the reign of John V (1399–1442), John IV was not exclusively dependent on the feudal service of his nobility, but hired English, Gascon, and other mercenary companies. There was a marshal and an admiral of Brittany. The duke was also among the first French princes to recognize the importance of gunpowder artillery, though it was under John V that major architectural changes would bring older fortifications into line with the most modern ideas on defence.

Finally, as far as the evolving 'ideology' of the Breton state is concerned, a few signposts can be noted. As early as 1336 advocates of John III were arguing in a succession dispute that 'Brittany is not like other peerages' and that it had once been a kingdom whose 'kings recognized no earthly sovereign'.[4] The allusion to the Roman law doctrine on sovereignty is clear. It was further argued that, by accepting his peerage in 1297, the duke had not forfeited his earlier 'regalities'. The same arguments were repeated and much adumbrated by Montfort's lawyers in 1341. They were taken up again by John IV and

[4] 'Item, que le Roy et les Roys de Bretaigne pour le temps ne recognoissoyent nul soverain en terre', Archives Nationales, K 1152, no. 49, m. 8.

his advisers on numerous occasions. Surprised listeners at the papal court in 1394 heard two Breton clerks claiming that the duchy was not part of the kingdom of France nor the duke subject to any secular ruler. Certainly by now Breton ecclesiastical affairs were almost exclusively regulated without any reference to the king of France and, if Roman law was being pressed into service to promote the duke's image and status, so too was divine dispensation. The notion of duke 'by the grace of God' was hesitantly announced by Charles de Blois and John IV on their coinage and in a few documents; it became part of the full style of John V from 1417. In 1401 John V was crowned in a ceremony that had ancient origins, but which had been specifically revamped on the model of the royal coronation service introduced by Charles V. At the same time, after a long period in which there had been little significant historical work produced in the duchy, from the late fourteenth century a historiography overwhelmingly sympathetic to the Montfort dynasty, written by men employed in the ducal chancery, emerges in works like the life of John IV by his secretary, Guillaume de Saint-André (c.1385) and the *Chronicle of Saint-Brieuc* (*c.*1398–1416). This tradition continued until the early sixteenth century; though on a modest provincial scale, it parallels the royal historiographical tradition of the *Grandes chroniques de France.* A panoply of distinctive practices that distinguished Brittany and its ruler with his 'regal' attributes was in full evolution by the time of John IV's death in November 1399.

The problem of Navarre

For most of the fourteenth century, the ruler of the little sovereign Pyrenean state of Navarre was also an important figure with extensive lands and rights within the French kingdom. In the first half of the century the problems to which this gave rise were chiefly legal. But as the war between England and France overflowed into new theatres, Charles II of Navarre (1349–87) played a central if devious diplomatic and military role which affected many provinces of France. Had he been alive in 1328 (he was born in 1332), his claims to the French throne might have been considered superior to those of either Philip VI or Edward III; as it was, he used every opportunity to advance his own interests by playing one side off against the other. In doing so, some of the richest and most strategically sensitive provinces of the kingdom were laid waste by soldiers fighting in his name, whilst a 'Navarrese' party made up of malcontents, hotheads, and would-be reformers briefly played a central role in the revolutionary movements that engulfed Paris and the Île-de-France after defeat at Poitiers (1356). The background to these important events illuminates the kaleidoscopic relationships between the crown and the provinces more generally as well as French foreign policy.

By his marriage in 1284 to Jeanne, countess of Champagne, the future Philip IV gained a life interest in the kingdom of Navarre, which was also part of her patrimony. In 1305 the couple conferred Navarre on their second son, the future Louis X. On his death in 1316 it passed to his daughter Jeanne, since female succession was accepted by the Navarrese. She in turn took it by marriage (18 June 1318) to Philip, son of Louis of Évreux, Philip IV's younger brother. But the terms of the Champagne succession, in which others like Eudes IV, duke of Burgundy, had an interest, were already disputed between senior and cadet lines of the Capet family. Both Philip V and Charles IV were reluctant to allow Jeanne and Philip full possession of Jeanne's extensive lands in France and procrastinated. To consolidate his own succession in 1328, Philip VI recognized the couple as king and queen of Navarre, but it was not until the treaty of Villeneuve-lès-Avignon (14 March 1336) that they agreed finally to renounce their claims to Champagne in return for Angoulême and Mortain and an annual rent of 5,000 *lt.* Philip of Évreux, king of Navarre, died in 1343. In 1348 Queen Jeanne agreed to release Angoulême and some other lands in Poitou in exchange for the *châtellenies* of Pontoise, Beaumont-sur-Oise, and Asnières-sur-Oise. This consolidated what the family already possessed around Mantes, Meulan, Étampes, and Dourdan. When she died the following year, Navarre and this motley collection of northern French lands passed to her ambitious son Charles II, known since the sixteenth century as 'the Bad'.

As king of Navarre, and married to John II's daughter Jeanne (1352), Charles energetically resurrected Navarrese rights to Champagne, displayed resentment at the loss of Angoulême, which had been conferred on Charles de la Cerda, constable of France, by assassinating him (January 1354), and negotiated a partition of the kingdom with Edward III. Charles's share was to be Normandy,

Champagne (see map 9), Brie, Chartres, Languedoc, and Bigorre (to which his family also had claims). Forced to act swiftly to prevent the disintegration of his kingdom through the treasonable designs of his son-in-law, John II brought Charles to the negotiating table at Mantes on 22 February 1354. Here he agreed to give up Pontoise and the other *châtellenies* in the Oise valley and to desert his English ally. However, this concession was bought at a high cost, since, partly to compensate for failure to provide sufficient dower for his daughter (another bone of contention), John II agreed to deliver the county of Beaumont-le-Roger and virtually the whole of the Cotentin to Charles II, further strengthening the Navarrese presence in Normandy and the Seine valley.

As the Anglo-French war developed from the 1350s, control of strongholds in these areas was a perennial concern to the major combatants, with the French and English kings continually wooing or threatening Charles, depending on the state of the war, while he or (during his absences in Navarre) his brothers Philip and Louis, acting as his lieutenants, played one side off against the other and allied with dissident local lords like the Norman, Geoffroi de Harcourt. The king's arrest of Charles and execution of his ally Harcourt in 1356 just made the situation worse. As a result, the late 1350s in particular saw much damage inflicted in Normandy, Picardy, and elsewhere by Anglo-Navarrese forces acting with or without the specific consent of the Navarrese king. After defeat at Cocherel on 16 May 1364 by Bertrand du Guesclin of an Anglo-Navarrese army led by the Gascon lord Jean de Grailly, Captal de Buch, Charles was temporarily reconciled with Charles V. At Pamplona on 6 March 1365 he ceded Mantes, Meulan, and the county of Longueville (already in Du Guesclin's hands) in return for the barony of Montpellier, though he kept his lands around Évreux and in the Cotentin, where Cherbourg was his main stronghold.

With the renewal of the Anglo-French war in 1369, Charles once again flirted with an English alliance, for which Edward III was enthusiastic but which Edward, prince of Wales, was unwilling to ratify. The conquest of some Navarrese strongholds in Normandy by royal forces, threatening the complete loss of his lands there, persuaded Charles to turn once more to the French. At Vernon in March 1371 peace was restored and the grant of Montpellier renewed, though it was now hedged about by much clearer statements on what prerogatives the crown had retained in making the grant, since it was nominally made by one sovereign to another. In practice these virtually prevented local officers from administering effectively the lordship in Charles II's name and certainly deprived him of most of its income from judicial and other sources. It is thus hardly surprising that throughout the 1370s Charles continued his intrigues. In 1378 a plot to poison Charles V was discovered, in which he was deeply implicated. The French king had already decided to end the military threat posed by Navarrese garrisons in Normandy by sequestration and systematic reconquest. But his efforts to capture Cherbourg, which Charles II leased to Richard II of England in 1378, failed. By late 1379 there were no Navarrese fortresses left in Normandy, and Charles's heir and his sisters were residing at the French court as 'hostages'. But even this did not halt their father's perennial scheming (a marriage alliance for one daughter with that other unreliable prince John IV of Brittany was agreed in 1385 and solemnized in 1386). Devious to the end, Charles II died on 1 January 1387. But it was 1393 before Cherbourg was returned to Charles III of Navarre (1387–1426) by the English, and it only came permanently into French royal hands in 1404, when he finally released his claims on it and other Norman lands for 200,000 *écus* and a pension of 12,000 *lt.* settled on various *châtellenies* in the Gâtinais and Champagne, now erected into the duchy-peerage of Nemours.

Estates and assemblies

So far this chapter has mainly examined the crown's relationship with those provinces that had princely rulers. However, fourteenth-century kings of France began to experiment with communicating with all their kingdom's provinces by summoning representative assemblies. How did these evolve, especially under the pressure of war?

Philip IV was the first French king to use large assemblies for political purposes. Contemporary theory, as well as common sense, dictated that a king should consult widely with his subjects. In 1302 Philip did so to seek backing against Pope Boniface VIII. At Tours in 1308 a large gathering, at which princes, clergy, nobles, and townsmen from all parts of the kingdom were present, deliberated on moves against the Templars. These two meetings have long been considered the earliest sessions of what was later called the Estates General, destined to have an intermittent history until the revolution. In August 1314 the king again called a general assembly, cleverly managed by Enguerran de Marigny. At one point in his own peroration he paused dramatically for Philip IV to rise from his seat to see more clearly those prepared to support his proposals. It appeared that France was on the verge of developing national parliamentary institutions like contemporary England; its subsequent failure to do so has been seen by many as critical in explaining the later divergent constitutional histories of the two states.

Such failure was not due to lack of experimentation with different forms of consultation. The half-century that followed the Tours meeting was one of continuous innovation. Philip V, in particular, summoned a very wide range of different assemblies in which townsmen were especially prominent and some meetings were attended by hundreds of delegates. But despite serious attempts to explain the government's plans, with the occasional dispatch of leading councillors like Henry de Sully to the Midi and Mile de Noyers to Champagne, the results were disappointing. Delegates, especially urban representatives, were unwilling to commit themselves even in principle to measures of which they could not easily foresee the full financial implications. The lesson that Charles IV naturally drew from his brother's laborious but unsuccessful efforts was that too much consultation was counter-productive, and he avoided large-scale meetings.

It was a policy to which Philip VI also adhered until financial difficulties in 1343 drove him to summon a general meeting of the estates, and another short period opened in which it seemed possible that central assemblies might find a permanent role in national affairs. On this occasion, in return for coinage reforms and to replace the tax on salt (*gabelle*) introduced for the first time in 1341, the towns of Languedoil agreed to allow the king a sales tax in which Languedoc also eventually acquiesced. Further large meetings in 1345–6 saw a formal division for consultative purposes between these two regions whose estates now met separately. The most pressing problems facing these sessions was the question of war finance and how to create and pay for an adequate army to meet the English threat. So far the solutions proposed had involved wide local variations rather than the establishment of regular and uniform taxation. A subsidiary theme which ran through these assemblies and culminated in the revolutionary meetings of the mid-1350s was mounting criticism of the royal administration, especially the excessive number of its officials and their abusive behaviour.

After the meeting of the northern estates at Paris in February 1346 Philip VI issued a comprehensive reforming ordinance reminiscent of that of 1303. This pattern was followed in similar assemblies until 1358. Following Crécy and the loss of Calais, the Estates General held at Paris in November 1347 accepted a programme of reform proposed by the crown. This entailed raising a large subsidy, expressed as the salary of mounted troops at a specified daily rate. Most of the precise details are unknown; characteristically they were to be worked out finally in local assemblies during 1348. But the scale of the grant was very large, and many of the conditions were to apply uniformly throughout the kingdom. Unfortunately, the outbreak of plague at this juncture proved disastrous: only a minute proportion of the subsidy could be collected and the crown lost a chance to stabilize its finances with the cooperation of the estates. No further assemblies representing the whole kingdom were called until 1468.

Under John II, whose experience of dealing with the estates of Normandy as duke had made him sympathetic towards such assemblies, the main regional estates were summoned to Paris and Montpellier in 1351 and the formation of several smaller provincial assemblies in the next few years was encouraged. But harmony between the king and the estates was undermined by the worsening financial and military situation between December 1355 and May 1358. The estates of Languedoil and Languedoc now briefly reached the zenith of their influence as the crown was forced to turn to central assemblies once more to obtain the resources necessary to fight the war. In December 1355 the estates of Languedoil agreed to raise 30,000 men to be paid for from a sales tax. But there was widespread resistance to payment. Subsequent meetings in March and May 1356 substituted other ways of raising taxes but with no greater success, while local assemblies resented central control whether exercised by the estates or the king.

Only a brief summary is possible here of the complex events that left the dauphin in charge of the government, after the capture of his father at Poitiers on 19 September 1356, but at the mercy of the estates of Languedoil, before he managed to break with them. The estates were in session every few months. In 1357–8 this body progressively fell under the revolutionary influence of Étienne Marcel and his allies, many of them supporters of Charles II of Navarre, calling for root-and-branch reform of the administration. They carried out a purge of the government (February 1357) and a year later executed some of their bitterest opponents in the dauphin's presence (February 1358). Continuing civil war, a marauding foreign soldiery, and a brief but bitter rural uprising, the Jacquerie (May–June 1358), that especially afflicted the Beauvaisis and Île de France, followed by the assassination of Marcel by his Parisian enemies (31 July), added to the political confusion. Relations between the estates of Languedoil and Languedoc also deteriorated as first one faction then another gained the upper hand in the struggle for power at court, in Paris or the provinces.

The eventual outcome was that although the central estates (those of Languedoil, now often reduced to an unrepresentative rump) voted money on several occasions, they had no means of ensuring its collection. As noted by Russell Major, two reasons particularly explain their failure: 'the growth of the local estates during the preceding fifteen years' and the 'alienation of a large part of the nobility whose cooperation was necessary if taxes were to be collected efficiently'. The inability of the estates to deliver what they had promised, coupled with vicious attacks on the dauphin, sealed their fate and ensured that, when free to act independently, the future Charles V would have little affection for the estates. It is thus not surprising that they played no part in the reconstruction of the kingdom after the disasters of the 1350s. The development, in response to demands for the king's ransom, of a system of taxation that did not depend directly on the consent of the estates, and the reconciliation of crown and nobility in the next few years, removed the need to call general meetings until the very end of the reign of Charles VI.

It is apparent that this period had demonstrated the impracticability of a single assembly as a regular solution to the pressing needs facing successive French kings. However, regional assemblies like the estates of Languedoil and of Languedoc, together with several provincial assemblies based on the historic regions or newer administrative divisions, like the seneschalcies to the south of the Loire or *bailliages* to the north, did establish themselves as more or less normal features of the late medieval political landscape. They allowed some dialogue between the crown and its subjects. Those of Normandy were active from 1339, Auvergne from 1345, Burgundy from 1352, Dauphiné from 1357, and Artois from 1361; in 1352 a meeting of nobles, clergy, and urban representatives, summoned to ratify a proposed treaty between Edward III and Charles de Blois, was a prelude to the later estates of Brittany.

Exercising varying degrees of authority and influence, giving counsel and consent, especially in financial matters, these provincial estates could never be entirely dismissed from the government's calculations in the later Middle Ages and required constant solicitation. The estates of Normandy later inaccurately claimed the charter granted to the Normans in 1315 as their warrant, and a comparable charter for the men of Auvergne (1318) may have had a similarly stimulating effect on their regional identity and its institutional expression in the form of a representative assembly. After 1360 there was a period lasting until Charles VI's reign in which the activities of the provincial estates were, like those larger assemblies, much reduced in comparison with the hectic years 1337–60, but around 1400 representative assemblies were a regular feature of political life in many provinces.

Often they are the most tangible evidence of a local identity. Those of Béarn (first recorded in 1391, but probably already of some antiquity) have been credited with playing a leading role in affirming their ruler's claims to sovereignty. They certainly defended the independence of their *pays*, which their viscount, Gaston Fébus (1343–91), had endangered by bequeathing it to Charles VI instead of his hated nephew Mathieu de Castelbon. Those of Normandy equally staunchly defended the province's privileges as announced in the charter of 1315 against royal encroachment, though when a meeting at Pont-Audemer in 1351 made a monetary grant it sparked off disturbances in Rouen. Those of Auvergne protested vigorously against the duke of Berry's attempts to tax them without consent, while (a perverse sign that he took their opposition seriously) on several occasions he used force against individual members, imprisoning them to bring them into line. In the 1380s the estates of Rouergue, Quercy, and the Auvergne occasionally joined with those of Velay, Vivarais, and the Gévaudan to tackle the endemic problem of hostile garrisons affecting these mountainous, central regions of the kingdom. Some of them were destined to survive well beyond 1400.

A united kingdom?

In late 1389 Charles VI successively entered Lyon, Montpellier, and Béziers in some of the first recorded royal provincial 'joyful entries' (*entrées joyeuses*). A journey by a reigning king of France to such distant parts of his realm was indeed a rare event and cause for celebration; Philip IV had once visited Bayonne and had toured the Midi in 1303–4. He also went twice to Lyon, paid at least five visits to Flanders, but never went to Burgundy or Brittany, though he reached Avranches and Mont Saint-Michel in 1307. The last Capetians reigned for shorter periods and had less reason to travel for diplomatic or military reasons, seldom straying far from the traditional heart of their kingdom. Philip VI fought at Cassel in 1328 and campaigned with his army at the beginning of the war with England, famously failing to come to grips with Edward III near Tournai in 1340–1, though they again came close to each other in Brittany in 1342–3 and he had to flee from the field at Crécy. Less belligerently, the papal court at Avignon sometimes attracted the king and the leading French princes, and John II visited Montpellier in 1351 shortly after its acquisition. But he was also the first French king largely to give up the habit of regular itineration, making Paris and its immediate environs his usual residence. The general sickliness of Charles V and insanity of Charles VI are undoubtedly other contributory factors encouraging the habit of royal stability by 1400. By contrast, when a king did make a royal progress, it was becoming a more structured event, presaging the theatrical presentations of French Renaissance monarchs to their subjects. Hence, in the continuously evolving 'religion of kingship' the significance attached by recent commentators to the fact that a canopy or baldaquin (*pavillon, poêle, ciel*) similar to that borne over the host in Corpus Christi processions was first carried over Charles VI as he made those southern entries in 1389.

However, the king was not alone in being fêted; other princes too were recognized as sharing Christ-like attributes of majesty on similar occasions. Philip the Bold and his wife, for instance, were met by the dean and chapter of Bruges on their 'joyful advent' to the city on 26 April 1384, when they swore on 'the book of privileges in which the count's oath is written . . . and then the duke opened a Gospel book and by chance he picked the Gospel, "But when the Counselor comes" '.[5] In 1379, for Louis I of Anjou's entry into Angers, tableaux were set up and allegorical presentations (*histoires*) were performed, that would become standard in all later princely or royal entry ceremonial. By the time something of their content can be discovered, this also frequently alludes to good government under a divinely chosen prince. No wonder that around 1400 most French princes were as eager to embrace the symbolic and ceremonial aspects of rule as the king and his advisers were.

By then, few great princes failed to attend court on a fairly regular basis; even a John IV of Brittany might condescend occasionally to come to Paris. His wife certainly bought some of her clothes and other luxury items there; counts of Artois, Flanders, and Hainault-Holland had done no less at the beginning of the century. But as their administrations or needs expanded and relations with governmental financial or judicial agencies became more complex, most princes kept permanent legal representatives at Paris, many employed other officers with experience in the royal administration or sought to place some of their own men in government posts, while messengers were constantly on the road between the capital and the provinces, transacting every kind of business for their masters. There was no lack of contact, whether formal or informal, between the centre and the periphery, but by 1400 the relationship between crown and many provinces had decisively shifted from the world that Philip IV had known. Put in the starkest terms, an age of princes had dawned. Could the monarchy reassert its authority, or would the trend towards independent and increasingly sophisticated, autonomous principalities in a period of continuing foreign warfare destroy the Valois kingdom? The fifteenth century would provide a decisive answer to these questions, but not before many twists and turns in a complex story in which 'unity under the king was not the only possible outcome' (Le Patourel).

[5] *Acta capituli*, Bischoppelik Archief, Bruges, A48, fo. 11^r, cited in J. M. Murray, 'The Liturgy of the Count's Advent in Bruges from Galbert to Van Eyck', in Kathryn L. Reyerson and Barbara A. Hanawalt (eds.), *City and Spectacle in Medieval Europe* (Minneapolis, 1994), 137–8, but translating *decanus* as dean not deacon.

4

France and the Hundred Years War, 1337–1453

Anne Curry

La Guerre de Cent Ans (Hundred Years War) is a French invention of the early nineteenth century. As far as can be discerned, the expression was first used by Desmichels in 1823 in his *Tableau chronologique de l'histoire du Moyen Âge*. Not surprisingly, the coining of a term to cover the Anglo-French wars of the later Middle Ages proved alluring, initially in textbooks aimed at the lycée and college (as in Boreau's *Histoire de France à l'usage des classes*, published in 1839), and subsequently in works aimed at the popular market. The first book to bear the title *La Guerre de Cent Ans* was published by Bachelet in Rouen in 1852. By the end of the 1360s the notion had crossed the Channel, as revealed by Edward Freeman's comment in the *Fortnightly Review* of May 1869: 'The French are perfectly right in speaking of the whole time from Edward the Third to Henry the Sixth as the Hundred Years War.'[1] Edward III had formally adopted the title king of France in Ghent in January 1340. Henry VI was crowned king of France in Paris in December 1431. The Hundred Years War appears, therefore, to be no less than a war waged by English kings for the crown of France itself.

While the term rightly emphasizes the long-drawn-out and insoluble nature of the conflict, it does have its drawbacks. It disguises the

[1] Cited in K. Fowler, *The Age of Plantagenet and Valois* (London, 1967), 13.

fact that the English and French had been at war on several occasions before 1340 because of issues arising from the tenure of lands in France by English kings. Such tenure dates back to the time of the Norman Conquest, but once Normandy and the other northern lands were lost in 1204–5, it was the duchy of Aquitaine (or Guienne), acquired through Henry II's marriage to Eleanor, which became the cause of dispute. There was no doubt that English kings held the duchy as vassals of their French counterparts. This was most famously confirmed by the treaty of Paris of 1259, following which Henry III of England performed liege homage to Louis IX in the garden of the palace on the Île de la Cité. In 1279 another territory, the county of Ponthieu, which straddled the Somme, was added to English royal possessions through the maternal inheritance of Eleanor of Castile, wife of Edward I. Try as they might to wriggle out of what was an awkward relationship—no king wished to be subordinate to another—it was impossible to do so because of the inherent nature of feudal tenure. The French king was undoubtedly the overlord of the English king as duke of Aquitaine just as he was overlord of any peer of France. This gave him the right to interfere in the business of the English king in his French lands, and, at worst, to confiscate such lands.

This was not merely local or even state politics as it might be in the case of other French peers; it was international relations, and a cause for war between the English and French people on behalf of their kings. Two wars had erupted in the wake of confiscations—1294–7 and 1324–7. In both it is hard to escape the conclusion that the French were bent upon removing the English from their soil but lacked the military power to do so. In 1337 Philip VI once again confiscated the lands of the English king, now Edward III. But the latter now had a new weapon to deploy—a claim to the French throne. In other words, the feudal wars of earlier generations were transformed into dynastic wars—into the 'Hundred Years War'. Although by 1453 the claim to the French throne had lost any real credibility following the final expulsion from Guienne, English rulers did not abandon their use of the title king of France until 1801. After 1453 it was no longer the holding of the title which stimulated and perpetuated Anglo-French wars, though rulers down to Henry VIII invoked it. Rather, the legacy of the bitter conflict of the previous 116 years, and the continuing interest of the English in the affairs of their near neighbour, ensured that relations remained sour for several centuries to come.

Recent historians have tended to question the 'dynastic' focus of the Hundred Years War, preferring to set it firmly within the context of earlier feudal problems and disputing whether Edward III, let alone his successors, were serious in their ambitions to make their claim to the French throne mean anything in practice. Although Desmichel's term-of-art has persisted throughout, the conflict has been seen as falling into different phases rather than being one single war. The first phase stretches from Philip VI's confiscation of English lands in 1337 (or alternatively from 1340, when Edward III formally took up the title king of France) to the treaty of Brétigny of 1360, which gave Edward an enlarged territorial holding independent of French feudal control in return for dropping his claim to the throne. The second phase is taken as running from the reopening of hostilities in 1369, when Charles V revived his feudal rights to declare Edward's lands confiscate, an act of war which prompted Edward to resume his French royal title. This phase sees the French recovery of most of the gains of 1360. By the end of the century a state of stalemate prevailed, prompting negotiation of a long truce in 1396. The third phase, stretching to the 1450s, begins with the renewal of war by Henry V's invasion of 1415. In 1420 the treaty of Troyes established Henry as heir of France, envisaging a prospective 'double monarchy' of England and France once Charles VI was dead. The English had, it seemed, almost won the Hundred Years War. Although Henry V predeceased Charles, his son Henry VI was actually crowned king of France in Notre Dame de Paris in December 1431. By then, though, French fortunes were beginning to recover from what might well be described as their darkest hour (although the capture of John II at the battle of Poitiers in 1356 had seemed equally bleak). The role of Jeanne d'Arc in this recovery remains contentious for the serious historian but has been universally accepted in French patriotic and popular literature. By the end of the third phase in 1453 the English had been driven out of Normandy and Guienne, leaving only Calais in their possession.

It is important to remember, however, that the cause and course of the Hundred Years War was not simply the result of English aggression. As we shall see, there is a strong argument for considering Philip VI rather than Edward III as the instigator of the conflict.

Furthermore, as will also be revealed, political divisions in France, between the Navarrese and royal party in the mid-fourteenth century, and between rival Burgundian and Armagnac (or Orléanist) factions in the early fifteenth century, also play a pivotal role in determining outcomes. France was a large country. Experiences of the Hundred Years War were both temporally and regionally varied, as many valuable local studies have demonstrated.

There is a strong argument that the conflict struck to the very heart of French national survival and that it affected all, high and low. Its intrinsic links with other events and trends of the period cannot be denied. In the late fourteenth and early fifteenth centuries, for instance, it took the form of a crusade when English and French, their allies ranged behind them, supported rival popes in the Papal Schism. In both centuries it impinged much on the relationship between the crown and nobility. But in the longer term the French crown's fight for survival in the face of a rival claim boosted its authority over its subjects and in particular led to royal incursion into the semi-independent principalities, discussed here in Chapter 3. The phoenix of absolutism, so to speak, rose from the ashes of defeat just as the long-drawn-out need to resist and to define an external enemy goaded the French into becoming a nation.

Historiography

It is no doubt this transition from 'darkest hour' to 'brilliant future' which helps to explain the place which the war has held in French historiography. Here we must return to the context within which the phrase 'Guerre de Cent Ans' was first coined in 1823. There can be little doubt that memories of the recent past, and in particular the defeat of France in 1815, were significant influences. France had moved from the abyss of self-destruction in the Revolution to the imperial domination of Europe—it was by treaty with Napoleon as First Consul in 1801 that George III had given up his French title—only then to find herself once more at the mercy of her enemies, and vacillating between monarchy and republic. Such circumstances invited reflection upon the peaks and troughs of France's history in an attempt to understand recent events and to remould national identity. Not surprisingly, the intelligentsia as well as increasingly well-educated middle classes of France were eager to receive the products of this historical, and often jingoistic and journalistic, outpouring.

The Anglo-French wars of the later Middle Ages provided readily instructive parallels. The humiliating capture of King John II by the English at Poitiers in 1356 had led to internal upheaval and peasant rebellion in the Jacquerie of 1358 as well as forcing the virtual dismemberment of France in the treaty of Brétigny of 1360. The equally demoralizing defeat at Agincourt in 1415 had exacerbated fissures within the political nation, escalating a civil war which brought the English to the crown of France itself. Yet from such past depths of suffering and shame the nation had recovered, in the fourteenth century through the wily realism of Charles V and his constable Bertrand Du Guesclin, and in the fifteenth through the inspiration of Jeanne d'Arc and the rebuilt confidence of Charles VII. In both scenarios the French had been forced to reunite and to redefine their existence in the face of war with England, and had managed to do so successfully. The period thus provided a positive image while by no means belittling the degree of pain and humiliation. This was a message which the French were keen to hear after 1815, not least, for instance, in the vicinity of Agincourt, where an English army of occupation had been rooting around for physical evidence of their victory of 400 years before—at least until the duke of Wellington responded sympathetically to local complaints and ordered the digging to stop.

As in the period itself the recovery of national identity and pride was in part predicated on slighting the enemy. In the 1830s Jules Michelet emphasized in both his influential public lectures and his best-selling *Histoire de France* the suffering of late medieval France, which affected all from high to low: 'the English left nothing behind them on the continent save in ruins'. They were natural aggressors, as he noted when introducing the section on the opening of conflict between Philip VI and Edward III.[2] Had he not seen with his own eyes in England the factories, and their workers, 'who subjugated nature by fire and steel . . . In the middle ages, the Englishman was almost what he is today, too well-fed, forced into action, warrior because there was as yet not enough industry to occupy him.' Yet, as

[2] J. Michelet, *Histoire de France* (Paris, 1837; 2nd edn. 1865), ii. 431.

Michelet concluded when discussing the loss of Normandy and Guienne, the English had rendered an immense service to France: 'France had searched, had dug deep, the lives of its people had sunk to the very lowest levels, but she had found what? She had found France itself. She owes it to her enemy to have discovered herself as a nation.' There was, he concluded, a strangely symbiotic love–hate relationship between England and France: 'long live their emulation of each other, their rivalry, if not their warfare'.[3]

By the 1850s this love–hate relationship was symbolized by the juxtaposition of a generally Anglophile emperor, Napoleon III, and 'Palmerston's follies', a ring of defences along the south coast built in fear of French attack and invasion, much as the early artillery defences of the same area had been constructed during the Hundred Years War—a lasting reminder that the French had tried to take the war to the English. But, just as the French had discovered to their cost in the later Middle Ages, pride comes before a fall. In 1870–1 France was once more brought to humiliating defeat and national upheaval. This gave interest in the 'Guerre de Cent Ans' an additional fillip, even if the enemy—now the Prussian—was a new one. It is striking how many historical works were coloured by the Franco-Prussian war. Not least, one can see a special emphasis on the role of Jeanne d'Arc as a liberator from foreign oppression. There was also an emerging emphasis on the physical damage wrought by the English, epitomized by the influential two-volume work of Henri Deniflé, *La désolation des églises, monastères et hôpitaux en France pendant la Guerre de Cent Ans*, published in 1897 and still the inspiration of studies of the impact of the war: 'an endless and grimly monotonous succession of massacres, fires, pillaging, ransoms, destructions, losses of harvests and cattle, rapes, and—to make an end of it—of every sort of calamity'.[4] It is significant too that the two kings given full-scale studies by French historians around the turn of the century (Charles V, the subject of a five-volume work by Delachenal published between 1909 and 1931, and Charles VII, the focus of Du Fresne de Beaucourt's six-volume study of 1881–91) were the two rulers who had done most to rid France of the English.

[3] Ibid. ii. 859.

[4] As translated in N. Wright, *Knights and Peasants: The Hundred Years War in the French Countryside* (Woodbridge, 1998), 6.

The most enduring work by a French historian on the Hundred Years War remains that by Edouard Perroy. It too was forged on the anvil of war, being largely written over 1943–4 as Perroy sought to resist German occupation. As he poignantly noted in his preface,

> it would be naïve to suppose that the tragic ups-and-downs of the Hundred Years' War can guide our action in the present or enable us to foresee our future nor can one even seek ground for hope in this story of failure, downfall and recovery in the past. But when a nation reaches the depths of the abyss, as was the case at that time and in our own, certain ways of behaviour in misfortune, certain reactions against fate, throw mutual light upon one another . . . certain actions have become more comprehensible; one is better placed to explain a surrender, or to excuse a revolt.[5]

The book was published after the Liberation of 1945. The context in which it had been written prompted David Douglas, in his introduction to the English translation of 1951, to draw further links between the Second World War and the Hundred Years War. Most obvious were 'Normandy landings' common to both, but Douglas also pointed to parallels between the treaty of Troyes of 1420, which envisaged a double monarchy of England and France, and the act of union suggested by the British government on 16 June 1940, in another of France's 'darkest hours'. Had either union been successfully implemented, then the course of west European history might have been rather different.

Perroy's book remains the best one-volume narrative of the Hundred Years War, although historians on both sides of the Channel have since contributed much through in-depth researches in primary sources of all kinds. Let us therefore consider some of the major phases of the war in the light of this work, concentrating particularly on the opening stages of the conflict where a French king had the unprecedented insult of his long-established enemy challenging the very basis of authority—the royal title itself. This determined for the French the whole of the late medieval conflict with England. While modern historians might debate the point, it surely mattered little to the French at any stage whether Edward III and his successors really intended to become kings of France. The important point was

[5] E. Perroy, *The Hundred Years War* (London, 1951; repr. New York, 1965), p. xxvii.

that they called themselves king of France and invaded the French nation under colour of that title.

The opening of the Hundred Years War

Until the death of Louis X in 1316 the Capetian royal house had been remarkably fortunate in that it had always had a direct male heir to inherit. The dynastic arrangements discussed in the Introduction led to the exclusion of one after another female heir in 1316, 1322, and 1328, not through an invocation of 'Salic law'—such 'law' was a later fourteenth-century invention to justify English exclusion—but for pragmatic reasons. On 2 April 1328 the regent, Philip, count of Valois, cousin of Charles IV, summoned an assembly. Given Philip's existing control of the government, his maturity (he was already 35 and had sons), and the fact that he was heir in the male line, Philip was the assembly's obvious choice as king, and on 29 May he was crowned at the traditional crowning place of Reims.

Yet it was clear in 1328 that there was another credible male claimant: the 14-year-old Edward III of England, whose mother, Isabelle, was the sister of Charles IV. On 16 May the bishops of Worcester and Coventry were appointed to go to France 'to show, demand, request and require for us and in our name all the right actions and possessions of the kingdom of France which have come down to us and belong to us . . . as to a direct heir of the said kingdom', 'to make requests and demands for the right of the said kingdom to those who are occupied on this matter', and 'to accept *journé* [debate?] with all those who dispute that the kingdom should come to us'.[6] One version of the *Grandes chroniques* tells us that the English did indeed put forward to the assembly that the kingdom should pass to Edward as nephew of the late king, in preference to Philip as cousin, and that some doctors of canon and civil law agreed with this view, no doubt because, in the inheritance of land, a nephew had precedence over a cousin.

A counter-argument was put forward in favour of Philip based on the fact that Edward's claim came through his mother: because

[6] Thomas Rymer, *Foedera*, Record Commission edn. (1816–69), ii. 743.

Isabelle was debarred from the succession herself because she was female, she had no claim to transmit to her son. This did indeed undermine Edward's claim. Although no formal pronouncement had been made in 1317 banning the transmission of royal title through a woman, it was surely implicit in that very decision. Although Jeanne, daughter of Louis X, was only 7 at the time of her father's death, it could not have been discounted that she might in time have a male heir (her eldest son, Charles of Navarre, was born in 1332). Moreover, it was apparent that Jeanne had a claim to the kingdom of Navarre which was heritable by and through women, having come into the hands of the French crown through the wife of Philip IV. Rather skilfully, Philip VI, soon after his accession, allowed Jeanne to succeed to Navarre, but retained Champagne, to which she also had a claim, offering her lands in Angoulême and Mortain in lieu. He also granted compensation for the territorial rights of his various royal nieces, for while the decision of 1317 might have prevented their assumption of the crown, their rights to land, by virtue of feudal law, were a separate issue. This raises the possibility that the claim to the throne put forward on behalf of Edward III in 1328 was made not at face value but as a bargaining counter for the land to which Isabelle, Edward's mother, as daughter of a king of France, might be considered due. In the context of continuing disputes over the status of English lands in France (the war which had followed Charles IV's confiscation of Guienne and Ponthieu in 1324 had only been brought to a peace settlement on 31 March 1327) it is tempting to suggest that the English were hoping to win concessions. Yet there is no direct evidence of any such arguments being put forward.

Once Philip was crowned king, one might have considered the matter closed. But there were some weaknesses in his position, not least because of an element of 'election' in his succession, and because a blood claim, such as Edward undoubtedly had, was not so easily disposed of. Research by Cazelles has shown how Philip had some difficulty in establishing a stable group of advisers. But, fortified by his victory against the Flemish at Cassel on 23 August 1328, he began to develop his own coterie and to put pressure on Edward to pay homage for his French lands in order to neutralize any future use of the claim. Edward's homage to Philip as king of France, performed in person at Amiens Cathedral on 6 June 1329 and confirmed in 1331, was a symbolic acceptance of one claimant by the other.

By 1331, therefore, the succession issue appeared to be at an end, but the issue of English lands in France did not. Edward's homage had been forced on him by French threats to confiscate the revenues of Guienne and Ponthieu. Philip's policy here was no different from that of previous French kings: to make the English territorial position in France vulnerable in the hope of bringing it to an end. Researches by Jusselin in the early twentieth century based on French royal financial records demonstrated how Charles IV had begun to prepare for an all-out invasion of Guienne in 1327. Over the course of the 1330s Philip lost no opportunity to undermine the English position whether in French-allied Scotland, where Edward was himself involved in a struggle for feudal overlordship, or in Guienne, where, as Vale has shown, there was 'an intensification of French jurisdictional activity' matched by an equal increase of defensive preparations on the part of the English and their Gascon subjects.[7] By 1336 matters had reached a head. The failure of the French and English to reach a settlement led Pope Benedict XII to cancel Philip's proposed crusade in March of that year—a blow to his pride and an incentive to move his fleet to the Normandy coast in order to threaten England.

There is no real doubt that it was Philip who started the war with England. At this stage all the military and naval advantages lay with him. Without allies, Edward's military potential was scarcely half as great as Philip's and he was already committed to a war in Scotland. On 26 December 1336 Philip sent a letter to Edward's seneschal of Guienne demanding that the English king, as a vassal, hand over Robert of Artois, the 'mortal enemy' of the French crown, whom Edward was harbouring. Although this request was debatable in feudal law (Robert was in England not Guienne), it served its purpose. On 24 May 1337 Philip declared the English king's lands confiscate, and within six weeks French troops had begun their incursions. By the spring of 1339 the capital of Guienne, Bordeaux, was threatened by French encirclement by land and sea. Already in the previous year Philip had commissioned raids on the Channel Islands and on the ports of southern England. That on Southampton on 5 October 1338 proved particularly devastating for the English, who, never previously attacked in this way, were lamentably unprepared. Meanwhile, Edward's search for allies and money had

[7] M. Vale, *The Angevin Legacy and the Hundred Years War* (Oxford, 1990), 257.

delayed his own crossing to the continent until July 1338, and it was not until 18 September 1339 that he was able to launch his first attack on France from Vilvoorde, near Brussels, into the Cambrésis. A week earlier Philip had taken the symbolic banner known as the oriflamme from the abbey of Saint-Denis. This was the real opening of the Hundred Years War in that it brought the two kings into potential personal conflict. Chronicle accounts suggest that battle was imminent on 22 October 1339 at Buironfosse, on the River Oise east of Guise, yet none transpired, and historians remain divided over which side chose to avoid engagement.

French politics and the Hundred Years War, 1339–1360

At this point, the end of 1339, we must take note of three important points. The first is that Edward had not, as yet, made an overt claim to the French throne. His choice of first theatre had been occasioned by the imperial vicariate which his ally, the Emperor Lewis of Bavaria, had accorded him in 1338: the Cambrésis was territory of the empire, and Edward's army had been boosted by many Low Country allies, subjects of the emperor. The second is that the campaign of 1339 saw much destruction and pillaging of villages. A papal almsgiving exercise in the following year reveals that forty-five villages suffered damage. Never before had French civilians been victims of war on such a scale.

In other words, right from the start the war was brought to the French civilian, much as Philip had already brought it to the citizens of southern England. It has been argued by Rogers that English strategy, now as in later campaigns, was consciously aimed at destruction so that the French might be brought to doubt the ability of the Valois to protect them. Taking this interpretation to its logical conclusion, the strategy of attacking the civilian is linked to putting forward a rival bid to the throne. We must remember, however, that Philip, as Charles V did later, used a scorched-earth policy in order to enfeeble the English army, which, fighting on foreign soil, would always have greater difficulty in acquiring victuals. This was a factor in all campaigns of the fourteenth-century phase. English armies lived off the land because they had to. Their actions hardly endeared them to the French inhabitants, nor made the latter keen to accept an English ruler as their own, but it is sometimes difficult to distinguish damage caused by English troops from that brought about by the French when Philip and his allies also indulged in a scorched-earth policy in order to deprive the English of supplies.

A third observation takes us back to the origins of the war and to the pivotal role of Robert of Artois, who was Philip VI's brother-in-law and one of the king's closest advisers in the first two years of the reign. Indeed, Philip had committed a misjudgement in supporting Robert's claim to the county of Artois, stirring up opposition from many other nobles, especially those in the coterie of the duke of Burgundy, another royal brother-in-law whose wife had a claim to Artois. The scandal emerged in December 1330 when it was revealed that Robert had commissioned forged documents to support his claim. Philip now cast him aside, and allowed a criminal prosecution to be brought against him. Robert fled from France, first to the Low Countries and then in 1334 to England. Philip hounded him at every turn, moved by the threats which Robert was making throughout his exile to stir up rebellion in France and to bring about the death of the royal children by necromancy. Philip was able, by his summons to Edward in December 1336, to attempt to kill two birds with one stone, to attack his brother-in-law and to create a pretence for the confiscation of Guienne. On the other side of the Channel there is little doubt that Robert did much to remind Edward of his putative French royal claim and to encourage a response to French aggression.

The role of Robert brings us back to an observation made earlier, namely that divisions within France played an important role in the Hundred Years War. If Edward was to meet with any success in his claim to the throne, or even to bring Philip to agree to territorial concessions, then support of nobles and communities within France would be essential. (As we shall see later, only when Henry V was able to achieve such support on a meaningful scale did the English come anywhere near putting their royal claim into effect.) As it turned out, the link with Robert did not bring as much advantage as Edward had hoped. In 1340, while Edward besieged Tournai, Robert was commissioned to the siege of Saint-Omer in the hope that he would attract a following from his supposed subjects in Artois. Robert's fall from grace within France had been so complete that he had no following there, and the plan proved ineffective. By this juncture, though, Edward had succeeded in gaining important support within France itself, and that was with the Flemish towns. The county of Flanders was a fief of the French crown, as well as crucially positioned on its northern frontier. Edward had earlier tried to gain the support of the count himself, but had failed, with the result that his initial base in the war with Philip had had to be established in Brabant, which lay outside France. However, over the winter of 1339, as the researches of Lucas demonstrated, Edward was able to exploit long-standing differences between the leading towns of Ghent, Bruges, and Ypres and their count, whom they had forced into exile in France. His ability to offer economic advantages through the promise of English wool, a commodity which formed the basis of the Flemish cloth industry, as well as to legitimize the urban rebellion, were the factors underpinning his acceptance by the Flemish townsmen as king of France. That explains why his formal assumption of the title was at Ghent on 26 January 1340. Although the count remained loyal to Philip, dying in his cause at the battle of Crécy in 1346, and Edward's support was limited to the urban groups, it was immensely significant that Edward's title had been accepted in at least one part of France.

Philip had little choice but to try to undermine Anglo-Flemish links by a naval blockade, but this went disastrously wrong. It has been calculated that up to 90 per cent of the French fleet was destroyed at the battle of Sluys on 24 June 1340, putting paid to any hope Philip had of continuing his aggressive attacks upon England itself, and thereby concentrating the war on land theatres in France. The Flemish alliance also dictated the focus of Edward's land campaign of the summer, which was devoted to the recovery of Tournai and other towns once in Flanders annexed to France under Philip IV. Part of his army was drawn from the Flemish militia, another reason why the Flemish alliance was of such potential value. The failure of Robert of Artois at Saint-Omer left Edward's besieging force at Tournai vulnerable, yet Philip failed to take advantage by refusing to engage, no doubt mindful of the defeat at Sluys.

Although, as it had turned out, the Flemish alliance had not brought as much advantage as hoped, it was not long before divisions elsewhere in France—this time in Brittany—offered new opportunities for Edward. Neither side had anticipated this, but the succession dispute in the duchy which followed the death on 20 April 1341 of Duke John III was to create a Breton theatre in the Hundred Years War which lasted, on and off, for most of the rest of the century, and which continued to play a role even in the fifteenth-century phase, contributing much to the development of Breton separatism through the pivotal role played in the determination of both French and English fortunes. Duke John III had himself been consistent in support of Philip VI, having fought in his army sent to the relief of Tournai, and having even proposed to bequeath his duchy to the French king, although, as Jones reminds us, 'his nobility energetically vetoed the suggestion' (above Chapter 3, 'The duchy of Brittany and the crown'). It none the less fell to the French king as overlord to hear the legal arguments of the claimants, Jeanne de Penthièvre, the niece of the late duke, who happened to be married to Philip's own nephew Charles, younger son of the count of Blois, and John de Montfort, the late duke's half-brother. Not surprisingly, Philip declared in favour of the Penthièvre–Blois claim, with the result that Montfort sought Edward's aid.

The potential significance of this was not lost on Edward, who invaded the duchy in person in October 1342 (interestingly, Robert of Artois had been one of the commanders of an advance guard sent in April). The ensuing war was one of attrition, waged largely by siege, counter-siege, and skirmish between garrisons, symptomatic, perhaps, of a conflict which was at base a civil war. As a result the duchy was effectively divided, with the north and east under the control of the French on behalf of Blois and the south and west under the English on behalf of Montfort. The latter, who had escaped from captivity in France, paid homage to Edward as king. His death at the siege of Quimper in September 1345 extended direct English control in the duchy, since the young heir, Duke John IV, was sent to England, not being allowed to return until 1362. Even so, there remained a persistent degree of stalemate in Brittany, which may have been one factor prompting Edward in 1346 to try another theatre—Normandy. Again, the potential offered by divisions in France seemed considerable. Geoffroi de Harcourt, sr. de Saint-Sauveur in the Cotentin, had defected to Edward and was present with the king as he prepared his invasion, encouraging him by speaking of the weak defences of the area and of the promise of further defectors (although these never transpired). Significantly, too, Edward sought at the very same point to call on the aid of the Flemish militias, perhaps in the hope of catching the French in a pincer move.

The events of 1346–7 are in themselves well known. Edward moved swiftly across Normandy, forcing the surrender and sacking of Caen, before moving as if towards Paris, where Philip lay. Rogers has recently argued that Edward hoped to draw Philip to battle there, but that he failed to do so. The latter hoped that by following Edward northwards he would cut off his return to England. What better, perhaps, than to defeat him within the county of Ponthieu, part of the feudal inheritance of the English crown. But this was not to be. At the battle of Crécy on 26 August the French were emphatically defeated. There can be no doubt that this put Philip on the defensive, forcing the withdrawal of his son's troops from the siege of Aiguillon, whose fall would have given the Valois entry into the heartlands of English-held Guienne, and persuading him against intervention to raise the siege of Calais, even though he had taken the oriflamme in March 1347 with that intention. The town fell to Edward in July 1347. Two months earlier Charles of Blois had been captured as his counter-siege of La Roche Derrien failed.

There can be no underestimating the psychological demoralization of the campaigns of 1346–7 on the French. Yet, importantly, divisions within France had not materialized. To cite but one small example, Geoffroi de Harcourt, having established a garrison at Carentan in Lower Normandy during Edward's invasion, soon found himself expelled by local French loyalists. He fled to Brabant, and by December sought pardon from Philip. Indeed, Philip's kingship was no more vulnerable in 1347 than it had been at the outset of his reign, in fact possibly less so, for defeat had generated a greater degree of loyalty, at least to the king himself. But there were mounting fissures early in the reign of his successor, John II (1350–64). These came from the Évreux branch of the royal family, headed by Charles of Navarre, son of Jeanne, daughter of Louis X (see Chapter 3). His rift with the king was occasioned by internal court politics rather than by any putative claim he himself had to the French throne, and focused on his opposition to the royal favourite, the constable Charles of Spain, in whose murder he was implicated in 1354. The king's reaction in April 1356, which led to the arrest of Charles of Navarre and the execution of four of his followers, did, however, play into the hands of the English. Navarre's power base was in Normandy, by virtue of royal donation. His fall led to the defection of other key Norman lords, most notably his brother Philippe, count of Longueville, and Geoffroi de Harcourt. It was at this point that Edward III began to call himself duke of Normandy, although distractions in Scotland prevented his campaigning in the duchy in person at this point. As Cazelles has shown, the pro-Navarrese faction in France was strong, with supporters in Champagne and in Picardy as well as Normandy. Thus the threat of destabilization was already great even before the major blow of the year, the capture of the king at the battle of Poitiers on 19 September.

This came in the wake of two of the most destructive raids undertaken by English armies, the *chevauchées* of the Black Prince, first in 1355 from Atlantic almost to Mediterranean, through areas of Languedoc previously unscathed by the war, and secondly northwards towards the Loire, this time with the objective of joining up with Philip of Navarre and the French rebels as well as the duke of Lancaster, who had himself indulged in much looting in the areas of Lower Normandy still loyal to the king. Given that the king's manoeuvres had prevented this coordination, and that he had forced the Black Prince to turn south, the victory at Poitiers ought to have been assured. But instead 2,000 French were dead, including several members of the royal council and both the constable and marshal, and another 2,500 taken prisoner, among them the king and two of his sons. As the researches of Cazelles and Henneman have revealed, the defeat led to an implosion in domestic politics. The dauphin, himself only 18 and with previously little role in government, was forced to call the Estates General, where demands for reform and for the release of Charles of Navarre soon emerged. A major problem was the declining value of currency, undermined by the impact of the Black Death and by King John's previous manipulations, and it was the dauphin's attempts at revaluation which prompted the bourgeois rebellion led by Étienne Marcel, *prévôt* of the merchants of Paris. When the estates of Languedoil met in the capital on 5 February 1357, the dauphin was forced to agree to the *Grand Ordonnance* prepared by Robert le Coq, bishop of Laon, which aimed at checking the perceived tyranny of the crown. The dauphin's authority was further challenged by the release of Charles of Navarre in November 1357. Indeed, it was no longer clear where authority lay.

The civil war which had begun in Normandy now spread east, but this was informal war, where military action and brigandage became indistinguishable. Indeed, several studies have revealed how much damage was caused to civilians in this period, more perhaps than in English actions. As Luce showed, peasants who were forced to pay protection money to brigands were then tactlessly fined by the government for having dealings with brigands. Wright's researches show how peasants began to take matters into their own hands, annoyed at being left undefended by the government—an important reminder of how the population as a whole perceived the duties of their rulers, and of the soldiers whom their rulers employed supposedly for the protection of the nation. Such pressures led in May 1358 to the Jacquerie, a peasant rebellion in Champagne, Picardy, and Beauvasis. But ironically, perhaps, it was reaction to these moves by the lower orders which forced the rulers of society to be reconciled with each other, and led to the discrediting of the bourgeois reform movement in Paris. Thus the dauphin and Charles of Navarre worked together to put down the rebellion. By 8 July 1358 Charles had agreed to swear loyalty to the crown in return for a large payment. Isolated, Étienne Marcel sent a plea for aid to the Flemish towns but was murdered at the end of the month.

The rapprochement between the dauphin and Navarre was short-lived. By the end of August the former was writing to the count of Savoy claiming that Navarre was intent upon seizing the throne. We know for certain that Navarre was involved in negotiations with the English at this point which envisaged a division of France. In return for recognizing Edward as king, Charles would gain Champagne and Brie, with the prospect also of acquiring Normandy and Picardy. The crisis in France was as great as ever, felt bitterly at a local level as demands for taxation were raised, and as the actions of *routiers* (essentially demobilized soldiers) escalated, for the formal armies had essentially collapsed and men looked to their own advantage, often ranging over wide geographical areas, including the Auvergne, which had previously seen little of the formal Franco-English conflict. Communities were increasingly reluctant to pay tax for central needs when they felt that they needed to look to their own defences, and when they were faced with huge ransoms to buy off the *routiers*. That which Sir Robert Knolles demanded of Auxerre in March 1359 was set at 40,000 *moutons*. Many towns, such as Rouen, began to levy purchase taxes in order to repair their defences.

By April 1359 another English invasion was imminent. The seriousness of the threat was great enough for the dauphin to call the estates of the whole kingdom for the first time in more than eleven years. This was the real moment for uniting. By the end of the year the levy of the salt tax (*gabelle*) was virtually national. On 21 August the dauphin and Charles of Navarre made peace at Pontoise. The dauphin even negotiated an alliance with the Danish king whereby the latter promised to invade England with 12,000 men in return for 600,000 *écus*. More significantly, he had enough intelligence to know that Edward was aiming at Reims and was thus able to warn the city. Knowing that he was too weak to give battle, he wisely pursued a scorched-earth policy, which prevented the English from sustaining a lengthy siege, impelling them in due course to negotiate. Here too it is important to note how Edward was damaged by his inability to control his *routier* captains such as Robert Knolles. Their tendency to hold individual places to ransom brought them individual rewards but contributed little to Edward's overall strategy, and undermined the possibility of his winning over the French at this crucial juncture. On 10 March the duke of Burgundy agreed that he would support Edward if the majority of peers did likewise. If not, then the truce which the duke had entered into with the English king would cease. Edward attempted to show his strength by taking Paris, but once again his looting and burning tactics proved counter-productive. The French lords showed every sign of answering the dauphin's plea for aid issued on 28 April. Faced with lack of food and heavy rain, Edward negotiated a settlement at Brétigny near Chartres.

The recovery of France, 1360–1390

Ironically, the Brétigny settlement worked in time to the advantage of the French. This may have seemed an unlikely outcome in 1360, faced as the French were by the loss of extensive territory and major financial problems. In order to hold out, the dauphin had been forced to devalue the currency on several occasions. Henneman notes that in Poitou and Saintonge Marshal Bouciccaut had even had to counterfeit money to pay his soldiers. Towns such as Reims had suffered repeatedly, not only from the English siege but also from the longer-term influx of local peasants in search of security, which Desportes calculates had boosted the population by 50 per cent, and by the repeated burdens of defensive costs, which were largely borne by local purchase taxes and which had necessitated the demolition of dwellings and religious establishments in the suburbs. Now there was a ransom of 3 million *écus* for the return of King John, to which Reims and other places were 'invited' to contribute loans. These were intended to be repaid out of later subsidies, but many were not, thereby giving rise to disputes for years to come. France remained ravaged over the 1360s by the actions of demobilized soldiers, both English and French. This was the main period of the Great Companies, who ranged as far afield as Alsace, Provence, and Languedoc. For the local population, it must often have seemed that the war was still going on.

But the need to plan for the ongoing payment of the ransom, given that the 'down payment' of 600,000 *écus* was to be followed by annual instalments of 400,000 *écus* for the next six years, prompted a new era in taxation and was an important element in the recovery of royal authority. Within two months of returning to France, John had issued ordinances stabilizing the currency and establishing the *aides* and *fouage* (or *taille*) as well as regularizing the salt tax (*gabelle*) inaugurated by his father in 1341 (see Chapter 7). Thus the crown gained the possibility of regular tax income without reference to any representative bodies. John was forced to end his days in England after his son Louis of Anjou broke prison in 1362. Furthermore, events over the 1360s increasingly redounded to the benefit of the French. Both John IV, duke of Brittany, and Charles of Navarre accepted French royal authority, the latter after military defeat at Cocherel in 1364. In 1367 Charles V secured the marriage of the heiress to Flanders for his brother, Philip, who was created duke of Burgundy. In Castile the French king's nominee, Henry of Trastamara, finally triumphed in 1369. Thus all English allies had been picked off, so to speak.

As with Philip VI in the 1330s, it was Charles who acted the aggressor in 1369, exploiting loopholes in the Brétigny settlement and disaffected lords in Guienne, most notably the lords of Albret and Armagnac. It would be all too easy to say that the latter were motivated by a sense of French patriotism, and that they had merely been biding their time under English rule waiting for an opportunity to return to their real allegiance. Yet what had prompted their volte-face was essentially their own interests and resentment at the Black Prince's tax burdens. Their own interests were easily fanned by promise of financial reward and royal marriage. Charles was already moving his troops into English lands even before war was formally opened, and by 1372 almost all the gains of 1360 had been recovered. By the late 1370s the war was once again being taken to English shores, with major raids on the Isle of Wight and the south coast towns.

Charles's reputation was much enhanced. Take, for instance, the Latin words of a motet composed by Philippe Roylllart in praise of the king celebrating his success against the English: 'Thou hast vanquished the enemy that plagued our innocent people.' Yet the success was not complete. The motet goes on to emphasize his subjects' desire for peace ('now bring back peace to us. Listen to us and make it happen').[8] We have here a reminder that Charles's policy of avoiding pitched battle with the English had its downside: it allowed English *chevauchées* to range widely in a geographical sense, even in the heartlands of northern France, causing much local damage. We may also have here an allusion to the continuing problem of the *routiers.*

Nonetheless, Charles was soon accorded the epithet le Sage (the Wise). As Christine de Pisan emphasizes, he was much assisted by his faithful military leaders, not only Du Guesclin but also members of the royal family, his own brothers, the dukes of Berry, Anjou, and Burgundy, and the queen's brother the duke of Bourbon. Although she exaggerates when she suggests that, thanks to Charles, 'the English no longer dare to set foot in France',[9] it was no longer likely, either in Charles's own reign or during the first thirty years of that of his son, that they would recover the ascendancy they had achieved in 1360. The last major *chevauchée* was in 1380, the year of Charles's death. Under such circumstances, prompted also by royal minorities in England and France in the 1380s, both protagonists were keen to negotiate a settlement which at least confirmed the status quo and created a cessation of hostilities. War effectively ceased in 1388, with a

[8] As recorded by David Munrow and the Early Music Consort of London, *Music of the Gothic Era* (Deutsche Grammophon, Archiv, CD 471 731–2).

[9] Christine de Pisan, *Le livre des faits et bonnes mœurs du roi Charles V le Sage*, ed. E. Hicks and T. Moreau (Paris, 1997), 194.

twenty-eight-year truce agreed in 1396. Desportes's study of Reims shows how there was a slow recovery of the urban economy after 1388. We also hear much less of *routiers* from the 1380s. Wartime conditions slowly subsided.

A divided France at England's mercy, 1392–1429

The experience of the last thirty years of the fourteenth century proved one important point. While the nobility of France remained united, neither English armed aggression nor their claim to the throne could damage her. Although the duke of Brittany and the Navarre line had been persuaded to offer the English support in the 1370s and 1380s, this was sporadic and was ended by the long truce. The French position was much strengthened once Philip, duke of Burgundy, came into direct control of Flanders in 1383 following the death of his father-in-law, Louis de Male. Prior to this point the English had attempted to revive their strategy of the late 1330s and early 1340s by exploiting the independent actions of the Flemish towns against their count. This was dealt a fatal blow by French victory over the townsmen at Roosebecke in 1382, and by the mid-1380s Flanders was serving as a base for further invasions of England.

The revival of English fortunes in the early fifteenth century, and the unprecedented successes of Henry V, were made possible only by the rise of divisions within France itself. These divisions stemmed essentially from the insanity of Charles VI, first evidenced in 1392, which encouraged a struggle between the king's brother Louis, duke of Orléans, and his uncle Philip the Good, duke of Burgundy, for control of the king and government, a struggle continued after Philip's death in 1404 by his son John the Fearless. The politics of this period, discussed in the Introduction, were complex and further complicated by the role of the queen, Isabeau of Bavaria, who was anxious to preserve her own rights, and those of her eldest son, the dauphin Louis (d. 1415), and by pressures for reform and an end to corruption in a faction-ridden government. Suffice to say that the feud escalated in the first decade of the new century, culminating in the assassination of Orléans by Duke John's agents in 1407. It continued with the new duke of Orléans, Charles, and became fully fledged civil war from 15 April 1410. On this date the dukes of Berry, Brittany, and Orléans and the counts of Alençon, Clermont, and Armagnac formed a defensive league at Gien, specifying how many troops each would bring against Burgundy and others whom they declared were damaging the king and kingdom. Orléans married the count of Armagnac's daughter, thereby giving rise to his party commonly being called 'Armagnacs'.

The gravity of the situation is revealed by the conflicting parties being prepared to seek the aid of the English. In 1412 the members of the League of Gien even went so far as to offer Henry IV full sovereignty in Guienne in return for an army of 4,000 men. On this occasion the involvement of the English army was cut short by the reconciliation of the League with Burgundy. Although technically both sides were at peace when Henry V invaded in 1415, there was much bad blood, and already violence, not least in Paris, over which the Armagnacs and Burgundy had already struggled. The battle of Agincourt saw the Armagnac party much damaged, not least by the capture of Charles, duke of Orléans. Whether Burgundy had deliberately held off from participation remains unclear. In later recriminations Armagnac supporters such as the poet Alain Chartier did imply he was to blame for the defeat by his cowardice, while Burgundian writers claimed that had the duke been there, Henry V would have been routed.

Similarly uncertain is whether Henry V and Burgundy came to a secret deal when they met at Calais in 1416. As prince, Henry had favoured the Burgundian group, sending armed aid in 1411 before his father reversed this policy in 1412. From the Burgundian perspective, it was useful to allow Henry a free hand in his conquest of Normandy in 1417–19 while he concentrated on gaining control of Paris, which he achieved in May 1418, subsequently taking control of the king and queen, while the last surviving dauphin, Charles, now deemed the leader of the Armagnac group, fled south. The *Journal* of the Bourgeois of Paris (more likely the work of a clergyman in the capital) reveals just how violent these factional struggles were, not only in Paris but also in many other areas of northern France. Of the Burgundian purge of Armagnac supporters in Paris in 1418 he writes:

'There was not one of the principal streets of Paris that did not have a killing in it . . . they were heaped up in piles in the mud like sides of bacon.'[10]

Only when Henry began to threaten the capital itself did the factions attempt reconciliation, but old wounds ran deep. At a meeting between Burgundy and the dauphin on the bridge at Montereau on 10 September 1419 which was intended to cement their treaty of friendship, the dauphin's entourage killed Duke John in an act which was in many ways a retaliation for the assassination of Orléans in 1407. With Henry continuing to advance on Paris, the inexperienced Duke Philip of Burgundy and the king and queen had little choice but to accept terms. By the treaty of Troyes, Henry became heir and regent of France. The dauphin was disinherited by his father in a formal *lit de justice* at the beginning of 1421. Unlike Brétigny, however, Troyes sought to preserve French integrity rather than to destroy it. Henry committed himself to preserving French institutions as well as to continuing the war against the Armagnacs until they were completely defeated. In this context, therefore, he perpetuated the French civil war, adding his might to that of the Burgundians. The seriousness of divisions in France is further demonstrated by the numerous French chroniclers who depict Henry as the only man capable of bringing peace to a divided nation.

Not all, of course, saw it this way. The treaty was not accepted outside those areas under English or Burgundian rule. Many in the north without strong factional leanings might wonder whether a king of England, the ancient enemy, was acceptable as king of France. Even in England there was some scepticism over a treaty which brought war rather than peace, and which forced friendships with those they had so recently been fighting against. The Normans, whom the English king had courted with notions of separatism, reviving old institutions and even dressing in the robes of the duke, were disappointed by Henry's promise at Troyes that the duchy would be reunited with the French crown once he succeeded his father-in-law. More significantly, the dauphin still lived, and was able to establish a rival administration south of the Loire.

It is all too easy, however, to see the treaty as unworkable because of its cavalier handling of French national identity. Had Henry outlived

[10] *A Parisian Journal 1405–1449*, ed. J. Shirley (Oxford, 1968), 114.

his father, who knows what further successes he might have won. But it was not to be. Although Henry VI was a credible heir to the double monarchy, much lauded as the descendant through his father of Edward the Confessor and through his mother of St Louis, he was too young to be the effective leader on which the treaty's success depended. Now the English were themselves embroiled in the French civil war, it was perhaps only a matter of time before divisions would emerge between them and their allies. Relations with Burgundy were soured by conflict in the Low Countries. The brother of the duke of Brittany, Arthur, count of Richemont, who had been captured at Agincourt, accepted English rule as party to a triple alliance with Burgundy and the duke of Bedford in 1423. But in 1425 he defected to the dauphin Charles, becoming the latter's constable.

Military advantage in the 1420s lay with the Anglo-Burgundians. It is certainly not impossible that an effective and long-lasting division of France into two kingdoms might have continued. After all, Charles's own court was ridden with divisions and uncertainties, as one might expect from the context of crisis. But for the treaty to be maintained the English needed to breach the Loire and attack Charles in his own 'kingdom of Bourges', and they needed to keep the alliance of Burgundy. They were able to achieve neither, as the events of 1429 demonstrated. Whatever the precise role of Jeanne d'Arc—and recent research by Roger Little has suggested that she may have been introduced to the scene by the Angevin faction at Charles's court—there can be no doubting her patriotism, probably fanned by her own experiences in her native Lorraine when Anglo-Burgundian troops came marauding. For while in the heartlands of Normandy relations between soldier and civilian were harmonious and peaceful, elsewhere anarchy and uncertainly easily prevailed, and as in the mid-fourteenth century, the line between legitimate warfare and brigandage became obscured. Once Charles was crowned in Reims, the English were forced onto the defensive, and the treaty of Troyes lost its force. The French had always placed much emphasis on the significance of the anointing and coronation rituals. There was therefore only one real king in France: Charles VII. The English were only able to have Henry VI crowned in Paris in 1431 (Joan's threat was regarded seriously enough for the young king to have been kept in Rouen throughout her trial, no doubt as a counter-force for God-given legitimacy). Although actors dressed as the dukes of Bedford and Burgundy supported Henry in his ceremonial entry to the French capital, Duke Philip did not deign to come in person, and was already involved in negotiations with Charles VII.

The French recovery, 1429–1453

In retrospect it is perhaps surprising that the war dragged on after 1429 for as long as it did. Several explanations can be put forward for this. The first was the reluctance of Duke Philip of Burgundy to withdraw from his English alliance, forged as it had been in revenge for the murder of his father. Significantly, he did not defect to Charles until the duke of Bedford, with whom he had a personal bond of friendship through the treaty of Amiens of 1423, died in September 1435. Even then, after a brief attempt to besiege Calais, he contributed little to Charles's subsequent war effort, but concentrated instead on expanding his territorial stranglehold on the Low Countries and on a projected crusade. The second was Charles's own hesitation when faced with the daunting prospect of taking Paris, into which the English had poured thousands of troops in 1429–30. Not until 1436, by which time the English were weakened and distracted by their loss of much of Upper Normandy as a result largely of local rebellion, did Charles move against the capital.

Once he had Paris, his eventual victory was assured. The English were now entirely on the defensive, and were facing increasing problems in Upper Normandy, not only as a result of the devastation caused by war and rebellion, but also by successive harvest failures and rural decline in the 1430s and 1440s. Guy Bois even went so far as describe this as 'Hiroshima en Normandie'. Such circumstances made it difficult for the English to raise the taxation needed to sustain a military presence. In the still peaceful backwaters of Lower Normandy the local estates increasingly resented paying for the costs of war north of the Seine. The Norman population was increasingly alienated from their English masters. No real inroads had ever been made into securing the support of the Norman nobility, many of whom had chosen exile with the dauphin in the 1420s, and the attempt to create a new nobility through land grants to English settlers had proved only partially successful. In Guienne, French incursions began in earnest in 1442, with economic problems following in their wake as vineyards were destroyed, taking years to recover. This was the first real threat to English interests in the south-west since the early years of the century, and also prompted defections to the French on the part of important local families hitherto accepting of English rule.

The rest of France was already restored to peace, and economic recovery under way, providing an important foundation for subsequent royal expansionism. But Charles VII's court was still faction-ridden, and the threat of armed rebellion by his nobles became reality in the Praguerie of 1440. The English were equally divided among themselves, and it is arguable that it was their weakness rather than Charles's strength that precipitated the denouement. His policies both in his own court and vis-à-vis the English became markedly more aggressive after the Praguerie. This is most notable after the truce of Tours of 1444, the first cessation of hostilities since 1417, when he made every effort to ensure mechanisms for the easy provision of troops (mindful, perhaps, of how the princes in 1440 had easily gained control of his resources) and where his international diplomacy became increasingly astute. By 1449 he could count on the aid of the duke of Brittany, and he had already persuaded the English to surrender Maine without a fight. The final campaigns of the war seem very much a damp squib. Henry V's achievements in taking Normandy in two years were eclipsed by Charles's recovery of the duchy, which took scarcely over a year. The taking of Guienne was equally painless, save for a brief rebellion in 1451 which put Bordeaux back in the hands of the English until the final defeat at Castillon on 17 July 1453.

By this date the French had, by defeating their ancient enemy, overcome internal divisions and sown the seeds of absolutism. The dark hours of the fifteenth-century phase of the Hundred Years War had done much to make this possible. As Colette Beaune has shown, the years of crisis, especially since the late 1350s and all the more so after 1420, had provoked an outpouring of patriotic lamentation. Personified on many occasions as a tear-stained woman whose robe had been torn and dirtied underfoot, or as a tree twisted and deformed by parasites, France's identity and that of her people had been forged anew. By the early 1450s France was now crowned and clothed in royal white, with a fine blue mantle peppered with fleur-de-lis, a virginal mother surrounded by her children—the king and the people. The paradise garden of France, symbol of both the country and its people, was restored to full splendour and integrity, with its rightful king as gardener.

5

Society and the economy: the crisis and its aftermath

Pierre Charbonnier

This chapter will first examine what the socio-economic crisis consisted of, then its results, and finally the new economic and social organization which followed. It was essentially made up of three violent elements and of a fourth, more insidious one.

Starvation

Corn famine was a harsh evil during the two centuries of the late Middle Ages. At that time there was no substitute for corn such as buckwheat and potatoes later provided, and speculation, as was pointed out in Chapter 2, made starvation harsher. The famine of 1316 can be thought of as the beginning of the crisis, and that of 1482 marked a setback in the recovery of the country. These two were general throughout France because their origin was climatic, the first caused by excessive rainfall, the second by damaging storms. Widespread starvation also took place in 1375 and 1438. In fact the climate of this period was midway between the fine weather of the eleventh and twelfth centuries and the little ice age beginning around 1580. As for the high corn prices in 1419–21, they seem to be explained by the extremely debased coinage of those years.

Local famines were much more numerous. They were caused by soldiers either ravaging fields or cutting trade routes. The author of the *Journal d'un bourgeois de Paris* (covering 1405–49, anonymous but probably by a clerk who was both pro-Burgundian and sympathetic to the poor) often mentioned difficulties in supplies because the town was surrounded by a succession of enemies, first the English, then the Armagnacs, and then the English again. He tells terrible stories of starvation, for example of women competing with pigs for food refuse thrown into the streets.

Nothing was done to cope with starvation on a national scale. Some towns tried to help their inhabitants. Taxing corn failed because it quickly disappeared from markets, but they had more success by buying up corn at high prices and selling it low. Town finances, though, were not unlimited, and to some extent individuals, clerics, lords, well-to-do men, and charities also helped the hungry population. A letter of remission of 1375 was given to a burgess tried for the death of an old woman found drowned in his courtyard well. In his defence he explained that she had been pushed in by the crowd fighting over some corn which he had ordered to be distributed. Indeed, astonishingly, starvation prompted movements of people from the country to the towns, where relief was more effective.

Plague

Plague was not the only epidemic disease of the late Middle Ages, but it was the most deadly. It was caused by the bacillus *Yersinia pestis*, which occurs naturally in a particular flea, *Xenopsylla cheopis*, which lives in the fur of rats. This process can break down, with the fleas biting people and infecting them with the bacillus. Plague can appear in three guises. By far the most common is bubonic plague, so called because of the subcutaneous haemorrhages or buboes that appear on its victims. Their skin becomes black, hence the name *peste noire* (black plague) given in France to the great evil of 1348, equivalent to the English term Black Death. The bubonic form is fatal in nearly 50 per cent of infected humans. It cannot pass directly from person to person but an infected person's house is liable to contain many fleas. These need heat to be active, so plague is a summer disease. The other forms, pneumonic and septicaemic, are contagious between people and almost 100 per cent fatal, but happily much rarer.

The black plague is thought to have started in Caffa, a Genoese harbour in the Crimea assaulted by Tatars. During the siege plague broke out in the Tatar army. The Tatar chief, perhaps the first known commander to conduct biological warfare, tossed victims' bodies into the town using catapults. Caffa was not taken, but Genoese boats brought plague back to Italy, whence it came into France through Mediterranean harbours. Plague was in Marseille in December 1347, and during the year 1348 it invaded France, striking Paris down in August and reaching Calais in December.

People were completely defenceless against the disease, whose nature was unknown. They thought that God was punishing them for their sins and that plague was transmitted by air. It affected even people of high rank, for example six cardinals died in Avignon as well as five municipal magistrates out of twelve in Reims. What was the percentage of mortality? One figure seems reliable: at Givry, a Burgundian village, the *curé* kept the acccounts for incomes from parish ceremonies. Whereas in an ordinary year the average number of burials was 30, in 1348 up to 19 November, when the count stopped, there were 649 deaths out of the 1,000 to 2,000 inhabitants. On the whole Froissart seems right when he said that 'a third of humanity died'. However, some places were untouched while in the same neighbourhood more than 50 per cent died.

In the following years plague disappeared, but it came back in 1361 and again in 1374. Indeed, from the end of the fourteenth century it should be considered an endemic disease and no longer epidemic. Every summer some areas were stricken and the next year others. The plague, though, was from then on less deadly. People who had previously been infected had acquired a certain immunity, and this explains why chroniclers noticed greater mortality among the young. Secondly, hygienic measures were taken which to some extent cleared out rats and fleas. Finally, the infected were kept in isolation, which had advantages, even though plague does not pass directly from person to person. Town authorities prohibited movement from infected areas, while great gatherings such as fairs were located elsewhere or cancelled. When plague was threatening a locality, its inhabitants were tempted to flee, but only those who owned property elsewhere, in effect the rich, could do so.

A letter of remission of 1468 expresses the tension people felt during periods of plague. The petitioner, a farmer, left his village, which had become infected, with his family, intending to go to another village. However, he was denied entry because he was suspected of being infected himself. Consequently, he returned and built a dwelling hut in one of his fields. However, a nobleman whose manor was nearby, fearing contagion, ordered the petitioner to go away, threatening to burn the hut down. The peasant obeyed and built another hut in a more distant field, but at the time of the grape harvest he brought some of his children back to the first hut so that they could watch over his vines. The nobleman became furious and ordered his staff to burn the hut down, and the sleeping children were burned inside. Some time afterwards the unfortunate father avenged his children by killing the nobleman's servant woman held responsible for the arson.

War

The events and military organization of war are discussed in Chapter 4. For our purposes, war often appears in letters of remission, but indirectly, because to kill an English fighter was considered praiseworthy and not reprehensible. In fact the Hundred Years War was not the only conflict of this period. There were many wars among Frenchmen: Burgundians against Armagnacs, princes against the king, and even little private wars. In addition, disbanded mercenaries strove to live off the land, notably the *grandes compagnies* (a company was an association of such mercenaries) after the treaty of Brétigny. On the whole, battlefield casualties were not numerous because soldiers were well protected, and moreover ransoming an enemy was more profitable than killing him.

So letters of remission linked to war were not always pardons for murder. They could be divided into three groups. The first covers treasonable actions, for example selling horses to the enemy, or towns making compacts with the enemy by paying not to be attacked. Equally, going over to the king's side needed his pardon for having fought against him. Secondly, many French soldiers after the end of the Hundred Years War had to beg for mercy because they had pillaged their compatriots as a result of the lack of a good supply system: soldiers might requisition supplies by right of *prise*, but this involved a payment so pillage was more profitable. The third group was connected to the second. Many peasants wanted pardons for slaughtering a soldier, justifying themselves on account of the excesses committed by the victim or saying that they thought he was the king's enemy.

Naturally war spread destruction. During his trial the English mercenary Aymerigot Marchès boasted that he had damaged the French realm because it was a meritorious act. Many documents describe places as being devastated, but most were devised to obtain tax reductions. There were in fact two types of case. Where powerful armies passed through an area, the devastation was obvious: towns were taken and the countryside not farmed. Where war was only made by small detachments of soldiers, the situation was different. They could not take the towns except by trickery, but they might settle in a castle and collect taxes on the neighbourhood; this was a new generation of lordships. However, defence was possible against them, notably in many villages where a *fort* (i.e. houses built in a circle connected to one another and closed on the outside, all openings facing a public inner court) was built.

As for the financial side, war might change individual situations particularly through the levying of ransoms. The principal royal tax, the *taille*, originated with war. Indeed, the vassals' military duties had become inadequate to face the huge demands of the wars against England and Flanders at the end of the thirteenth century. So the king wanted all Frenchmen to contribute to the war effort by making payments. These were at that stage tiny and required only in war years, but the *taille* became permanent after 1360 and reached a peak of 4.5 million *lt.* in 1482 (see Chapter 7). One important debate concerns how far royal taxes played a part in the reversal of the economic trend at the beginning of the fourteenth century.

Economic depression

The trend during the thirteenth century had been clearly one of expansion in most sectors. For example, at the beginning of the thirteenth century the price of wheat in Paris for a *setier* (a measure of 120 kilos) was about 6 *st.* During the second decade of the century its average price rose to 15 *st.* In 1316 it shot up to 60 *st.* because of scarcity and speculation. Suddenly, at Easter 1318 it fell heavily 'without harvesting' as one chronicler noticed. Indeed speculators, knowing the coming crop would be abundant, began to sell off their stocks. More surprisingly, though, except in starvation years corn prices stayed low, at less than 10 *st.* per *setier*, after 1318 until the end of the fifteenth century.

Industrial prices and incomes did not follow the same pattern. The former remained at a high level and the latter went up after the plague. However, the overwhelming importance of corn justifies the late Middle Ages being described as a period of depression. Depression was bad for businessmen, in contrast to inflationary periods, during which they automatically sold at higher prices than they had bought. Several explanations for the depression have been given. The demographic setback, first in 1316 and more so in 1348, had diminished the demand for bread while the supply of corn was almost maintained, except in devastated areas, because production was concentrated on the best soils with more seed. As for industrial prices, these generally reflected higher incomes, with demand for manufactures growing since the better-paid workers could afford to buy them.

The scarcity of precious metals is another explanation. This was related to a decline in mining, significant hoarding connected with wars and royal monetary changes, and expensive trade with the East, which exported to Europe more than it imported. Since price corresponds to the quantity of coined precious metal given in exchange for an item, if the precious metal is scarce it becomes costlier, so in the exchange less precious metal must be given and the price of the item goes down.

However, a social historian of this period, Guy Bois, has put forward another theory. He argues that the crisis was structural and was not tied to events such as the Black Death, to which he gives little or no importance. Bois considers that in about 1300 the country was so overcrowded that many lived wretchedly and production could not be improved. Thus the imposition of royal taxation would have been the last straw and would have set the economy back because poor men could not pay the new taxes. Bois accepts that the starvation of

1316 played a small part in the economic reversal, but he insists that it started before 1316. However, his figures for taxation, i.e. 30 *st.* per hearth in 1348, are not reliable and were not levied before, but long after, 1316. A hearth in Normandy had to pay 2 *st.* in 1328, which is a tiny burden. It is, then, preferable to return to the two previous theories, which can be combined. In any case, depression is by no means the worst aspect of the crisis.

Population during the crisis

There was undoubtedly a decrease in the population during the crisis. After the plagues, marriages and births were certainly very numerous, as chroniclers observed, but they did not compensate for the plague mortality, to which war casualties should be added. Figures may be given for well-documented regions. In Provence and Dauphiné, where there had been 100 hearths in the first half of the fourteenth century, there were only 40 to 45 in the second half of the fifteenth. However, the second half of the fifteenth century is not the nadir of population levels, which is generally situated around 1400, though a little later in Normandy and the Bordelais, which were fought over until 1450 and 1453. At this lowest point the population may have fallen to only 30 per cent of that of around 1300. According to the global figures for Dauphiné, town and country were nearly equal in terms of their losses. Towns were perhaps slightly less depopulated because they were protected by their walls and could better face grain shortages, but on the other hand they were more exposed to plague as a result of their overcrowded and unsanitary conditions.

Outbreaks of disease in the countryside might result in the complete depopulation of a village, which thus became deserted. Most of the deserted villages, though, were little hamlets, where farming had been difficult in good times; the parish centres were hardly affected. Indeed, this phenomenon was quite different from the English experience, which saw a move to pasture and sheep-rearing as a result of the enclosures. In France this outcome was accidental and strictly dependent on the two elements of the crisis: war and plague. So some deserted villages were subsequently reoccupied and saved from being 'lost villages'.

Another consequence of the demographic crisis was the numerous population movements, either from a devastated region to an undamaged one or from the countryside to a nearby town which had walls and could distribute bread. These two factors were combined in the motives of the drowned old woman mentioned above, who had fled from Limousin to Clermont in Auvergne. Thus, at Périgueux and Dijon local studies have shown that there was a continual turnover of householders. Among migrant people there were some who sought better work since the labour market was unbalanced, as shown below.

New social conditions during the crisis

The Black Death changed employment conditions overnight since labourers were now in a position to dictate their terms. King John II therefore tried to avert this social turnaround by enacting a law in 1351 with three principal points. First, he strove to force everyone to work by prohibiting help to beggars. Secondly, he revoked the craft regulations, permitting anyone to engage in any craft he wanted. Finally, he restricted wage rises to one-third. While the success of the first two provisions remains uncertain, it is certain that he failed completely in the third one, for wages commonly doubled and remained at this high level thereafter. This is in sharp contrast with England, where the king, supported by Parliament, kept wages almost at their level before the Black Death, at least until the Peasants' Revolt of 1381.

Northern France was also shaken by a peasants' revolt in 1358, called the Jacquerie after the mocking name for peasants, Jacques Bonhomme. Its origin was quite different from that of the English revolt. As has been pointed out, wages had risen and waged workers were not numerous in the countryside. In fact this revolt was related to war. It started with a routine scuffle between peasants and soldiers about requisitions in Saint-Leu-d'Esserent (on the Oise, north of Paris) in which some soldiers were killed. To avoid punishment the peasants hoped to conceal their guilt in a major movement against all fighting men and especially lords, whom they accused of not protecting them and even of burdening them; besides, lords were blamed for the defeat at Poitiers. The revolt spread widely and became cruel: Froissart relates that one nobleman was spit-roasted and his family made to eat his flesh. Thus, as contemporary texts suggest, this could look like a 'war of the non-nobles against the nobles' and some credibility might be given to an explanation of it based on the theory of class struggle. However, the origins of the movement were not entirely social, and besides many of the rioters were not poor. The Jacques got some help from townsmen, although the aims of Étienne Marcel's party in Paris were rather different from theirs. Finally, at Clermont (Oise), they were crushed by a professional army at the first onslaught.

The mysterious Tuchin movement was also, at its beginnings in the 1360s, related to war. The Tuchins were patriots who rejected compacts with enemies and secretly fought against them. For example, the city council of Saint-Flour, an important episcopal town in the Cantal, was in difficulties because some Tuchins of the town had stolen a horse from Englishmen of a neighbouring castle with whom the city had negotiated. Consequently, the city had to compensate the soldiers for this loss. Later on, in the 1380s in Languedoc, other Tuchins set themselves against excessive taxes.

Farmers who stayed in their original areas changed their production patterns by abandoning labour-intensive farming, such as viticulture and continuous farming. Both meadows and woodland were on the increase; indeed, a proverb of Saintonge said 'Woodlands came thanks to Englishmen'. Peasants could bargain with their lords by threatening to leave, so they got their rents reduced and eventually obtained their freedom. Seigneury, though, was not destroyed and provided the framework for the recovery of the countryside.

Recovery: towards a national economy

The recovery of French society from the crisis began at different periods in different regions according to when military operations came to an end: much sooner in Burgundy and Auvergne than in Normandy and the Bordelais. Besides this, economic and social changes, which will be stressed later, were different from region to region. The region that improved most was Brittany, the first to emerge from the travails of war. Its navy became particularly important.

As regards the rural economy, there is little to be said since there was minimal change. The part played by small farms managed by their owners as perpetual tenants increased since some of them took the place of demesne-farming made difficult by expensive labour costs. Moreover, these small farms increased in size because land was plentiful for fewer peasants. This provided the opportunity for new commercial agricultural production to appear, such as woad, the dye produced in the region of Toulouse.

Craft regulation by *métiers* was spreading, and henceforth the monarchy looked to it to control labourers. As the population decline reduced demand, competition became harsher. Established masters strove to prevent too many people from becoming masters. For instance, a letter of remission was given in 1481 to a young locksmith of La Roche-sur-Yon who wanted to set up on his own account. The story relates how he killed his previous master, who had refused to return his own tools to him so that the petitioner could not establish himself. More generally, according to new *métier* statutes, a candidate for mastership other than a master's son had to produce a masterpiece, which was very difficult and expensive. As a result, mastership was tending to become hereditary.

Some technical progress took place during the fifteenth century in industry, especially in mining, through better pumping galleries, which allowed deeper digging, and in iron metallurgy, in which the changeover from crude iron to cast iron was fundamental. Cast iron could be poured and so used to make many previously wooden articles. Consequently, metallurgical industry was very active, and mining and metallurgy were two branches in which Jacques Cœur invested much capital.

Jacques Cœur (1395–1456) was a prominent figure in the French commercial recovery. Of humble origin, he made a considerable fortune by lending to the king and the princes, for instance advancing more than 100,000 *lt.* for the campaign for the recovery of Cherbourg in 1450. His vast wealth, though, led to his downfall. Like many others before him, he was tried in 1451 on a trumped-up charge, in this case of having poisoned the king's favourite, though he might have been guilty of fraud. However, exceptionally, he was not sentenced to death since Charles VII admitted that he had done France good services. Indeed Cœur strove to take French Mediterranean trade out of the control of Italian merchants, though this was not fully achieved, largely because France still lacked a good harbour. Marseille (under the counts of Provence) was still outside royal control.

The successor to Cœur in making economic policy was King Louis XI himself. Louis aimed to prevent precious metals from flowing out of France, especially as the monetary shortage had still not ended. His main instrument, like that of his predecessors, was legislation, but unlike them he injected money into new businesses. His endeavours to get Levant goods carried only by French ships were rather unsuccessful, nor did he succeed in his aim of getting noblemen to take part in trade. However, he was more successful with developing silk and arms factories in Tours, which was becoming his chief town, and with fostering the Lyon fairs, where European businessmen met as they did formerly at those of Champagne. Louis's political ambitions, though, compelled him to raise taxes excessively at the end of his reign so that they dealt a blow to the well-being of his subjects.

An easier world

The main feature of the recovery in the countryside was the availability of land, even in the less damaged regions, and at lower rents. However, in regions where the effects of the crisis had been slight, so that lords had not had to make substantial concessions to their tenants, dues related to serfdom proper, *taille à volonté* and *mainmorte* (tax on inheritance) were undiminished, and many peasants were still held as serfs. This was the case in Berry, Bourbonnais, Marche, and Burgundy. Among war-stricken regions two types of case can be distinguished at the end of the fifteenth century. Those that had lately emerged from war were in the full phase of reconstruction. In the others, such as Auvergne, the period was almost a golden age for peasants. They could send their sons to study and they were able to acquire a horse for riding, not for ploughing. A problem arose for his children at the death of a peasant who had participated in resettlement. Did they have to share his large lands? One solution often opted for, particularly in central France, was that of remaining together and forming an extended family living 'at the same pot and at the same hearth'. Letters of remission from the second half of the fifteenth century show many such families, especially when there was a clash between members, for example in allocating tasks or about the inequality of their work.

Good times for peasants did not mean misfortune for the lords. Indeed, in spite of concessions to their subjects, they maintained their incomes and even increased them through concentrating several seigneuries in one hand. For example, Guillaume de Murol in Auvergne had six seigneuries, as against the two his father had held. Many noble families died out, some members having been killed in fighting and others becoming ecclesiastics, and the new lords who replaced them included rich townsmen or lucky former soldiers, among whom there were Scots who had fought with the French army.

The Church still provided attractive livings, although it suffered much from the crisis. Indeed, it had suffered a fifth evil, the Great Schism, which put it in an awkward position in having to respond to calls for reform. Ecclesiastical establishments in any case had difficulty in restoring their incomes, but the call for reform exposed their weak points. These were not removed in spite of individual attempts at reform by bishops who founded schools to teach their priests. Meanwhile, other abuses were growing, not least the famous indulgences, which reformers would come to think of as the blatant sale of salvation, as well as the holding of abbeys *in commendam* (when the abbot was an absentee prelate who only took the income). More rigorous Christians were hoping for a profound reform which would affect both Churchmen and laymen. Some preachers commended this to their listeners, and the Bourgeois of Paris admiringly relates how in 1429 a friar, Brother Richard, converted Parisians to a radically ascetic life, so that men burned their gaming tables and women their luxurious clothing. But the Bourgeois went on to despise him when he learned that Richard leaned towards the Armagnacs, and he thought it unsurprising when all these Parisians returned to their sins.

In the towns society was not very different from what it had been like at the start of the fourteenth century. Workers certainly received higher wages after the plague, but these did not continue to rise, and the trend was unfavourable to labourers at the end of the fifteenth. For example, the length of the working day was often increased for the same wage. Town government was controlled by much the same families, provided they had made small concessions. Having paid out a great deal as *bonnes villes* during the wars when the countryside was ravaged, by obtaining exemptions towns obtained a better tax regime and became to some extent fiscal paradises.

Men of law and also officials were more numerous and established a good place for themselves in society, particularly members of the Parlement, who could aspire to noble status. So, in dividing society into twelve groups, the poet Eustache Deschamps listed first the *clergie*, a word encompassing all educated men. Indeed all officials, now overwhelmingly laymen, aimed to make their function hereditary, especially when, at the end of the Middle Ages, *vénalité des offices* (the possibility of handing on one's office through payment) appeared. Thus a new class was created which became very influential.

Some members of this class took part in court life. The court was also a new social element (as will be seen in Chapter 7), whose composition and glamour varied according to the personality and financial means of kings and princes. The royal court was at its most elaborate under Charles VI during the truces with England and before the outbreak of civil war. During the fifteenth century the most sumptuous courts were those of Philip the Good, duke of Burgundy, and of René, the titular king of Sicily, who held his court in Anjou and Provence. Writers and artists flocked there because they hoped to profit from the master's generosity. But, as Eustache Deschamps, who lived at Charles VI's court, put it, 'He who stays at court takes too many risks' for 'he has to sham fellowship with those injuring him'; it was a place where courtiers lived an artificial life 'sleeping in the daytime and . . . sitting up at night'. In fact, the court, even if it was closely tied economically to the rest of the country, was really a special case, to some extent a world apart.

Conclusion

The crisis of the fourteenth and fifteenth centuries inflicted brutal damage on France, but it did not change it profoundly. As for the seigneuries, it seems that where they were weak before the crisis, they became weaker, but where they were sound, they were unaltered. France remained a country of peasant landowners, a country relatively little oriented towards commercial exchange, where the well-to-do preferred to invest in lands and offices. The main consequence of the crisis was to improve the lot of poor people, but population growth and inflation were soon to cancel this out in the sixteenth century.

6

The crown and the provinces in the fifteenth century

Graeme Small

In the course of the fifteenth century the terms 'crown' and 'province' achieved wider currency than ever before in the history of France. The first, used in the abstract sense, appears already in the work of Abbot Suger of Saint-Denis in the twelfth century. The crown subsequently became the supreme embodiment of royal public authority, quite distinct from the king (who was its minister, defender, even husband) and from the kingdom (the geographical extent of the lands which could be counted among its territorial possessions). It was a set of inalienable dominions and rights, a source of continuity from one reign to the next, and a focus for loyalties through difficult times. By contrast the idea of the province, although familiar to Churchmen as a subdivision in ecclesiastical organization and to readers of Roman histories, was a relative newcomer in French political thought. Usage is said to have increased through the fifteenth century in chronicles and royal documents, alongside or even in place of words such as 'pays', 'contrée', and 'terre' previously used to designate different parts of the realm. While it is possible that more frequent talk of provinces was stimulated by the vogue for Latinity in Renaissance France, it could also be argued the development acknowledged political change. Just as the towering abstraction of the crown had been augmented by the victories of Charles VII (1422–61) in the Hundred Years War, by the absorption into the royal domain under Louis XI (1461–83) of lands once ruled by great princely houses, and by the French descent into Italy under Charles VIII (1483–98), so the subordinating concept of the province, a term that flattened distinctions between regions and denied them an autonomous political identity, had gradually become more relevant.

It is possible to write a history of fifteenth-century France which emphasizes the extremes present in the idea of a powerful crown and dependent provinces. Such a history would be royalist in perspective and would divide the period into roughly two halves. In the first, the crown's powers would appear to have been usurped in the provinces by princely rulers of apanages and great fiefs who sought to form states within the state. 'Usurpation' would be too strong a term to characterize the actions of municipal authorities in many larger towns and cities (*bonnes villes*) of the realm, but the financial, military, and political autonomy they had begun to acquire in the fourteenth century did not diminish and in many cases increased. This first period also witnessed the vast majority (twenty-seven out of thirty-one) of the supposed or known meetings of the Estates General and regional estates of Languedoil (northern France) which were summoned by the king in the fifteenth century, suggesting once more the crown's reliance on provincial forces. In the second half of the fifteenth century, however, change would be emphasized, particularly the variable fortunes of ruling houses in the apanages and great fiefs, the sharp intervention of Louis XI in the affairs of the *bonnes villes*, and the decline of the estates. In royal correspondence the term 'subject' began to oust 'vassal' as a means of describing leading princes of the realm. The rule of dukes and counts gave way to the administration of royal governors. The 'pays' or the principality became the province.

But change can be overestimated and continuities neglected. To George Chastelain, a Burgundian commentator writing on the periphery of the kingdom at some point between 1461 and 1475, it seemed that Louis XI sought to govern 'through absolute power', that is, unfettered authority bordering on despotism. Whether the king was capable of achieving such an objective in the fifteenth century is far from clear. As we shall see, the monarch's need to govern through and with forces in the province was arguably as strong at the close of our period as it had been at the start.

Princes and noble affinities

The territorial lords who mattered most were those princes capable of exerting control over noble affinities, the *bonnes villes*, and the Church within a substantial part of the realm. The extent of their lordship occasionally coincided with regions which had acquired a sense of cohesion and identity over time. In practice there were two types of prince, although intermarriage had made them virtually indistinguishable: those of the blood who held an apanage from the crown, either of old (most notably the dukes of Burgundy, Bourbon, Berry, Anjou, and Orléans, whose apanage grants went back to the fourteenth century), or of more recent standing (such as the sons and brothers of fifteenth-century monarchs to whom new grants were made); and, secondly, the great fiefholders, the most important of whom were the duke of Brittany and the counts of Armagnac and Foix.

The aggrandizement of princely territories continued to develop from the fourteenth-century resurgence described elsewhere in this volume. The spectacular gains made by Philip the Good, duke of Burgundy (1419–67), in the empire, most of them prepared by his father and grandfather, can obscure the fact that Burgundian territorial ambitions found some satisfaction in the kingdom of France during the fifteenth century. The grants of the county of Champagne (1430) and the great city of Tournai (1423; see below) during the period of his alliance with the Lancastrians turned out to be ephemeral, but the cession of the strategically important Somme towns and the county of Ponthieu in 1435 by the treaty of Arras was longer-lived, likewise the acquisition of the Picard towns of Péronne, Mondidier, and Roye. More permanent still were grants or confirmations concerning the counties of Boulogne (1423) in the north, of Mâcon and Auxerre at either end of the duchy of Burgundy, and, close by, of the castellany of Bar-sur-Seine (all 1435). By the terms of the treaty of Arras, Philip the Good was personally exempt from homage for his lands between 1435 and 1461, and his son Charles eventually sought to evade this responsibility also. Elsewhere in the kingdom the most successful empire-builders in the fifteenth century were the counts of Armagnac and Foix, both vying for supremacy in the south-west.

Divided like the lands of Burgundy into two main blocks, the Armagnac possessions were augmented—owing mainly to the predacious Bernard VII (1391–1418)—by the acquisition of the counties of Pardiac (c.1403) and l'Isle-Jourdain (1421) west of the Garonne; the important viscountcy of Fezensaguet on the same side, along with those of Creissels (c.1403) and Murat (1415), and the baronies of Meyruis and Valleraugue (early fifteenth century) to the east. Along the Pyrenees and towards the Mediterranean the counts of Foix, who were exempt from homage to the crown for their possession of Béarn, obtained the substantial county of Bigorre in the face of Armagnac opposition (1429) and the viscountcy of Villemur (1422) under Jean I (1412–36), as well as the restitution of that of Lautrec (1425). In 1453 the crown managed to keep the county of Comminges from Gaston IV of Foix (1436–72) as well as his rival Jean V of Armagnac (1450–73). However, Gaston did make the valuable purchase of the viscountcy of Narbonne (1448) which brought his lands full circle around Roussillon. A similar drive to round out or extend the borders inherited from one's predecessors motivated the acquisitions of the last princely house to have significantly increased its domains in the fifteenth century, the dukes of Bourbon. The complex of Bourbon lands in central France was established under Louis II, 'the Builder' (1356–1410), who acquired the large lordship of Beaujolais to the east in our period (1400). He also made possible the eventual acquisition of the even larger duchy of Auvergne to the south (1425) by his son Jean I (1410–27). With the return of the county of La Marche (1477) to the possession of the dukes, the Bourbon lands were extended significantly to the west. In 1510 Charles III, duke of Bourbon, constable of France, was second only to the king in the extent of his territorial lordship.

Princely expansion in the provinces was clearly a feature of our period, but it is above all the consolidation and exaltation of their authority which has commanded the attention of historians. A stark list of the seigneurial rights of the counts of Armagnac suggests that the fifteenth century witnessed an appropriation of public authority to match or even surpass any earlier 'age of principalities' in French history. The counts could grant letters of legitimization, ennoblement, remission, and safe conduct, and rights pertaining to taxes, tolls, mining, and markets; they issued municipal charters, summoned the local estates, and appointed all officers in matters of justice and finance. In fifteenth-century Brittany the duke could do all this and more, such as minting silver and gold coin. Given these and other circumstances discussed below, it is little wonder that Édouard Perroy believed 'the political problem of fifteenth-century France is not a feudal one; the state is swallowed by rival and smaller states'. The tentacles of princely power reached deep into the provinces of fifteenth-century France to bind other forces to their ambitions and fate. The development of the princes' relations with the towns are discussed in a later section; here we may consider local nobilities and the Church.

Noblemen, noble families, and wider affinities were aware that a local princely dynasty could usually reward loyalty and punish challenges to its authority. The Pot family was one noble clan which clearly understood the value of serving the prince. Renier (d. 1432) was the founder of the family's fortunes, serving successive dukes of Burgundy and through them Charles VI as a royal governor in Dauphiné and Languedoc. Renier's grandsons Philippe and Guyot took different routes, one in France (Guyot Pot served Charles, duke of Orléans (1407–66), and intermittently Philip the Good, and was later a royal *bailli*, councillor, and the main beneficiary of the confiscation of the county of Saint-Pol), the other in Burgundy (where Philippe Pot became first chamberlain of Philip the Good). The brothers' career paths crossed once more when the collapse of Burgundian power brought Philippe back into French royal service. In this capacity he made a famous address to the Estates General of 1484, arguing that a strong Estates General was necessary to counter the power of the princes. There is some irony in this fact, given that Pot, like many a provincial nobleman, had built his career through a princely household.

The Pots were a buoyant noble family who prospered in ducal service, but there were also victims of the entrenchment of princely power in the provinces. Those who suffered most were old families of second rank with sufficient territory and tradition to harbour ambitions but insufficient resources and connections to withstand the prince. Louis II of Chalon-Tonnerre was one such nobleman; he unwisely made a stand against John the Fearless, duke of Burgundy, had his lands confiscated, and eventually died without male heir, leaving his family unable to recover the bulk of his estate. Unless he could count on a large affinity, outside help, or the weakness of his princely adversary, the recalcitrant provincial noble was in trouble. In the duchy of Bourbon, it is said, not a single noble castle of note was built in the course of the fifteenth century. It is doubtful in any event that noble castles would withstand the artillery pieces which some princes could muster by this time, most famously Charles the Bold, duke of Burgundy (1467–77).

Princely control over the affairs of the Church in provincial France could also be extensive, not least because benefices afforded valuable patronage for friends and family. Charles II, sire d'Albret (1415–71), did not have to worry about providing for his son Louis in his will: he had already obtained the bishopric of Aire and a cardinal's hat for his offspring. Another cardinal, Pierre de Foix the elder (d. 1464), brother of Jean I and uncle of Gaston IV, created, in Gazzaniga's words, a 'veritable monopoly of benefices' for the house of his birth. Among his more audacious exploits was an attempt to have a scion of Foix made bishop of Tarbes at the age of 12. The fifteenth century marked a turning point in the ability of princes to impose their nominees upon vacant posts; by the early sixteenth century the king is described by Guenée as 'the sovereign of a strong state and master of a loyal church'. But some princes were slower to renounce control than others, and some did not do so at all. For most of our century the bishopric of Tournai was held by candidates promoted by the dukes of Burgundy. Each of the bishops served in the ducal council, the vast majority at its head, and many of the cathedral canons held lands and other benefices in the Burgundian dominions. In Brittany, meanwhile, the Church established its own rapport with Rome irrespective of the Pragmatic Sanction of Bourges. Relations between Francis I, duke of Brittany (1442–50), and Pope Nicholas V were good enough for the latter to permit the creation of a new bishopric at Redon for the son of the grand master of the duke's household, although in the end the erection of the see proved unnecessary thanks to an alternative falling vacant at Saint-Malo.

The competence and autonomy of institutions of princely government in the provinces of France reached a high point in the fifteenth century after the long period of development described elsewhere in this volume. Along with Brittany, the most striking example is surely Burgundy under Charles the Bold. In the last years of the reign several reforms placed the duke in a position to do his duty 'to God the all powerful and to the lands, principalities and lordships which, by His esteemed bounty He has submitted to us'.[1] The separation of the ducal dominions from the jurisdiction of the Parlement in Paris began in the county of Flanders long before Charles's reign, as much at the instigation of the towns as of ducal government. But Charles greatly accelerated the trend: first, in 1468, when he secured restrictions on the Parlement's jurisdiction at Péronne; again, in 1471, when he raised the ducal council at Dijon to the status of a sovereign body (saving appeals to his own Great Council); and, finally, in 1473 by the creation of a sovereign court for all his northern lands at Mechelen. Centralization of finances was promoted by the creation of a single Chambre des Comptes for the northern lands, replacing those of Lille and Brussels. Two new bodies were established to deal with ordinary and extraordinary revenues, known respectively as the Chambre du Trésor and the Chambre des Généraux. Charles's financial reorganization was linked to the military reforms he initiated in 1471 and completed two years later. The core of a permanent army now emerged with clear regulations on command and discipline, lodgings and leave, drill and exercises. By 1473 Charles the Bold was a king in all but name.

As princes of the blood and as benefactors of earlier marriage policies, several princes (Gaston IV de Foix in Navarre and René of Anjou in southern Italy) could indeed claim to be monarchs in their own right. Pursuit of such claims may have deflected princely attention away from the temptation of state-building in the French provinces. Others simply came to regard their own powers in quasi- or overtly regal terms. The list of those who styled themselves rulers 'by the grace of God' is remarkable, from the dukes of Brittany and Burgundy to the counts of Armagnac, Foix, Comminges, and Astarac. As rulers of Rodez, the counts of Armagnac wore a crown. The dukes of Brittany adopted a complex coronation service from 1401, and on their death lay in state beneath a royal gown. Like the dukes of Burgundy, they came to believe that the crime of *lèse-majesté* could be committed against the person of the prince, not just against what Cuttler calls 'public authority as represented by the person of the king and as symbolized by the crown'. The appropriation of royal prerogatives by these dukes may even have seemed historically justified to

[1] Preamble of the ordinance of Thionville (1473), trans. R. Vaughan, *Charles the Bold* (London, 1970), 186.

their most fervent supporters. As Breton chroniclers were wont to recall from an early stage, Brittany had formerly been a kingdom in its own right. Similar (although less confident) views began to emerge in Burgundian court historiography, in works such as the *Chronicle of the Kings, Dukes and Counts of Burgundy from 14 AD to the Present.* The reign of Charles the Bold, for whom this short history was compiled, witnessed the only really serious attempt by a French prince to create a kingdom incorporating his French lands. The duke's plans quickly came to nothing in 1473, but it is clear he viewed his power wholly independently from the kingdom of France by that stage. At a meeting of the estates in Dijon in 1474 Charles announced that the French had usurped the ancient kingdom of Burgundy and had wrongfully reduced it to the status of a duchy. Later that year he signed a treaty with Edward IV of England which envisaged a division of France, with all his lands in the kingdom, plus a few others he had long coveted, held in full sovereignty. The clause is a measure of the seriousness of the coalition of 1475 which, in the end, the king was able to contain.

In the matter of princely authority and aspirations in the provinces of fifteenth-century France, however, the example of Charles the Bold cannot stand for all. A process of state formation was clearly occurring in parts of the kingdom under the aegis of ambitious princes who profited from the king's difficulties. The process can be studied in terms of territorial expansion, centralized institutions, an emerging ideology of princely power, and a coincidence of interests between princes on the one hand, and local nobilities, towns, the estates, and the Church on the other. But the extent and trajectory of princely state formation varied very considerably across the kingdom, and its strengths can be overestimated.

From the outside, the robustness of princely states was tested—and often found wanting—by the interventions of crown officers in everyday governmental affairs. The action of the Parlement was perhaps the most obvious sign of royal authority in the provinces. This sovereign court might be an irritant to princes whose subjects could appeal against their executive decisions or the judgment of their courts. In 1456 a wealthy Lille brewer protested to the Parlement against Philip the Good's decision to marry off a ducal archer to his daughter. The duke had the girl abducted and placed under the guard of the sire d'Antoing outside the boundaries of the kingdom, but the Parlement nonetheless summoned Philip's vassal to give the girl up. Stories of this kind are common, and imply an habitually conflictual relationship between royal justice and princely power in the provinces. It is relevant to remember that there were disincentives to those who would appeal against a judgment handed down in their lord's court: a complete trial at the level of the castellany in our period could cost around 5 *lp.*, while at the Parlement expenditure might amount to between twenty and 100 times that figure. We should also remember that the Parlement was a court of law whose interventions could be useful to princely authority: in fact, it upheld the original decision of the council in Flanders in over 90 per cent of the appeals which reached Paris from the county. For princes whose conception of their own sovereignty was pragmatic, it made sense to leave the door open to the king's justice; for those who perceived its action as an intolerable interference, their options were limited. In matters of justice the princely state—even one as autonomous as Brittany—was ultimately permeable.

In matters of finance this was less uniformly the case. By the start of the fifteenth century the king's taxes were already a distant memory in Brittany and were becoming so in the duchy of Burgundy. Elsewhere the picture is quite different, owing mainly to the ordinance of Orléans (1439), which sought to reserve for the crown the right to levy *tailles*. In the duchy of Anjou the weight of royal taxes became so great in the 1440s that Duke René (1434–80) presented a series of grievances to Charles VII on behalf of his subjects. René began by noting the privileges of Anjou, its status as an apanage, and his own as a peer of the realm, and spent the early part of his submission complaining of the interference of the royal *bailli* of Touraine. Such grievances were far from unique: the dukes of Bourbon bore similar grudges against the royal *baillis* of Saint-Pierre-Le-Moûtier, Montferrand, and Mâcon. The bulk of René's complaint, though, focused on the unequal fiscal burden of the *taille* for the king's army, which, he claimed, left his subjects paying 100–150 per cent more than the inhabitants of Touraine. The king's answer, full though it was, offered little comfort to René or his subjects. The dukes of Bourbon did not bother with such noble protestations, but they did face similar difficulties. The presence and action of the king's financial officers in key ducal towns like Moulins, Montluçon, and Vichy were, as Leguai notes, 'proof for the Bourbonnais that the duke was not their sovereign; it reminded them they were part of the Kingdom of France as much as the Bourbon state'.

Despite the more spectacular examples of their state-building, princes were also very much part of the realm. Royal office was desirable because it could yield far greater influence than that afforded by territorial lordship alone. Louis de Chalon, prince of Orange (1418–63), held a small proportion of his lands from the king when he was appointed a royal commissioner in the Languedoc after the death of John, duke of Berry (1360–1416). He was eventually forced out by Jean I, count of Foix, but not before he had amassed, according to a contemporary, 'a very great treasure . . . said to be worth around two hundred thousand *écus*'. Far wealthier and more autonomous French princes than Louis de Chalon regarded the king as the ultimate dispenser of status or reward. When Philip the Good came to Paris in 1461 to crown the new king Louis XI, he appears to have believed—despite the murder of his father and subsequent relations with the French crown, despite the territories and rights he had since acquired in the Low Countries—that a return to the heyday of Burgundian influence in the kingdom of France was imminent. The scramble for royal office among ducal servants which followed was distasteful to some Burgundian observers, but the pattern of behaviour was no different from that which followed the princely coups of Charles VI's reign, or that which was feared during the minority of Charles VIII. The result in the early fifteenth century had been the emergence of servants of two masters, men who made careers in princely service and who found favour by that route with the king, or vice versa. Dual allegiance grew dangerous as the autonomy of princely masters and royal resistance increased, but it never disappeared entirely, and indeed at some courts it remained very strong. It was still possible in 1470 for a Breton to describe himself to the king as a 'bon Breton et bon Françoys', and for the king to reply, equally without fear of ridicule, that many Bretons had made a name for themselves in the service of the crown. The dukes of Burgundy and Bourbon had to contend with powerful nobles whose attachment to the court of France made their loyalty a relative matter—most famously the seigneur de Croy and the seigneur de Sully respectively. The cathedral chapter of Angers was a rich source of talent for the Angevin administration, but it also produced many servants of the crown—even if Dean Jean de La Vignolle discovered in 1470 that he could not retain Duke René's favour 'because he was richly provided for in the service of my lord the king'. On top of the rewards of service the king tied a great many to him by grants of pensions. In 1470, it has been calculated, 35 per cent of the king's revenue was disbursed in this way. For a prince like Jean II, duke of Bourbon (1455–88), this money was essential for the running of his affairs.

Above and beyond the development of princely states in the provinces there existed a French body politic in which the crown's jurisdiction, fiscal powers, and ability to bestow preferment and reward were of very great value. As peers of the realm, princes swore an oath on the king's coronation 'to uphold and defend the rights and noble privileges of the crown of France and its sovereignty'.[2] Their interpretation of the king's rights no doubt varied from the monarch's view and again from those of the crown's servants in the Parlement. But princes were participants by duty and birthright in the political community of the realm. To judge from the advice he reportedly gave to his son in 1482, even Louis XI learned to recognize the value of princely counsel—or at least the dangers of ignoring it. It is instructive to note here how the great noble coalitions of the fifteenth century were not concerned with protecting provincial privileges or securing charters for local institutions like the Leagues of 1314–15, but rather with the degree of influence their members exercised in the kingdom. The rebels of the Praguerie (1440) and the princes who met at Nevers two years later were particularly concerned at the composition of the king's court and his council. The League of the Public Weal (1465) went further, proposing the seizure of an incompetent king whom it was the rebels' public duty to replace. During the minority of Charles VIII, Louis of Orléans and his princely allies hoped to substitute the regency powers of the Beaujeu by their own. Seen in this light, the problem of fifteenth-century France was not, in the first instance at least, that the state would be swallowed by rival and smaller states, or that the kingdom might be dismembered and its ruler left to one side with a role comparable to the emperor's. The danger, as Chevalier has put it, was that a 'princely polyarchy' would succeed in running the kingdom. Dominance of core and periphery was the ideal scenario for princes who would have it all.

[2] Charles V's *Livre du sacre*, cited in P. Desportes, 'Les pairs de France et la couronne', *Revue Historique*, 282 (1989), 337–8.

The most extreme princely conception of how France should be ruled did not come to fruition. The crown had a part in this outcome, perhaps less through the use of military force (despite much-vaunted reforms of the king's army, the battle of Montlhéry during the War of the Public Weal was inconclusive) than through the enforcement of the law of treason. The highest-ranking princes to be convicted were Jean II, duke of Alençon, in 1458, Louis de Luxembourg, count of Saint-Pol, in 1475, and Jacques d'Armagnac, duke of Nemours, in 1477 (the first being reprieved, the last two publicly executed). The threat of a treason trial could also intimidate princes into respecting the king's wishes, as René of Anjou discovered in 1476. In the provinces the trials had the practical effect of reminding all of the king's authority, as illustrated by the dispatch of the four limbs of the executed Burgundian agent Jean Hardi to the four corners of the realm in 1474, or by the destruction in effigy of Jean de Chalon, prince of Orange, in Paris, Dijon, Mâcon, and Caen after his conviction *in absentia* in 1479. The resulting confiscations also redistributed territory in the provinces to the benefit of men the king then considered to be loyal, such as Alain the Great, sire d'Albret (1471–1522), who received his uncle's property and lands in this way, and later the viscountcy of Fezansaguet on the death of Jean V of Armagnac in 1473.

The greatest damage to princely rule in the provinces of France, most of it occurring in the last quarter of the fifteenth century, was in fact done by failing blood lines. Charles of France, brother of Louis XI, was as troublesome to his sibling as Louis had been to their father, but his early death in 1472 removed a focus for disgruntled princes and noble affinities and led to the reversion of the apanage of Guyenne to the crown. Five years later another untimely death, that of Charles the Bold, left the Burgundian succession without a male heir and allowed Louis XI to attempt to impose royal rule in the territories the duke had held of the crown. The fatal riding accident of the duke's only daughter, Mary, in 1482 further hampered his dynasty's recovery. In Anjou, Duke René lost his son and grandson in quick succession; his nephew's prospects were diminished by laws governing the transmission of lands through the female line, and his elderly brother survived him by just over a year. Louis XI exploited this insecure succession to extend the crown's possessions within the kingdom and into Provence. Finally, Francis II, duke of Brittany (1458–88), left two girls, the eldest of whom eventually married

Charles VIII in 1491, thereby initiating the gradual absorption of the duchy, which was completed in 1532. Of the main rebel houses of 1465, only Bourbon held significant territorial possessions by the reign of Louis XII.

The imposition or restoration of royal rule in provinces formerly governed by princes of the blood could be a difficult process. Sporadic rebellion broke out in the towns of the duchy of Burgundy in 1477–8, riots against the king occurred in Angers in 1478, and when Louis XI died in 1483 there was celebration and insurrection in Picardy. Whether these rebellions indicate there had been a fusion of princely power with regional identity in the provinces is a moot point deserving further study. Resistance could be strong enough to compromise royal attempts to absorb the province, as happened in Artois. But whatever the problems which the crown faced, there is no escaping the fact that Louis XI augmented the kingdom by more than 40,000 square kilometres of territory, most of it formerly in the hands of the great princely houses of France. In the end the extension of princely state-building in the provinces, such as René of Anjou's application of French administrative models in the county of Provence, had worked to the benefit of the monarchy.

The *bonnes villes*

The proportion of the king's subjects who lived in the *bonnes villes* was relatively small, but it was not so much the size of the towns that made their affairs a frequent matter of interest or concern for the king and his officers. What interested them were the judicial, financial, military, and administrative functions that municipal authorities exercised to varying degrees, acting alone or in conjunction with local royal servants, and supported by the authority of renewable royal charters or ad hoc permission from the king. Well into the sixteenth century many municipalities continued to provide the court of first instance for crimes which fell into the categories of high, middle, and low justice. These courts could be distinct from (and sometimes in conflict with) those of local royal officers, and were under the overall jurisdiction of the Parlement of Paris or its regional equivalent. In the

Picard towns of Abbeville or Noyon the municipal court could in theory pass sentence of death for a crime as serious as *lèse-majesté*. The development of municipal revenue-raising powers from the second half of the fourteenth century, primarily in the form of indirect taxation of consumables like wine and salt, continued apace through the fifteenth century. Mints were also located in the towns. The *bonnes villes* looked to their own defence even after the creation of the standing army in the 1440s. Municipal authorities resisted efforts to garrison the new companies of the ordinance within their walls—in Tours riots broke out in 1465 at the mere rumour that a garrison was planned. Civic governors preferred to rely on the service of the watch, urban archery confraternities, the purchase of artillery, and continuing fortification programmes to preserve their security. In the thirteenth century the jurist Philippe de Beaumanoir advised the king to treat his *bonnes villes* like children; by our period they could look after themselves.

The centrifugal forces which had contributed to the emergence and growth of urban autonomy in the provinces of later fourteenth-century France were still in evidence in our period. Many *bonnes villes* could describe themselves as frontier communities and claim that freedom of manoeuvre was justified to preserve their status and interests. Such towns were obviously to be found at the extremities of the realm (Caen after 1450, for instance), but they also existed much nearer to the geographical centre (Chartres after its recapture in 1432, or Angers in the 1480s, uncomfortably close to the theatre of the Breton wars). In such circumstances the traditional role of the *bonne ville* as 'a relay point for central authority' became all the more important, through the dissemination of royal edict and news, as a military force and as a focus for loyalty.

The crown and municipal authorities were also keenly aware of the preponderant influence which the *bonne ville* could exercise within the province directly and by example, particularly in crisis periods. In 1417 the *consaux* (aldermen) of Tournai were accused by Queen Isabella of setting a bad example to their counterparts in Arras and Reims by their reluctance to accept her Burgundian-sponsored regime. Concerted action by *bonnes villes* could pose a serious obstacle to the fulfilment of the crown's wishes in the provinces, most often over the king's fiscal demands. At Saint-Flour in the Auvergne, the consuls responded to Louis XI's tax demand in 1466 by delaying tactics: lengthy consultations with their counterparts in Issoire and Clermont-Ferrand were initiated while the king's deputy was kept waiting; these discussions completed, more deliberations were held with the authorities in Aurillac and further afield. When faced with a unified body of urban resistance, servants of the crown had to move cautiously, patiently, or with decisive force to achieve their goals in the provinces.

The interdependence of the monarch and his *bonnes villes* in later medieval France is clear, but interpretations of the relationship between them differ. It was long believed the period witnessed an alliance between town and crown which ultimately saw off the older forces of the feudal aristocracy and the Church; through the unquestioning loyalty of their *bonnes villes* and the talent and wealth of their citizens, successive kings, Louis XI in the van, took a decisive step towards the creation of modern France. Without disputing the role of the *bonnes villes* in the restoration of the Valois monarchy (especially under Charles VII), Henri Sée traced a different trajectory in the relationship. Once dominant in the realm, the king sought to exert a 'tight administrative tutelage' over the towns and cities of France. The trend appeared most marked under Louis XI, whose interference in municipal privileges, government, and finances seemed by turns erratic and brutal, as evinced by his decision to revoke charters of the city of Troyes in 1474 just four years after granting them, or by his announcement in 1475 to the authorities of Beauvais that they would no longer be permitted to hold municipal elections.

With the benefit of many enlightening case studies (including his own of Tours), Bernard Chevalier saw things a little differently. The *bonnes villes* of the realm did not offer unadulterated loyalty to the ruling king, at least during the period of internal strife down to about 1440. Towns had to look to their own interests in the absence of a monarch who could provide them with secure, sustained protection; for this among other reasons, a firmer relationship with princely power in the provinces often seemed a sensible option. In the second half of the century, however, a significant shift occurred. Few instances of urban support for princely political action against the ruling king could be cited. An age of harmony between the monarchy and the *bonnes villes* now dawned and would endure well into the sixteenth century, fuelled by shared needs, mutual respect, and—contrary to Sée's view of a monarchy set on subjugating its urban ally—by a concerted charm offensive aimed at the towns by Valois kings. The monarch who showed greatest favour to his urban subjects was arguably Louis XI, whom Chevalier calls 'the protector, not the executioner, of the *bonnes villes*'.

That some civic authorities in the provinces should have wavered in their support for the ruling monarch, if not in their avowed loyalty to the crown, is readily understood when one considers the circumstances which confronted them. In the early decades of the fifteenth century, in particular, princes pursuing their own agenda wielded a bigger stick in the provinces than their royal master. In 1423 Philip the Good was granted the *bonne ville* of Tournai, then fiercely loyal to Charles VII, by his English ally Henry VI. Unable to make good his claim in the face of Tournaisien opposition but unwilling to give up any financial benefit, Philip eventually settled for a substantial annual sum which was paid to him by the municipal authorities. The duke's threats against Tournai were taken seriously because princes had the means to damage towns materially and economically. A partisan of the count of Armagnac believed his master could destroy Millau, Toulouse, and Montpellier if he so chose; after that he could simply make his peace with king and council. In the end the count was charged with treason for his attacks on Millau, but the monarchy was not always so vigilant or consistent. Despite his coronation oath not to alienate parts of the domain, the king could be persuaded to cede towns and cities to princes altogether. For his role at the battle of Agincourt in 1415 John V, duke of Brittany, was granted Saint-Malo, a concession which was wholly at odds with the city's previously successful efforts to resist ducal hegemony. The municipal authorities of Épinal protested in 1465 against Louis XI's decision to grant the city to the marshal of Burgundy, Thibaud de Neuchâtel, claiming that their new ruler would be too weak to protect them. In reality it was often the king of France who was too weak to protect his *bonnes villes*, particularly in the first half of the fifteenth century. Municipal authorities had to act accordingly.

It would be wholly misleading to characterize the relationship between princes and *bonnes villes* in the provinces as one based purely on intimidation and control. Within the principalities, long-established relations between the prince and urban authorities made for close relations which could elevate cities to the de facto status of regional capitals. Pau under Gaston IV, count of Foix, or Lille under Philip the Good, duke of Burgundy, were two such *bonnes villes* in the fifteenth century, both benefiting from the establishment of princely organs of government in the town, visits by members of the dynasty, and the building or upkeep of extensive palace complexes. Many a prince found favour among civic governors beyond the boundaries of his lands. Support for John the Fearless in Paris and many northern municipalities in 1417 surely stemmed in part from the belief that he was capable of restoring order to a chaotic realm. Towns could also benefit from the influence which princes exercised at the level of the kingdom. The authority of Philip the Bold, duke of Burgundy, at the court of Charles VI may well explain the presence of so many prominent Lille citizens in membership lists of the Cour Amoureuse, a literary circle around the king made up of the most influential men in the realm. In Lyon the rise of the consul Jean II Le Viste to the position of royal adviser during the same reign was made possible by the access he gained to the king's service through his post as chancellor of Louis II, duke of Bourbon. In the county of Champagne the *bonnes villes* of Troyes, Reims, and Châlons cultivated the Burgundian connection down to 1429. The relationship was grounded in mutual needs, the prince maintaining support in a region bordering his patrimony, the Champagne towns counting on the importance of the dukes to the Lancastrian regime. Peace and economic stability, the advancement of careers, and access to networks of sociability and influence were just some of the advantages the authorities of the *bonne ville* might hope for from their relationship with a prince; in the provinces the latter could dangle the carrot as well as wield the stick.

In the second half of the fifteenth century, however, particularly away from those territories where princely power remained dominant, the *bonnes villes* reached a beneficial and enduring understanding with the monarchy. Evidence for this entente has been sought in the weakness of urban support for the aristocratic rebellions of the Praguerie (1440) and the League of the Public Weal (1465). That said, kings could not take it for granted that *bonnes villes* would shun princely factionalism in the second half of the fifteenth century. Jean Maupoint felt the princes had turned their full might against the unified force of 'King Louis and the city of Paris' during the War of the Public Weal,[3] but it is clear that the programme of the dissident princes enjoyed some support in the capital, and indeed, as Krynen notes, 'the Parisian elites had begun to betray the king'. Any change in the capital's allegiance would have had a wider impact in the kingdom, just as Rouen's fall to the League contributed to a royal reverse in the province of Normandy. If towns were more likely to support the king, perhaps this was because municipal authorities had come to believe the monarch was more likely to prevail over princely opponents and thereby guarantee peace. As Charles VII's envoy announced rather grandly to the *consaux* of one northern city after the impressive first reconquest of Guyenne, 'since Charlemagne, no king of France had been more powerful than he'.[4]

The growing strength of the monarchy was accompanied by changing attitudes towards the *bonnes villes*. The change was not, as was once thought, towards an ever more draconian policy of intervention and subjugation on the part of the crown: in this respect Louis XI's more extreme actions were not typical of his reign as a whole or of those of his successors. The occasional judgments of the Parlement of Paris or its regional counterparts in Toulouse, Bordeaux, or Grenoble against municipal authorities were not representative of some wider crown policy of hostility towards urban autonomy either: indeed, in many such cases the Parlement was acting as an arbitrator in disputes within the *bonne ville*. It was arguably such internal conflicts within ruling urban oligarchies, rather than external pressure from the crown, which posed the greatest long-term threat to urban autonomy in the provinces. At Tournai in 1452, Orléans in 1485, and Bayonne in 1489 internal disputes between rival parties seeking supremacy in the town opened the way to royal interventions that would not otherwise have been necessary.

By contrast, the crown's change in attitude certainly included a far greater degree of favour shown towards the *bonnes villes*. Historians of urban communities on the periphery of the kingdom or adjacent to it have tended to contrast the greater privileges and autonomy granted there by local princes with the circumstances of royal *bonnes*

[3] Jean Maupoint, *Journal parisien*, ed. G. Fagniez, in *Mémoires de la Société de l'histoire de Paris et de l'Île-de-France*, vol. iv (Paris, 1877), 52.

[4] 'Extraits analytiques des anciens registres des consaux de la ville de Tournai, 1431–76', ed. A. de la Grange, *Mémoires de la Société historique et littéraire de Tournai*, vol. xxiii (1893), 181.

villes under later Valois kings. But the contrast can be overstated. Awards of exemption from the tax of *franc-fief* (the fee payable to the crown by commoners acquiring a noble fief, justified in theory by the fact that the king lost the traditional feudal services of the nobleman in the transaction) became widespread in the later fifteenth century, benefiting the well-off provincial townsman who acquired country estates. Exemption from direct taxation in the shape of the *taille* is another royal favour which was more common by the close of the fifteenth century. In its place the royal administration came to rely on gifts and loans requested from the *bonnes villes* and secured by municipal authorities from wealthier inhabitants against the future income of the city. While these requests could generate even greater revenue than the *taille*, there was the possibility of negotiating the final amount awarded: in Angers the municipality paid out around 54 per cent of the taxes requested in the period 1489–96, dropping to around 48 per cent in 1500–13. Moreover, there was an economic benefit in the transaction for provincial elites. The majority of the townsfolk gained little and rural dwellers lost out as the *taille* continued to be levied on them in increasing amounts, but the ruling oligarchy of the *bonne ville* was more important to the king than the bulk of the provincial population. Louis XI's interview with a deputation from Amiens after that city returned to the royal obedience in 1475 has become famous as an example of that monarch's courting of urban groups in power: the deputation described with some pride how they had been taken aside to consult with the monarch, 'not as ambassadors', as the king reportedly put it, 'but as friends'.

Perhaps the changing attitude of the monarchy towards the *bonnes villes* is best characterized as one of greater trust on either side. If French kings from Charles VIII to Francis I intervened infrequently in provincial urban politics, this may have been because municipal authorities got on with their job in a manner that was generally acceptable to the crown and its officers. In Tournai exercising justice on the king's behalf was a matter of pride to the aldermen's bench; the city's authorities also kept the king's peace, took a hand in minting his coins, raised archers in his name, and considered their own banner a true representation of his power—so much so in fact that they refused a proposal to add the royal emblem of the lily to the city's coat of arms. Writing of local pride in a regional Parlement, Bernard Guenée states that 'it is symptomatic that at the close of the fifteenth century a French province could find no more appropriate way of affirming its personality than by means of a royal administrative institution'. Through the exercise of office and the interests of their personnel, royal institutions in the provinces often had a profoundly local flavour; their ability to function depended on a status acknowledged and sustained by the periphery as much as by the centre. Tacit assumption of this fact goes some way towards explaining why 'perfect harmony' (or at least the absence of serious conflict) can seem to characterize relations between the king and his *bonnes villes* in the provinces of later fifteenth-century France.

Under such circumstances the need for sustained direct contact between the monarch and his towns was less pressing. The most effective way of dealing with an important matter in the province was to send a commissioner from the centre, as happened when the Somme towns were returned to the duke of Burgundy in accordance with the treaty of Conflans. From the perspective of the *bonne ville*, best results were achieved by men who represented the city in Paris or, more commonly, by representatives sent to persuade a patron in the entourage of the king to bring their concerns to the fore. The classic example here is the 'expert fixer' Raymond Queu, one-time alderman of the Saintonge community of Saint-Jean d'Angély who frequently travelled 'to Paris to wait upon the king and his council upon the town's business' in the early decades of the century. To judge from the numbers of letters patent issued to towns by the royal council from 1422 to 1498, the *bonnes villes* took up relatively little of that body's time. As we progress from the reign of Charles VII, the proportion of new and pressing matters dealt with in the correspondence declines: by the accession of Louis XII the vast majority of letters concern the renewal of urban charters, a standard act at the start of any reign. The means of contact between the centre of the crown's political activity and the *bonnes villes* in the provinces were therefore personal, informal, and irregular. This fact helps explain some aspects of the development of the estates in fifteenth-century France—the last provincial force to consider here.

Estates and representative assemblies

The potential dynamism of representative assemblies had the greatest opportunity to express itself when the ruler was at a low ebb: hence the impact of the Estates General in the 1350s and the early years of Charles VI's reign. The provincial nobles (usually the majority of those present), clergy, and townsmen who attended assemblies in the fifteenth century could find themselves considering a wide range of matters. In the ruler's eyes, however, there were two main reasons for calling them, both of which became less pressing as the century wore on: to obtain consent to taxation and to influence public opinion. It is tempting to conclude on this basis that the fifteenth century witnessed the 'failure of the French medieval estates', particularly at the level of the kingdom, and especially when compared to long-term developments in England or the empire. At a provincial level, however, the picture is more complex, and any history of the estates is obliged to reflect on the survival of representative assemblies into the sixteenth century and beyond.

The struggle against Lancastrian and Burgundian France during the early years of Charles VII's reign led to the most concerted royal effort in the fifteenth century to seek the support of estates. The king had only limited success in summoning the Estates General, but those of Languedoil met frequently (either as a whole or in their eastern and western subdivisions), and elsewhere it is possible to detect the revival (Touraine), growth (Poitou), and even the first emergence (Bourbonnais) of provincial assemblies through a process of dialogue with the crown's representatives. In Languedoc the estates' authority reached a high point with the creation at their request of a regional Parlement at Toulouse (1420). The king's willingness to work through the Estates General or their subdivisions diminished once his circumstances improved. Already after his coronation at Reims in 1429 Charles appears to have favoured local estates over central assemblies. The last of these general meetings for his reign was summoned in 1440. The king's exasperation with a provincial estate is recorded in 1442, and around the same time he is famously reported to have dismissed proponents of the estates as worse enemies than the English. The only other known meetings of the Estates General in the fifteenth century, both held at Tours, occurred during times of royal weakness. In 1468 Louis XI secured the support of the Estates General against his brother Charles and his princely allies. Sixteen years later it was the turn of Louis's daughter and son-in-law to seek support from the same source, this time against princely efforts to control the young Charles VIII. In the course of the deliberations in 1484 some of the deputies voiced radical views which, had they been implemented, would have greatly increased the weight of assemblies in the relationship between crown and province in fifteenth-century France: a more permanent role for the Estates General in future tax-raising was sought, along with the creation of new provincial estates. Meetings of general assemblies may have been less frequent, but the crown could still find them useful and challenging.

That kings had reason to be wary of the Estates General was surely one reason for the latter's decline. The ability of *bonnes villes* to pursue their goals by the informal channels discussed above was another contributory factor (although outside Flanders or Languedoc, it should be noted, the towns had only a limited influence within the estates). To these elements we can add the disincentives felt by the king's provincial subjects when confronted by a summons to a general assembly: the distance that they might have to travel, the costs, discomforts, and dangers of the road, the unpredictable length of time involved in deliberations, the limited ability to effect change, and the inevitable request for money that would ensue. Provincial feeling could also work against the establishment of general assemblies in France. There is no better example of this than the oft-quoted dismissal of central estates by the Rouergois deputies at Chinon in 1428: 'the *pays* of Rouergue [is] accustomed to having an assembly of its own'.

But if particularism weakened central assemblies, clearly it could enhance the attraction of their provincial counterparts. At this level the pattern of decline is less uniform. Representation had often grown strongest in princely France for a variety of reasons: the origin and nature of the assemblies (for they were often very different from one another), the smaller size and cohesion of the territories in question, or the circumstances and inclinations of the local dynasty. In Brittany meetings of the estates appear to have been frequent in the first three and sixth decades of the fifteenth century, although some historians believe they were more regular than that; they ratified decisions of the duke and his council in matters of taxation and wider political concerns, and unlike many French estates they had a judicial function. In the duchy of Burgundy the estates are said to have met ninety-four times in the period 1440–1500 to consider demands for taxation, as well as monetary and (occasionally) judicial matters. Representation was well established in the dukes' northern lands, where in 1464 an Estates General was held for the first time at Bruges. A gathering of this body in 1473 was informed by Chancellor Guillaume Hugonet that they were lucky not to be living under Louis XI, whose tax demands, it was claimed in all seriousness, far exceeded Charles the Bold's. The assimilation of Brittany, Burgundy, and other great *pays d'états* (such as Provence) into the kingdom towards the close of the fifteenth century did not bring about the destruction of the estates. In Brittany they continued to play a role in fiscal and other governmental matters under the Valois kings. In Burgundy the estates adopted the same robust approach to Charles VIII's tax requests as they had to Philip the Good's. In some principalities, indeed, the estates played a part in the assimilation of the territory into the kingdom, such as Guyenne (where the military reductions of 1451 and 1453 were settled by consultation with representative assemblies) and Provence (where the estates helped define the terms of the union of the county to France in 1482 and 1486). Elsewhere in the kingdom the estates of the later fifteenth century appear more subdued than they had been under Charles VII. Henri Gilles wrote of the 'steadily increasing tutelage' which Louis XI exercised over the estates of Languedoc. However, he also acknowledged the gradual institutionalization of the same body, the emergence of its own personnel and archives, and its continuing relevance to local government and interests. In Auvergne the estates had been particularly dynamic, contributing between 1430 and 1438 to a scheme of self-defence in central France which prefigured the arrangements for Charles VII's standing army. The assembly declined after 1452, when the king began to rely on the *élus* to raise taxes. In the lower Auvergne, however, the estates met at least once a year after the 1470s to grant taxes to the duke of Bourbon, and acted in a range of local concerns from the upkeep of waterways to the reduction of the fiscal charge. Perhaps, looking from the centre to the periphery, these seemed marginal issues; from the opposite perspective, however, they assumed greater importance. The mere fact of their survival into the early modern period warns against overestimating the inherent fragility and fifteenth-century decline of the provincial estates.

The failure of monarchs to rid themselves of regional representative assemblies is said to have been the result of their personal failings: Charles VII's weak will when confronted by the resistance of a regional assembly; Louis XI's mental instability, which led him first to favour provincial estates at the expense of royal machinery for raising taxes, then to reverse that policy. But even if they had cause to feel threatened by provincial estates (and it is arguable whether they did), fifteenth-century French kings were not obliged to 'root out rival sources of influence and authority'; such things were not necessarily 'incompatible with firm rule'.[5] Kings had to reach a consensus and achieve cooperation with provincial forces which existed on their accession and continued to play a role in their reigns—a point which, although applicable to the estates, leads on to wider conclusions regarding crown and provinces in fifteenth-century France.

Conclusion

On the face of it our period did provide decisive answers to questions left hanging in 1400: the crown eventually reasserted—indeed, extended and developed—its authority; the threat of the territorial principalities grew stronger but ultimately faded; the *bonnes villes* of the provinces stood by later fifteenth-century kings; and the estates never again enjoyed the level of influence attained in the fourteenth century. The kingdom may have been lightly administered, but itineraries show that Louis XI saw a good deal more of it than Charles V had done. Communications between centre and periphery had never been faster or more regular. If a fourteenth-century king really did have difficulty 'imagining what his kingdom was like', as Robert Fawtier famously thought, this was less true of his later fifteenth-century successors.

Out in the provinces, however, change may not always have been quite so apparent. Servants of the crown usually had to work through

[5] D. Potter, *War and Government in the French Provinces: Picardy 1470–1560* (Cambridge, 1993), 11.

and with local powers to achieve their ends, including—as we have seen—municipal authorities and some estates. The influence of local princes could still be extensive. In the south-west Alain d'Albret supplanted the waning houses of Foix and Armagnac and at times proved as impervious to royal command as they had been. Noble affinities—to descend another level—were neglected at the monarch's peril. Louis XI discovered this in Normandy during the War of the Public Weal, when the Brézé affinity was instrumental in causing the duchy to go over to the rebels. Royal governors may have replaced apanaged princes of the blood, but many of these appointees were princes themselves, and all tended to attract local networks of support based on patronage and clientage. One type of potentially awkward potentate had therefore been replaced by another. Even at the centre the distribution of key provincial offices (*bailli, sénéchal*) remained in the hands of a powerful oligarchy: the Burgundian and Armagnac factions at the start of the fifteenth century had given way to the so-called 'masters of the kingdom' at its close—perhaps more amenable to the reigning monarch's will, but no less acquisitive or potentially obstructive. 'Forms change, but the structure remains and the polyarchy holds fast, despite the progress of the monarchy.'[6] *Plus ça change, plus c'est la même chose.*

[6] B. Chevalier, 'Gouverneurs et gouvernements en France entre 1450 et 1520', in W. Paravicini and K. Werner (eds.), *Histoire comparée de l'administration (IVe–XVIIIe siècles)* (Munich, 1980), 304.

7

The king and his government under the Valois, 1328–1498

David Potter

Popular tradition has tended to settle on the idea that the French state was finally consolidated from the middle of the fifteenth century onwards, after a lengthy period of chaos, by Charles VII and Louis XI, 'new monarchs' ready to sweep away feudal survivals and usher in a new age. This is not how the victories of these monarchs would have been viewed in their own time. In the half-century after the death of Charles VII, after all at times a highly loathed and controversial figure, his reign became a touchstone for good governance, due reliance on wise noble advisers, and, most astonishingly, taxation by consent. For Francis I, Louis XI, feared and hated as he was in his life, may have been the predecessor who got the kings of France 'out of their leading strings', but his reputation remained one for tyranny. Like all such simplifications, the notion of these kings as 'new monarchs' has a nugget of truth in it, but at the same time it conceals the fundamental fact that both in theory and in practice the kings of the late fifteenth century built on a long process of consolidation which had in some ways been stimulated by the disastrous foreign and civil wars of the period 1340–1450.

Public administration

In considering the organs of central government we must first remember the recurring tension between two principles: first, the concept of *potestas absoluta*, which concentrated legitimate authority in the hands of a divinely ordained monarch; secondly, the idea of government by good counsel which was expressed in practical terms during the period by the notion of the kingdom as a family enterprise in which all the princes had a legitimate role. The tension was marked by savage upheavals and political violence on the grandest scale—at its most severe in the first two decades of the fifteenth century—but was also to some extent in the process of reconciliation through the construction of a state in which the highest and middle nobility as well as the grand bourgeoisie had a central part to play in government and which became a crucial source of profit for them. Late medieval monarchy was highly personal but paradoxically impossible to exercise alone. In the later fourteenth century the royal letter-close headed 'De par le Roy (By the King)' became a routine instrument for the conciliar and financial officialdom (the traditionalist Philippe de Mézières thought them 'a waste of time and ridiculous'). For the king to indicate his own personal action, he had now to add his own signature and preferably a word or two of instruction; otherwise the letter would be subject to judicial challenge and investigation. A royal secretariat at court was therefore increasingly necessary, and the vast printed corpus of Louis XI's letters missive gives a fair idea of the range of his understanding of the *métier du roi*.

The term 'state' for the late Middle Ages is replete with anachronism, of course. Late medieval statesmen saw the essence of government as external relations (including war) and the giving of justice (including remissions for crimes). 'Finance' was thought to entail the costs of the royal household and ordinary revenues (derived from feudal incidents and the royal demesne). Extraordinary revenues (aids and other taxes) were only reluctantly seen as part of normal activities. Government was still a minuscule affair at the centre. While its personnel became more stable in the mid-fourteenth century, nine ordinances sought to restrain numbers between 1346 and 1413. This permanent central officialdom was reduced by an ordinance of

January 1360 to 175, and in the late fourteenth century (excluding the court, the army, and extraordinary revenue receivers) stood at little more than 200. There it remained until the mid-fifteenth century; around a hundred of these were employed in various functions in the Parlement. Of course, if the royal household is admitted, we get a much larger figure. A ruling of 1389 suggests a figure of 700–800 persons for the entire household, but this is deceptive. Only on grand occasions and military expeditions would such numbers have been assembled. In 1387 only two of the seventeen *chambellans* were required to serve each month. The guard increased from 1418, and the entire complement of the court under Charles VII has been estimated at 2,000 (10,000–12,000 is a reliable guide for the mid-sixteenth century).

There are a number of reasons for the small size of the central government. First, the king was always keen to economize on salaries; money was a constant problem. Secondly, bureaucrats were always regarded as bloodsuckers, and controlling them was bound to be a popular move. The idea of 'reform' since the thirteenth century had constantly referred to the 'time of St Louis' as the ideal; so, whenever a new tax was demanded, demands for the reduction of officials from the local *sergents* upwards were made. Even with the small numbers involved, about 1389 Philippe de Mézières could denounce the inflation of Chambre des Comptes officialdom. Thirdly, with the massive drop in population we have seen in the century from 1350, fewer officials were needed. At Amiens 120 of the 260 *sergents*, the most locally visible and resented royal officials, were cut back under the 1396 ordinance. One of the consequences of all this was that many law graduates entered the service of princes and the Church; another was the employment of supernumeraries to carry out basic administrative tasks, especially in tax collection.

All officials from the chancellor down to *sergents* and *tabellions* in the localities were 'officiers du roi', yet, of course, they were not viewed in the same way. For some great officials there was much preoccupation with 'election' in the second half of the fourteenth century. This did not mean anything like democracy or meritocracy. Though it was much talked of as a 'reform', in fact, as Françoise Autrand has pointed out, it served to strengthen both the status of those officials and royal power at the same time. The time had not yet come when officials constituted a semi-independent oligarchy as they did by the seventeenth century. In any case, the theoretical desirability of election was constantly coming up against human nature and practical politics. In the Châtelet it was argued in 1394 that to choose officials by 'impetration' (i.e. by special request leading to royal letters of gift, sometimes made out to rival lobbyists) would lead to 'many insufficient [men] being received' and, even though officials had been elected, 'since then their office has been sold to inadequate candidates and many appointed by lobbying, the importunity of petitioners and by impetration'. An ordinance of 1389 extended the desirability of election to a wider range of local legal officials, but the practice of impetration, with all its attendant disorders, continued despite the distaste for it on the part of the Parlement.

From the late fourteenth century royal officials were increasingly visible in terms of specific dress, which underlined their special status as representatives of the king; hence the formalization of specific robes for members of the Parlement, Chambre des Comptes, as well as liveries for members of the royal households. From the same period the inviolability of royal officials in the exercise of their functions, hitherto only covered by a general royal safeguard, was established from the highest to the lowest. This was not yet the principle that to attack an official was treason (as argued by Charles Loyseau in the seventeenth century), but it was very close to it. That idea had been mooted in a submission in Parlement of 1369 but was not accepted. Then in 1393 a disgruntled litigant attacked and wounded a councillor of the Parlement with a knife; he was condemned, on the basis of Roman law, to have his hand and head cut off 'because the lords of the Parlement, especially when exercising their office, are part of the king's body'. On the other hand, with privileges went responsibilities. Aggrieved individuals could take officials to court, though this was less the case than before, and the latter could no longer count automatically on being given immunity from prosecution. But they could only be condemned for the inadequate or fraudulent exercise of their functions, as many *fermiers* were in the years around 1400, and not for carrying out legitimate commissions.

All this gives a distinctive image to the originally small network of families which owed everything to royal service and staffed the royal institutions which had become stable from the middle of the fourteenth century; they assumed political power with the 'Marmousets' in 1389. These had a coherent point of view on public affairs: the strengthening of royal power. They have been described by Henneman as 'architects of the French state', while Autrand has argued that their rule 'consolidated decisively the foundations of the state'. The concept of security of tenure in office was in its formative stage during the late Middle Ages. It was aided by the self-perpetuating tendencies of bodies of officials allowed to 'choose' their new colleagues and gradual disappearance of the payment of officials through 'fermes', that is the periodic auction of the rights to profits from an office (especially prevalent among local officials such as *prévôts* and *tabellions*). The replacement of this by salaries was a slow and hesitant process but clear by the later fourteenth century. The fact that salaries remained fixed for decades if not centuries explains why the pension became a necessary supplement. Open venality was as yet confined to the levels of court ushers and notaries, not officers of justice, where it was condemned by canon law; as long as the purchasers proved competent, judges were not over-concerned by it. How far venality at higher levels was hidden, though, is impossible to say. Stability was also promoted by jurisprudence, which, while it argued that no royal office could be held for life and that all were revocable at royal will, in practice largely left officials in peaceful possession. The dismissals of local *sergents* in 1396 were only carried out with due regard for ability and on good advice, i.e. the principle that 'none be deprived of his office without being heard' and that dismissal should only follow formal court judgment, not an act of discipline by a superior. The next step was to be the ordinance of 1467 on the irremovability of officials. That said, it is certainly the case that the turnover in *baillis* and *sénéchaux* during the Burgundian–Armagnac struggles of 1410–18 was substantial, if only because of the circumstances of civil war.

An embryonic stage of the 'robe' milieu, personnel serving the crown in justice and finance, may be observed, and by 1400 the phenomenon of families of royal servants is well established. This was shaped by shared cultural and educational training in the faculties of arts and then of law, both canon and civil, the latter typically studied at Orléans in view of its prohibition at Paris. Studies, financed for ambitious or well-connected scholars by the Church or occasionally by the crown at a college, created an attitude which prepared scholars for integration into the official world. The latter was to a large extent self-selecting, especially as the process of nomination through election by existing officials gained favour in the Parlement during the period 1370 to 1420 as a remedy for the conferment of offices through lobbying and favouritism. Only with the schism in the royal administration after 1418 did this mode of preferment give way gradually to the regime of venality which was to become characteristic of the Ancien Régime. At first, traffic in offices was a private matter permitted by the crown. By the reign of Francis I it had become a formal state practice. With the end of the wars in the mid-fifteenth century, the numbers of officials increased. This was partly at any rate the result of the incorporation of some of the major fiefs into the royal demesne (see Chapter 6). By 1515 the number of officials in the Parlement of Paris had scarcely changed since 1360, but *parlements* had been extended throughout the kingdom and their total officialdom was nearly 200. In 1328 there were thirty-six *bailliages* and *sénéchaussées* but in 1515 just over 100, each with a full complement of officials. The appearance of the whole apparatus of 'extraordinary' finance since the mid-fourteenth century created a complement of 1140 officials by 1515, and there were now aristocratic governors in all the provinces. In that year, then, the total number of royal officials stood at a minimum of 4,000, probably a few hundred more, to whom should be added the staff of secretaries and commissaires. Central and local officialdom was then on the verge of substantial increases, though still modest in comparison with the era of Louis XIV.

The royal household

It used to be assumed that, before the sixteenth century, the royal court was no more than a household which expanded on ceremonial occasions by the attendance of great princes and lords and which was overshadowed by them. The role of the household in access to real political power in late medieval monarchy is now, though, increasingly apparent. The term 'cour' for the royal entourage appears in the writings of Philippe de Mézières and Christine de Pisan, where it is a real cultural force. It was customary to decry the corruption of life at court, its life of ambition, rivalry, flattery, and adulation. The *Songe du vergier* mocked this: when the prince might say 'I'm hot', the courtier says 'I'm sweating', when 'I'm cold', he says 'I'm shivering'. This was the common coin of anti-court literature through the centuries. In reality the servitude of courtiers was accompanied by pleasure and the opportunity to learn the rules of courtly life and deportment which marked off the true courtier from the townsman or rustic; few would have given it up voluntarily. Philippe de Mézières denounced favourites of princes ('Mahomets', in the language of his time), who ensured that 'if by chance there is an honest man in the court who tells the truth . . . they will not rest until by one means or another he is driven out', and, while he acknowledged they had always existed, thought they should only exist for the public good.

The court was not only the place where the personal needs—religious, physical, recreational—of the king's daily life were looked after; it was also a centre of government and, in the words of Bernard Guenée, 'the theatre of royal magnificence'. Formal ceremonies of state took place in the Palais at Paris, with its Sainte-Chapelle built by St Louis to house the crown of thorns. Formidable fortresses fitted out for domestic use were available west of the capital at Saint-Germain and east at Vincennes, while in the city itself there was the rambling Hôtel Saint-Paul near the Bastille as well as the Louvre. Elaborate court ceremonial had been formalized in the 'Estats de France' by Charles V and then transmitted to the Burgundian court. The upheavals of the Armagnac–Burgundian wars led to a return to simplicity in the manners of the French court which, by the sixteenth century, was elevated into an ideology of frankness and liberty in the relations between the French kings and their nobles. When Charles V refitted his *logis* in the north wing of the Louvre, he had seven rooms at his disposal. After the great upheaval of 1418 the court transferred its centre to the Loire, first of all at Bourges and then, even after the recapture of Paris, to Tours, though not in the city itself but at the country manor of Montilz. The *logis* of the king in the later fifteenth century seldom involved more than a *salle, chambre*, and *retrait.* George Chastelain, visiting the court in 1454, was struck by the envy that the luxury of the Burgundian nobles provoked, while the Milanese ambassadors received by Louis XI remarked that 'in this court there is no pomp'.

In the king's chamber, which gave the tone to the whole court, the nobility dominated. Whereas Mézières at the end of the fourteenth century was concerned about excessive numbers and thought the 'magnificence and glory . . . of your court will shine forth not in large numbers but in silence and good regulation pleasant to wise men', Robert de Balsac in the 1490s suggested that one of the finest ornaments of a prince's rule was to have a 'mass of fine knights, men of experience and clerics at his court', so that visitors would see that he was a 'sufficient prince and his household one of prudence and good government'. The chamber was both a central department of the household and a location, the king's bedroom which, as continued to be the case down to the seventeenth century, constituted the bulk of the king's living space and was widely accessible. Its staff were called the king's 'familiers', members of his *famille* and *maisnie*, stressing the personal relationship. The 'Marmousets' who came to power in 1388, though effective administrators, were not essentially bureaucrats but men 'of the king's chamber', in other words Charles V's favourites (that is what 'Marmouset' or 'Mahomet' meant in this period). One other interesting facet of their modus operandi: they were very much a collective group who shared ideas and indeed may have been linked by oaths of personal loyalty, 'alliance and friendship'. The hostile Chronicler of Saint-Denis noted that they 'joined in all the court intrigues and offices and tax farms could only be obtained through their intervention; court offices could only be obtained by promising them devotion and friendship against all comers'.[1] Under Charles VII the king's closest confidants, André de Villequier, Guillaume Gouffier, and Raoul de Gaucourt, were called his 'mignons'. The post of 'master of requests of the household' had long been a stepping stone to higher positions in the officialdom for rising men and still in the fifteenth century remained in the household to sift the cases to be retained by the king's direct justice. By the mid-fourteenth century more and more nobles were seeking appointment as chamberlains for the access given to the king. Mézières suggested that this had happened under Charles V 'because of the weakened state of the ship of France and to win over the love of the knights whom he needed'; hence the fact that the number of chamberlains had grown to forty-five in 1387, when it was reduced to twenty. The chamberlains, in daily contact with the king because they 'protected the king's body' and slept in his chamber, were present at his *lever* and *coucher*, held his confidence, knew his secrets, and (much as the gentlemen of

[1] F. Autrand, *Pouvoir et société en France, XIVe–XVe siècles* (Paris, 1974), 42.

the chamber from the reign of Francis I) were used to convey his will. They were what the Chronicler of Saint-Denis called the king's 'familiarissimi'. At this stage to be *conseiller et chambellan du roi* was not, as it was to become by the end of the fifteenth century, largely honorific; it conveyed real power. Bureau de La Rivière, first chamberlain to Charles V and in whose arms the king died on 16 September 1380, owed his substantial power to household influence and only became a royal councillor later. The chamberlains did not look after the bodily needs of the king; this was done by the *valets de chambre*, fifty-two of them in 1378, regarded by Mézières, who thought no more than six were needed, as 'men of low estate . . . who will not be very loyal or discreet'. They should not for that be underestimated; present at the king's *lever* and *coucher*, they heard many of his secrets and they too could aspire to be 'curials'.

Like the chamberlains, the *maîtres d'hôtel*—thirteen of them in the late fourteenth century—who held a leading position in the chamber, were both administrators at court and military men at need; Robert de Boissay (appointed 1383) was killed at Agincourt. The *grand maître d'hôtel* could sometimes, as in the era of Jean de Montaigu (1401–9), hold serious political power as well as a dominant role at court. The post of *maître d'hôtel* was highly prized and conveyed real influence; hence the tendency for a limited hereditary transmission to appear in the fifteenth century. Boissay's cleric son became *maître des requêtes, grand maître d'hôtel* to the dauphin Charles, *conseiller et chambellan*, and ambassador. A minor post at court could lead on to greater things. Pierre de Fenin, a minor nobleman of Artois, began as *panetier* to Charles VI and ended as *prévôt* of Arras in 1433. Raoul de Gaucourt, son of a Picard noble who was a royal chamberlain, was *valet tranchant* to Charles VI at 13 (1384), and became governor of Dauphiné and captain of Rouen in 1449.

The royal council

If the court was the focus of political power, the royal council was the essential organ of central government, more so than the great officials (whose influence depended largely on their presence in it) or the sovereign courts. The theory of government by good counsel was one of the most durable of late medieval society, and to be someone's councillor implied being among his most faithful followers. An ordinance of Charles V had declared: 'Where great matters and affairs are dealt with by the counsel of several wise men, so they are done more surely and certainly . . . We and our predecessors have always been governed in all our business by the advice of a great number of wise men, clerical and lay.' Gerson added: 'a king without prudent counsel is like the head of a body without eyes, ears or nose', and Guillaume Fillastre (1468): 'what prince or king was so ever wise that he presumed to govern his kingdom by his own understanding?' Robert de Balsac in a work published in 1502 suggested that 'the prince has only his own understanding like any others which by weakness or lack of care can fail to penetrate'.

We are well informed about frequency and membership for the period 1345–63, and for the reigns of Charles VII to Louis XII. In certain periods (the 1350s and 1390s–1410s) membership was heavily influenced by the relative power of great princes and barons. In times of political crisis, when it brought together the needs of daily administration and the demands of malcontents, in the words of Raymond Cazelles, 'the Council was not an instrument of royal power. On the contrary, it was a means to control and oversee that power, a most flexible instrument, as were most things to do with the monarchy, without rules or constitution.' This, he argued, was why the revolutions of the mid-fourteenth century were not more bloody and disintegrating. However, in normal times the personality of the king largely determined how he would use his council. In the earlier Valois period kings had tended to reach decisions with small trusted groups. Charles V's council saw fewer working meetings; his style was on one level to place important decisions before larger meetings—'great councils' of forty to seventy people. In 1373 he held a 'great and general council' of 105 at the Louvre to nominate a chancellor. No council could have worked effectively in routine matters with such large numbers. This perhaps is the reason that led Cazelles to argue that the political style of Charles V was to rely on his household. Most of his acts are countersigned by one or two favoured individuals—what Cazelles calls a 'small multi-tasked team'—which isolated the king from pressures either of council or of estates. The inner council as such does not seem to have met as a group under the king's chairmanship. Charles VII attended meetings only very rarely; for instance, only three out of thirty-nine sessions in April–June 1455. The king tended to retire to deal with matters apart with a few individuals when questions of high drama were to be dealt with. Robert de Balsac, by contrast, encouraged Charles VIII 'to attend the Council as often as he can and when he is not there appoint a great personage who will report to him what has been done'. He nevertheless assumes that there will be 'secret matters and of great weight' which can only be discussed in private with a small number of reliable and wise men.

In the mid-fourteenth century the frequency of meetings varied according to the nature of the problems facing the crown. In crisis years eighty to a hundred meetings have been recorded; in others, as few as seven. What were those crises? Externally they concerned either the threat of war or the difficulties attendant on the implementation of peace or truce; internally, serious political upheavals such as the Navarrist movement or meetings of the Estates General. Years of active campaigning saw relatively few meetings. Under Charles VII we see a much more institutionalized structure. The council, meeting roughly five times a week, dealt with practically all matters of state. The register of 1455 reveals that it dealt with international diplomacy, internal politics, the Church, justice, finance, and military affairs. This was the norm for the period; in addition Charles VII was accustomed to place before the council such matters as the nomination of a marshal, the reform of the army, and decisions for war, as in 1449.

The title 'king's councillor' could mean either an active executive member of government or possession of a number of eminent offices in the centre or the provinces—councillors of the *parlements, maîtres des requêtes, baillis,* and *sénéchaux.* These were the people who, Mikhail Harsgor has suggested, gravitated in orbit around the king. Of the 370 known councillors of Charles VII, eighty-seven (24 per cent) never sat in the council. Under Louis XI there were fifty-one honorific councillors out of 462. The council was thus meant to embrace as wide a range as possible of the king's servants in the centre and provinces. This wider council was still called the Grand Conseil before, at the end of the fifteenth century, that name was attached to the royal councillors who attended to the king's reserved jurisdiction. There was always the nucleus of a directing group; in the reign of Louis X a Conseil Étroit and late in the reign of Philip VI a Conseil Secret. In the crisis of the late 1350s the small inner group of John II's early years were displaced by many newcomers, including several princes. Their regularity of attendance was much lower, indicating the absence of much direction, even though meetings were frequent. In principle, the king designated whom he wished to sit in the council without much surviving formal documentation. The active council consisted of ten to twenty men. By 1484 this inner working group was known as the Conseil Étroit and generally consisted of a dozen or so members. Members were usually men with a range of specialisms, and councillors were normally active in a number of different fields. Under Charles VII the most influential forty-nine councillors included sixteen military men, nine financiers, and eight bishops.

In the mid-fourteenth century the main regions from which councillors were drawn were Île-de-France, the north, and the west. Burgundian councillors, important at first (at 22 per cent) under Philip VI, went into a sharp decline in the late 1340s. The central provinces maintained a steady representation around 10 per cent throughout. Languedoc and the eastern regions were very poorly represented. Under Charles V there was a shift to the eastern provinces stretching from Flanders in the north to Auvergne and Dauphiné in the south, precisely the areas left to French control after Brétigny and favoured by the close relations between France and the empire in the period. Charles VII's reign clearly reflected the reliance of the king on his lands south of the Loire. Then we find large numbers (fifty-five) from the pays de Loire (Touraine, Anjou, Orléanais, Berry), thirty-eight from the centre (Bourbonnais, Auvergne, etc.), and twenty-one from the west (Poitou, Angoumois). These were the bedrocks of royal support. This included members of princely or aristocratic families who remained loyal: the Bourbons, Anjous, Orléans (including Dunois), Lavals. There were Normans and Parisians despite English domination, but the areas least represented were the remoter border ones (Dauphiné, Languedoc) and those under Burgundian domination (Burgundy itself, Picardy, Artois, and Flanders). Under Louis XI the leading role of the pays de Loire and Centre continued from the reign of Charles VII; these were the regions in which the king travelled most frequently and in which the most reliable princely families, the Anjous and the Bourbons, dominated. Some changes are observable: the northern provinces produced more councillors (7 per cent) with the recovery of lands from Burgundy, and Languedoc begins to play a larger role.

The centrality of the council in government and politics meant that its composition and access to it are highly revealing of the political process. In the mid-fourteenth century the council was dominated equally by nobles and clerics, though nobles, especially military men, tended to predominate in years of crisis, when there were greater numbers who were not members of the judicial or financial bureaucracy. There seems no reason to think that, in the years when 'reform' of the kingdom was on the agenda, nobles were thrust aside. Despite Noel Valois's assertion that the bourgeoisie (with whom he assimilated clerics) were dominant, modern research has tended to reveal the continuing importance of the higher and middle nobility including princes such as Dunois, Richemont, Maine, and the Bourbons. The number of princes attending fluctuated slightly under Charles VII and Louis XI and, though there was a growth in the numbers of commoner councillors in the latter reign, this should not be seen as a 'rise of the bourgeoisie' in government.

Princes and aristocrats were still numerous in the council, but this to some extent limited their independence; most were in need of the pensions and salaries they received. Until 1477 former followers of the house of Burgundy were not encouraged, even after the 1435 treaty of Arras. Charles VII retained a deciding voice; twenty-two of the councillors were officers of the royal household and six courtiers in the sense of being called 'mignons'. Yet birth and clientele counted for most after the king's trust. After the fall of the Armagnacs in 1425, the clienteles of the houses of Anjou, Orléans, Brittany, and Bourbon took care to insert significant numbers of their *fidèles* into the council. Under Louis XI the king's will in appointments continued to predominate. As under Charles VII, royal pensions were vital to the princes (Duke Jean of Bourbon seriously needed his 50,000 *lt.* pension). Princes continued to be called to the council, then, though there is some reason to think that fewer of them were among the most influential members, and Louis XI was clearly less amenable to the lobbying of princes for their servants to be appointed to the council.

In the fifteenth century there was a move from sharp changes in personnel to much greater stability. Louis of Orléans aimed to secure his domination through appointments to the council (he controlled over half the members of the fifty-strong body in 1406, twenty out of the reduced council of twenty-six in the spring of 1407); domination of the councillors-general of the *aides*; and influence in the Chambre des Comptes. Locally, the *baillis* and *sénéchaux* were changed as the regime changed hands at the centre. Changes in royal policy were always reflected to some extent in the composition of the council. With the elimination of the Armagnac councillors in 1425 only four out of fifteen of the new councillors belonged to the former ruling group. The fall of La Trémoille in 1433 was less stark in its effects since after that ten of the eighteen influential councillors had been there before. The Praguerie (1440) was slightly more dramatic, with only six out of the sixteen influential councillors from that year continuing from the previous team. The most dramatic moments were the ends of reigns. Louis XI notoriously excluded many of his father's councillors. Of the fifteen most influential, he retained only Jean, duke of Bourbon, his brother-in-law (then only briefly), and the finance expert Jean Bureau (d. 1463). The War of the Public Weal excluded many of his new councillors and brought back many who had been dropped in 1461. It was long thought that a similar clean sweep was made on the death of Louis in 1483, under pressure from the Estates General reacting against his unpopular policies. In fact, in all some 66 per cent of Louis's councillors survived into the new reign. There were further upheavals during the 'Guerre Folle', but 59 per cent of Louis XII's councillors had experience in the previous reign.

The Parlement

Most observers who thought about power would have asked the same question as St Augustine: 'Remota . . . justicia, quid sunt regna nisi magna latrocinia?'[2] ('Without justice what are rulers but great robbers?'). In France from the late thirteenth century, as has already been seen (Chapter 1), justice was assured above all by the body of king's councillors known as the Parlement. By the late fourteenth century this was called 'part of the king's body', representing 'the image of our royal majesty' and some even likened it to the Roman senate.

The Parlement remained ill-defined—a series of *parlements*—until the ordinance of 11 March 1345 gave it stability of membership,

[2] *City of God*, bk. IV, ch. iv.

regular salaries, and a means for controlling recruitment. The seventy-eight councillors and three presidents (the numbers fluctuated slightly over the next century) with the ushers and royal lawyers made up roughly half of the 200 central government officials until around 1450. There seems little doubt that by the end of the fourteenth century the Parlement had taken on the role not only of supreme law court but of the forum for the most formal acts of state in which the king sat 'in the throne of his royal majesty and holding his justice'. By the reign of Charles VI this had become the context for the most formal appearance of the king of France as legislator and justiciar.

In the same period the stability of appointments opened the way for the consolidation of a 'milieu parlementaire' between 1380 and 1420. Social mobility, though inevitable, was always fraught with difficulties; long legal studies had to be followed and then the vested interests of those in place had to be confronted. It paid more and more to be of a *parlementaire* 'lineage'. The influence of families in the process of ascent into what would later be called 'sword' or 'robe' dynasties increased. A sense of this emerges from the reform ordinance of 1413, which aimed to prohibit the appointment of new judges within three degrees of consanguinity. There had been disquiet well before this, especially about the insertion of princely servants in the court, and the encroachment of lineages was obvious; President Henri de Marle was accompanied by his brother and three sons-in-law. Of the ninety-four members in 1413, forty-nine had at least one relative in the court. However, the sense of solidarity created by the social interconnection of *parlementaires* was crucial in the development of a collective sense of identity of the court as a 'corps'. Collective consciousness in the court was fostered by the idea of the members as a whole as 'part of the king's body', the sense that all members were dispensing the king's justice and had common interests.

In this period two chancellors of France were anchored in the Parlement, closely allied and surrounded by relatives also prominent there. Guillaume de Dormans (chancellor in 1372), a self-made man who made his career in the law, entered the Parlement in 1345, becoming one of the most trusted advisers of Charles V. He placed cousins, dependants of his brother the cardinal, there; two sons became bishops and the other a knight. Through his daughters he allied himself to another group around Pierre I d'Orgemont, chancellor in 1373, founder of lines of both sword and robe nobility in later generations. These networks ensured that, despite the profound divisions which had led to the creation of parallel *parlements* between 1418 and 1436, the court could reunite after Charles VII's entry into Paris with a surprising degree of effectiveness.

The Chambre des Comptes and *gens des finances*

The operation of royal finance was made up of a complex series of courts and offices which had issued out of the royal household. The rare attempt to create a 'souverain gouverneur des finances' in the persons of Jean de Montaigu and Pierre des Essarts in the early fifteenth century in no sense presaged the emergence of a finance minister. Collective authority remained customary until the end of the monarchy and the Chambre des Comptes was the central financial organ of the monarchy by the middle of the fourteenth century. Like the Parlement, it was a court and fixed from the early years of the century at the Palais in Paris, with a growing archive at its disposal. Charged with the audit and verification of the accounts of all royal receivers—*baillis, trésoriers, maîtres de la chambre aux deniers, trésoriers des guerres*, etc.—its remit expanded to registering acts of provincial officials in financial matters and in participating in the royal council. By the early fifteenth century it had a high view of itself as 'sovereign court, chief and of final appeal in all matters of accounts and finances, repository of the titles and knowledge of the crown and of the secrets of state, guardian of the regalian rights and preserver of the royal demesne'. It entitled its decisions ordinances 'by the Council being in the Chambre des Comptes', stressing its origins in the Curia Regis. A number of early depictions of this institution have survived. One in particular shows the Chambre under Charles VII: in the midst of a room hung with the royal hangings of blue and gold sit eight men around a table with a green cloth. Four of them are reading the accounts, two others, probably the *maîtres*, are listening and manipulating counters. The numbers involved were few, then, for such a great task. From 1320 there were eight *maîtres*; then from around 1360 the royal supervision was shared by one clerical and one lay 'souverain' (later there was to be a 'souverain' established as first president). There were also eleven clerks (*auditeurs*), as well as *greffiers* and *correcteurs* (instituted in 1410). In 1389 there were in all thirty officials of the court. Clearly, this was a seriously understaffed office to deal with the audit of the finances of the entire monarchy, so not surprisingly the mid-fourteenth century saw the detachment of part of its duties by the creation of the Chambre des Monnaies (1348) and the Cour des Aides (1356–7). Even so, the finance officialdom at the centre was meagre and forced the Chamber to work long hours seven days a week, much to the discontent of the clerks. Up to the late fourteenth century the Chambre had been staffed by men who held a wide administrative brief and political role. From the 1390s the Chambre was more and more a specialized administrative body, its officials strictly confined to finance.

The nucleus of administration for 'extraordinary' taxes goes back to the college of the nine *généraux élus* of 1355 charged with the assessment and collection of taxes by the estates. It took definitive shape with the three *trésoriers généraux* appointed in December 1360 to oversee the collection of John II's ransom money. In December 1363 there were added three more 'généraux élus sur le fait de la guerre et de la défense du royaume'. These were reshaped as the twelve 'councillors-general of war and the aides' in 1369, nine of whom were policy-makers and members of the royal council (later simply called *généraux des finances*). In most cases these were men who worked closely with local interests. Their function of judging disputes was hived off to a special Cour des Aides from 1389.

The years 1436–50 saw a significant further transformation of the financial machinery with greater institutional clarity. This involved a stricter separation of expenditure and accounting procedures and the geographical formalization of the four great 'charges': Languedoil, Languedoc, Outre-Seine-et-Yonne, and Normandye. Henceforth we can identify more clearly the parallel working of the *généraux* and their staff for the management of extraordinary finance, the *trésoriers* for the demesne, etc. These functions accounted for about twenty offices of prime importance to the state. By the last quarter of the fifteenth century the classic organization of the finances under the aegis of *messieurs des finances*, an oligarchy of closely related nobles of bourgeois origin, had taken shape and was to remain in control down to the 1520s.

The king's revenues

The development of the taxation powers of the French crown lies at the heart of any discussion of the defining characteristics of the monarchy. Inevitably it is controversial. Martin Wolfe, in *The Fiscal System of Renaissance France*, seeking a point of departure in the move to 'taxation absolutism', found it in the reign of Charles VII. Yet even Wolfe had to admit that many of the instruments of taxation used under Charles VII were similar to those of his immediate predecessors' reigns. Wolfe's argument here was that the hiatus of the civil war and English occupation meant that a new start had to be made from about 1430 onwards. In fact, the essential features of a 'modern' tax system were in place by the end of the fourteenth century.

The convention that the king should 'vivre du sien' (live of his own) remained a powerful one but faced insuperable problems by the late fourteenth century, especially in the light of the demands of *causa necessaria* and *utilitas publica*, the core of the idea of reason of state. In reality, extraordinary taxation had become routine by the middle of the fourteenth century. Around 1250 the monarchy could count on an average of 250,000 *lt.* per year; by the mid-fourteenth century that sum had increased to 2.5 million. Money of account had fallen in value, but the population had slumped so this represented probably a fourfold increase. The driving force of fiscal change in late medieval France was deficit in the face of war. The wars of the period 1294–1356 were largely financed by many forms of special war subsidy. From the summoning of the Estates General of Languedoil (1355) and the battle of Poitiers onwards, the necessity to pay the king's ransom and the failure of the Estates General to provide the necessary mechanism for raising funds ultimately forced a complete re-evaluation of the crown's financial potential. From then on a regular basis of taxation began to emerge. By 1412 it was possible for a royal official to declare 'that the King can levy *tailles* and *aides* on his kingdom as an emperor, for its defence and guardianship; nor may any lord whoever he be levy anything without the king's consent'. Christine de Pisan, on the reform side of the political debate, in the *Livre de la prod'hommie de l'homme* (1406), accepted that it was legitimate to raise taxes 'if you receive what is due to you by well ordained and ancient custom stemming from the rights of lordship', but if levies are made rapaciously 'for private profit without just cause or for the public good . . . such people are not ministers of justice but of the devil in hell'.

The genesis of taxation had important consequences for the shaping of political society. Although at first exemption was not automatic, it was quickly established for the higher clergy and 'nobles of noble lineage, professing arms and living nobly'. Indeed, a proportion of taxes was remitted to the holders of great fiefs and apanages, so that under Charles V and Charles VI as much as one-third was transferred in this way. The exemption of royal officials started on an ad hoc and personal basis as a means of supplementing meagre official salaries but gradually became generalized in all the major administrative and judicial bodies. In other words, the defining characteristics of Ancien Régime taxes were set down by 1400. Exemption, started as a custom, became fixed and then a privilege which defined status.

The revenues of the royal demesne—the Trésor properly speaking—jealously guarded as they were by a range of institutions such as the Chambre des Comptes, were not particularly promising during the demographic collapse of the fourteenth century. The danger of infringing interests was too great, and the tendency to create apanages out of the royal demesne continued throughout the period. Its administration by the *trésoriers de France* constituted the core of the demesne system, working through receipts in each *bailliage.* The yearly receipts in the late fourteenth and early fifteenth centuries varied from 180,000 to 200,000 *lp.* A series of ordinances in the late fourteenth century sought to eliminate burdens on the demesne such as *rentes* (annuities) and pensions. In 1388, under the Marmouset regime, a serious effort was made to improve the condition of royal estates by an investment of 25,000 *lt.* In the disturbed economic context of 1388–90 this policy had little chance of success and had failed by 1391. Repeated attempts to do the same over the next generation, for example a solemn reform ordinance of January 1401, came to nothing, even when economic and political conditions were more favourable. John the Fearless made reform of the demesne a key item in his 1405 manifesto and renewed the 1401 economies in the demesne after his coup of 1409; once again the plan was swept away, this time by civil war.

The constraints on tax revenues were fairly obvious. The king and his ministers had no clear understanding of the numbers of taxpayers or of their wealth. They had no permanent officialdom to assess and collect taxes. They had therefore to rely on the collaboration of communities in the payment of taxes. There was a further constraint: the fundamental shortage of specie. France had no great resources of its own in gold and silver and thus had both to recirculate its supply and seek to acquire new supplies by a proto-mercantilist trade policy. The temptations of debasement were ever present. As a result, a form of revenue could be created at the expense of taxpayers whose income was fixed in a money of account that declined in value as the coinage in circulation was debased. In addition, in certain periods, for instance between 1435 and 1485, virtually no new coinage was minted and this added another difficulty for taxpayers.

Late medieval officials still observed the archaic formula of dividing taxes into 'ordinary' and 'extraordinary'. So, when war and government demanded new taxes, they were 'extraordinary' but quickly assimilated into routine administration. By the last decades of the fourteenth century extraordinary taxes had become more or less permanent and essential to the monarchy. The origin of such levies was the requirement to 'aid' the king in the urgent discharge of military and other duties. In 1324 the first export duty (*gabelle*) on salt was levied, extended in 1343 to trade within the kingdom. The clash with Étienne Marcel and the reform movement of the 1350s came essentially over the issue of the proper use of such revenues rather than the principle. From the late 1340s the crown had resorted to sales taxes throughout northern France voted annually at *bailliage* level. These had not in the end proved viable but had indicated a major possible source of revenue. The estates of 1355 voted in principle a sales tax and *gabelle* which would bring in about 5 million *lt.* but it could not compel the local estates to accept it. Charles V after 1360 needed to pay his father's ransom and established a general network of retail and wholesale consumption taxes—*aides*—as well as the *gabelle* on salt. When war began again in 1369, they were simply re-employed for military defence and joined by a series of special levies on the towns and the countryside called 'fouages' (hearth taxes) first raised in 1363/4 to deal with the *routiers* and then reaffirmed in 1369 as a basket of taxes designed to maintain a permanent army. These were abolished by Charles V on his deathbed, an act often thought to show the king's short-sighted view on the need for permanent taxes. He had, though, acquired a budgetary surplus by the reconquest of most of the English territories and was aware of population decline. In January 1381, at the request of the Estates General of Languedoil (which voted in principle for a new tax), the new government abolished the *aides*, only to be forced to bring them back in January 1382 without a further vote of the estates. After savagely crushing the consequent uprisings, the government was thus able to re-establish permanently the regime of the extraordinary revenues: 5 per cent taxes on all retail transactions, 25 per cent on drink, 5 per cent on exports. Drink taxes were much higher than under Charles V, but then he had levied *fouages* as well. They were collected by *fermiers*, given the contract to do so by *élus*, substantial regional notables who also had a duty of inspection. The *gabelle* at this stage had not developed into the great state monopoly of the Ancien Régime; it was a consumption tax like the others but at a higher rate and organized differently. In 1360 it was fixed at a quarter of the merchant's price (thus salt of 20 *st.* value was sold at 25 *st.*, 5 *st.* going to the king) but from 1366 at a movable rate according to the needs of the crown. The king could thus double the wholesale price, which would be collected at the point of sale.

The network of collection for indirect taxes had evolved essentially after 1345 in the course of horse-trading with *bailliage* communities, who feared that the taxes would be embezzled by corrupt officials. The *élus*, then, were originally meant to be guardians against this and were revived by the estates of 1355 as 'upright and solvent men' chosen by local estates as agents to collect the *aides* they voted. Only later did they develop into regular royal officials. This underlines the fact that, for efficient revenue collection, any late medieval government needed local cooperation; this could take place with estates (though Charles V was rather reluctant to call these) but was more likely to be through local notables. How much did the *aides* bring in? The total revenue around 1390 from Languedoil and Languedoc was about 2 million *lt.*, though a third of that never reached the central receipts. Given the estimation of crown expenses in 1372/3 at 1,650,000 *lt.*, the margin was very small and the *aides* clearly could not cope with urgent expenditure.

The inception of new burdensome taxes in the form of *tailles* was noted by Froissart for the year 1386 (chroniclers rather than government used this term) and the practice of raising them over the previous thirty years was ponderously attacked by Philippe de Mézières in book II of the *Songe du vieil pelerin* when he likened it to an operation of being 'taillez de la pierre' ('cut for gallstones'), stones then transmuted into gold and palaces. Mézières was writing in a well-established tradition that insisted that free men could only pay taxes by their own consent and that, once the causes of taxes ceased, so should the taxes. By then, though, the idea of such a tax was not new. The Estates General of March and May 1356 had proposed to replace sales taxes with taxes on income (though of a regressive kind), but this had not been generally put into effect. How did the new *tailles* of the 1380s differ from the existing levies, the *aides ordinaires*? The latter were thought inadequate for ambitious war plans and the *fouages*, as hearth taxes, were undermined by the population decline of the 1370s. In October 1384 we see the first of the 'aides pour le passage de la mer' (the *tailles* were, confusingly, called *aides* at first) and in the following two years nearly 3 million *lt.* were raised in this form even though the objective, an invasion of England, was put off. Then in 1387 came demand for levies for problems in Spain and with the frontier of Guyenne. Despite the relaxation of fiscal pressure with the inception of Charles VI's personal rule, the conclusion of a long truce with England brought demands for another such levy, and thereafter they became a regular feature of the years when Orléans and Burgundy were struggling for control.

These levies were deemed at first to be temporary and raised directly as taxes on communities in northern France (in parts of the south they were levied at first as a hearth tax). The idea of special contributions was slightly older and went back, as we have seen, to the meetings of Estates General in the mid-fourteenth century, but there was no such meeting between 1381 and 1413, so the *tailles* developed essentially as non-voted levies (the dire necessity of the government prompted it to call a meeting of the estates in 1413, which in fact refused a demand for *tailles* and fatally undermined the stability of such government as there was). The *tailles* were not paid in Brittany, Burgundy, and Flanders, and in those *pays* that had developed local estates they were voted by them.

The crisis of 1418 led effectively to a collapse of the indirect taxes, the *aides*, as both sides sought popularity by remitting them. This left the Bourges government in particular in a difficult position, which was alleviated by the frequent grants of taxes in principle by meetings of the Three Estates for large areas during the 1420s. There has, though, been much misunderstanding here. It has often been argued that the crown 'seized' absolute power in taxation by continuing to raise taxes granted by the estates without further consent. However, as has been seen, the tradition that taxes be voted by an Estates General had never become established for the simple reason that it was always easier to deal with local estates and towns. Charles VII was doing no more than this. Nevertheless, it is important that Charles was able to resume collection of the *aides* after the vote in principle of the estates from 1428. The successes of the king prompted the Estates General of Languedoil to renew the grant of *aides* in 1436, in a form which was then consolidated by a great royal ordinance systematizing all the indirect taxes operated since the reign of John II: a 5 per cent tax on all provisions and merchandise, 12.5 per cent on retail alcohol, and 5 per cent wholesale (in the south the estates won the right to vote an 'equivalent' for these *aides*).

The famous Estates General of Orléans in 1439, which voted the king a *taille* of 100,000 *lt.* 'for war needs', has similarly been seen as one of the great constitutional landmarks, for after it no king felt the need to ask the Estates General for a grant of the regular *taille*, Charles VII proceeding to collect around 420,000 *lt.* This was the result of war and revolt in the years immediately afterwards, and the crown continued to insist that calling together the estates would only be a 'burden' to his subjects. However, the formal grant by estates had only ever been seen as a matter of political wisdom in difficult times, not a question of constitutional principle. Juvénal des Ursins's 1452 diatribe against the raising of taxes without consent was unable to offer any answer other than that the king, though *legibus solutus*, 'ought' not to place himself above the law. The November 1439 ordinance on the *taille*, while prohibiting seigneurial *tailles* on free men, confirmed noble exemption. It also proscribed the private use of military force, obviously a major development, but it was not until 1445 that the organization of the existing aristocratic cavalry into twenty regular companies (at a cost of 720,000 *lt.* a year) put the usual demands of military expenditure onto a clear and regular basis.

This resulted in an additional *taille* for the military, producing near enough the 1.2 million *lt.* in total generally regarded as the norm for the *taille royale* by about 1460. Of course, in two-fifths of the kingdom various assemblies of local estates continued in principle to vote these *tailles.* The implications of this are discussed in Chapter 6.

Louis XI just modified these arrangements while in certain periods towards the end of his reign massively increasing the burden. By 1480 the *tailles* were bringing in 3.9 million *lt.* compared with 655,000 for the *aides.* The main long-term consequence of his period was the confirmation of the trend towards exemption from the *taille royale* for the *bonnes villes,* thus confirming the image of the tax as essentially one upon the peasantry. The 'reaction', if it can be called that, at the end of Louis's reign, though it seemed to presage a renewed role for the Estates General in voting taxes, only managed to secure a reduction to 1.5 million *lt.* Any hope of this depending on renewed votes by the estates had gone by 1486. The level of the *taille* thereafter only crept up to about 2.5 million by 1498, to be slightly reduced by Louis XII, the 'père du peuple', who also made a serious attempt to improve demesne revenues. Nevertheless, Louis XII's total revenues stood at an average of around 3.5 million *lt.* (2 million from direct taxes). We can observe from all this a series of taxation 'pulses' which largely reflected the ups and downs of royal power. Direct taxation had become an absolute necessity, and yet it remained controversial at times of royal weakness.

The emergence of a governing elite

Kings needed councillors, and their government was transmitted through a network of interests—financial, landed, family—which were gradually consolidating around the monarchy as a directing group. At the highest level this was already taking shape in the fourteenth century and, as Raymond Cazelles has shown, is clear enough in the 1350s with the coteries of 'councillors and governors' under John II. During the Estates General of October 1356 there were complaints that when King John II came to the throne he chose those 'to whom he entrusted much of the government of the kingdom . . . who together constituted a league and alliance' to the extent that 'what one wished to propose another would in no wise impede' and from which 'great ills have happened and could happen in time to come'. The Chronicler of Saint-Denis described in 1388 how the Marmouset councillors brought in by Charles VI 'made a pact of alliance and friendship among themselves and promised by oath to support each other with all their power and, in fortune or adversity, to act with the same mind, will and objective'.

This tendency to an administrative solidarity was usually expressed within the council but also on a much wider scale; the councillors were drawn from an 'oligarchy', as it has been called by Mikhail Harsgor, of a few dozen favoured families drawn from the middle nobility and 'peuple gras', the wealthy bourgeoisie, which took a more recognizable shape under Louis XI. At the death of Louis the transition to the regime of Pierre de Beaujeu and Anne de France was assured by Jean d'Estouteville, Jean de Baudricourt, Philippe de Crèvecœur, and Pierre de Rohan, mostly members of old families but all of whom owed everything to Louis. Beaujeu's elder brother, the constable Jean, duke of Bourbon, by contrast held prestige but little real power within the government.

Court and council were the great sources of enrichment for these oligarchic families such as the Amboise, Batarnay, La Trémoille, and many others among the middle nobility and the dozen or so families which constituted the 'group of Tours' who had emerged during the royal residence in the Loire. The ruthless pursuit of enrichment by them became an essential part of the political process. This took the form of royal pensions, salaries as officials, concessions of the royal demesne and rights, and military commands. Jacques de Luxembourg, seigneur de Richebourg, wrote that 'I have no other revenue than that which comes to me from the King.' The count of Maine, bemoaning the war damage to his county of Guise, asked in addition to his pension for further funds, 'otherwise without your help I shall not be able to carry on'. Pensions were a well-established form of supplementing officials' salaries as well the incomes of grandees (in 1398, 250,000 *lt.* out of 934,050 money spent from the *aides* in Languedoil went on pensions). There was criticism of this, of course. In 1445 Jean Juvénal wrote, 'Alas, poor taxes, go off to the wars! God knows why the princes of the blood and the officials should have those pensions; they are the king's relatives, therefore they must have what the king needs to fight his enemies with. Everyone wants a pension now.' Peter Lewis showed in his analysis of the royal pensions lists under Louis XI how significant were these payments in binding a larger elite to royal service at the end of the fifteenth century; 950,000 *lt.* was paid out in 1480–1 to 760 individuals, but half of it went to sixty of them. Members of the council held thirty-seven out of the seventy-three *bailliages* and *sénéchaussées* between 1483 and 1515, and these the most important. From the reign of Charles VII onwards a pattern had been emerging by which the posts of *bailli* and *sénéchal* had been taken over by the greater barons and members of the royal council. The Church also became an obvious battlefield for patronage. Of the 109 bishoprics outside Brittany, only thirty escaped the control of councillors or members of their families, which in turn strove sometimes violently to make good their promotions. Promotion to benefices became a major buttress to the power of these oligarchic families.

This oligarchy was composite: middle nobility, a few grands and families of origin which had taken care to rise into the ranks of the nobility. Within it there are certain identifiable groups such at that of the Tours financiers. The Briçonnet, Beaune, Poncher, Ruzé, Hurault, Bohier were all destined to play a lasting role in the administration of the monarchy, though it was only after the War of the Public Weal that they emerged centre-stage in public administration. Guillaume Briçonnet was the central figure in their conquest of the upper reaches of the financial administration. Son of a *receveur* of Languedoil, son-in-law of Jean de Beaune, he spent his early years in the family enterprise as court provisioners. In 1480 he became *secrétaire des finances*, 1483 was *général des finances* of Languedoc, and in 1484 a member of the council. Thereafter, this closely intermarried milieu of royal servants increased their grip on the central agencies and by the end of the fifteenth century were leaving their bourgeois origins behind. The Tours financiers, like many other oligarchs, played the game of Church benefices. On the death of his wife, Guillaume entered the Church, starting as bishop of Saint-Malo in 1493, and attaining the archbishopric of Reims and many other benefices as one of the great pluralists of his time. The Tours group may not have equalled the princely aristocracy in wealth but were certainly more wealthy than most middle-ranking nobles and made good their status by acquiring knighthoods and constructing spectacular country estates.

With the absorption of great apanages in the late fifteenth century, the monarchy was transformed. This transformation, though, was one of degree, not of type. The basic building blocks of the Renaissance state had been assembled since the early fourteenth century, and the driving force was the idea of a composite political elite dominated by aspiration to noble status which perceived that the crown was a source of profit and security to be served and milked at the same time.

8

The later medieval French *noblesse*

Gareth Prosser

Noblesse is ancient and international, and the historiography of its origins and trajectory is vast and fissured. Key concepts in the modern study of the European nobility—Germanic origins, the rise and fall of chivalry, class conflict with bourgeois capitalism, domestication by centralizing monarchies—now seem simplistic or ideological. The abandonment of the great edifice of 'feudalism' alone might easily monopolize this discussion, and few implications of it for the period after 1300 have been pursued. What half-formed new paradigms share with their predecessors is power: no longer 'private' enemies of a nascent 'public' state, nobles have been reincorporated into the 'personalized' states finally smashed by revolution between 1789 and 1914. Nobility was from antiquity the privileged and legally recognized social class from which governing elites derived. Born into a landed aristocracy, its members made careers in princely service or the Church. They wore the Roman *cingulum* to symbolize their participation in the public power of late and post-Roman princes. Springing from Gallo-Roman and Germanic aristocracies, held in an honorific hierarchy of titles linked to office, subject to quasi-military discipline whether soldiers or administrators, personally bound by oath to the prince, this *nobilitas* monopolized the offices or *honores* in which power inhered. It was not merely an integral part of the Roman, Merovingian, and Carolingian state, but synonymous with it.

Until the 1960s historians associated the disintegration of the Carolingian empire with the rise of feudal institutions and the anarchic replacement of an old aristocracy by new elites of knights and vassals. Thereafter, it was realized that the Carolingian aristocracy survived in many regions, to be joined by a rising class of knights with whom they intermarried, creating a two-tier nobility with a common lifestyle. Non-feudal elements—birth, wealth, delegated command—were more important for nobles than the receipt or render of services for property. Historians had used the language of feudalism and vassalage so variously that it was leached of meaning, giving way to an understanding of how dextrously princes exploited what had been thought of as the privatization of public power. In fact the *féodalité* restored rather than destroyed public power in 1050–1250. Capetian kings, participants in this process as territorial princes in the Île-de-France, benefited from it as their rivals failed in the thirteenth century. Characterized by knighthood, exhibiting wide variations in wealth, instrumental in strong Capetian kingship, a single unified nobility had emerged in France before 1300.

Defining *noblesse*

Noblesse was so basic a social category that contemporary definitions tended to the banal. Nobility was a recurrent motif in literature, poetry, song, religious life, drama, and ceremonial events. With such material, much has to be inferred, but noble status itself became an issue in the fourteenth century. Much writing on the subject was a programmatic response to the crises affecting the crown and social order, but some evidence directly addresses definition. Established nobles had to prove their status in many situations, even to religious institutions like the Order of St John. This became ever more common in this period as nobles' relationships with their communities and superiors became entangled in judicial processes and official inquiries. The criteria which emerged for determining whether an individual was noble have tended to be neglected in favour of literary treatments, so it is not yet possible to relate intellectuals' theoretical notions to the developing concerns of lawyers and officials. The assumption here is that the literature condensed views conventional in wider French society.

The earliest royal ennoblements under Philip III and Philip IV were basically permissions to become a knight, but the chancery quickly settled on a more elaborate formula, which thereafter changed little. Françoise Autrand counted over 1,500 letters of ennoblement for the period 1290–1483. The chancery's definition of *noblesse* was contained within the concessions made to the *anobli*. He was to join 'the company and union of nobles of our realm', and, to be reputed noble, might arm himself knight if he wished, was to enjoy the judicial and other privileges of nobility, might acquire and hold noble fiefs without being subjected to the penalties applied to commoners.

The chancery rightly perceived the *noblesse* as a community. In lawsuits over *noblesse* the issue of noble sociability was critical. Self-styled nobles tried to bring as many nobles to testify to their status as possible, regardless of the issues of fact they could speak to. Had this man hunted with other nobles, ridden with them, been received in their houses, drunk and eaten with them, married among them? Marie-Thérèse Caron recognized that noble sociability was important in Burgundian suits and conflated it with *commune renommée*. To be noble was to be reputed noble, for nobility was not a private technical matter: public acknowledgement was essential. Many elements came together in the testimony of Breton peasants as to the status of a Vannetais lady: they knew her, she lived on her own property, behaved as a *demoiselle* should, clothed herself as a noblewoman ought, socialized with other nobles, was addressed by them as cousin, and sat with them at mass. In her daily life she exhibited herself as noble. Nobles were visually distinctive in ways so obvious that hardly anyone bothered with specifics: a murderer at Château-Landon in 1336 was 'wearing the clothes of a knight'.[1] In 1493 a peasant explained that the 'chapperon large et estendu' unfamiliar to his Norman audience was that worn by Breton gentlewomen. In conferring the right to knighthood and *alia nobilitatis insignia*, the crown encouraged all to accept the right of new nobles to proclaim status in public ways. They might assume the customary dress, and place arms upon their houses, tombs, and in the stained glass of the churches they patronized.

Birth was necessarily absent from the definition of nobility implicit in ennoblements. The chancery sometimes mentioned maternal

[1] 'Soy portant en abit de chevalier'; *Confessions et jugements de criminels au Parlement de Paris (1319–1350)*, ed. M. Lanhers and Y. Langlois (Paris, 1971), 115.

ancestry, but this was legally irrelevant in most provinces and the issue was sidestepped by envisaging ennoblement as recognition of intrinsic virtue rather than conferment of status. These evasions were necessary, since lineage was clearly important to most people's conception of *noblesse*. It was usually central to inquests into status. The putative noble set out his ancestors, and witnesses testified to the genealogical facts and the status of fathers, grandfathers, uncles, and cousins as revealed in their careers, wealth, dress, marriage partners, property, and social connections.

Inquests into noble status began as examinations of whether individuals were undermining the lord's (thus the crown's) right to service. The notion that only nobles might hold fiefs was rooted in fear that non-nobles could not render the military service owed on them. Itinerant commissions of *franc-fiefs* or *nouveaux acquets* fined non-nobles they discovered holding fiefs. Philippe Contamine found an inquest of 1312, and they became a frequent financial expedient for the crown. Hence the fourth element of Autrand's chancery definition of *noblesse*: the right to hold noble property without hindrance. The commissions became a routine venue for policing the cusp of *noblesse* as their regularity increased. In much of Languedoil this happened in the late fourteenth century, but in some areas ordinary courts retained their importance until much later. Landowners could escape the commissioners by showing that their ancestors had performed military service, enjoyed tax exemption, and practised the customs locally reserved for nobles. The first two questions were factual, but the last element touches the moral and economic framework around the exercise of power in the community. These customs were linked to property management and inheritance. Because the fragmentation of property threatened the status of their lineages, nobles gradually abandoned equal distribution of property among children. Male primogeniture and the reservation of most of the inheritance for the eldest boy was a device for preserving the wealth of at least the elder line. When officials or peasants referred to a family's *gouvernement noble*, they often had these tools for preserving the patrimony in mind.

Gouvernement noble merged with *vivre noblement*, however: it meant observing a prescribed lifestyle and avoiding behaviours regarded as derogatory. When in 1408 witnesses in the Vivarais defined nobility, they ruled out a range of economic activities, and stressed military service, wealth, and a lay lifestyle which they characterized as 'living nobly'. A 1336 survey into the status of individuals rendering homage to the Dauphin Humbert II, in the Valentinois, was precise, adduced fewer proofs, and made little distinction between personal freedom and nobility—a commonplace also in parts of northern France. Seventy-two years and a revolution in extraordinary taxation separated these Rhône valley surveys. Taxation had risen, but nobles had remained exempt, so taxpayers had pressed for greater rigour in determining their status. Officials developed criteria of definition from social conventions and practice before the *franc-fief* commissions. Fiscal pressure was general, undermined local customary variation, homogenized the definition of *noblesse* across the realm, and sharpened awareness of its military *raison d'être.*

In 1441 Burgundian nobles were exempted from taxes if they were 'descended from noble lineage, *item* living nobly, *item* apt to bear arms'. Failure to qualify did not mean loss of *noblesse*, but did mean paying tax.[2] Tax privileges did not define the *noblesse* (some non-nobles were exempt), and they were not novel: the notion that nobles made their contribution through military service was already old in 1304, when Philip IV taxed nobles not serving alongside commoners. But fiscal pressure forced the development of institutions to control passage into the nobility. The process can be demonstrated at opposite ends of France and from the beginning and end of the period. Montpellier was torn during the 1320s over how to deal with the crown's growing fiscal demands. In the 1320s a 'popular' movement extracted concessions from the city's controlling elite. Taxation would be levied on the basis of urban property, rather than through levies on consumer goods. The rich, unable now to negotiate exemption with the town's government, began claiming exemption as nobles, generating litigation.

While in the south ordinary royal courts kept a strong role, in northern France the usurpation of nobility was increasingly policed by those administering extraordinary taxation—the *élus* and their regional superiors the *généraux de la justice.* They judged all disputes

[2] T. Dutour, 'La noblesse dijonnaise dans la seconde moitié du XIVe siècle (1350–1410)', in P. Contamine, T. Dertour, and B. Schnerb (eds.), *Commerce, finances et société (XIe–XVIe siécles): recueil de travaux d'histoire médiévale offert à M. le Professeur Henri Dubois* (Paris, 1993), 321.

over tax liability, including exemption and thus its most important social category, *noblesse*. Nobles found themselves before these courts when their neighbours refused to recognize the tax exemption their status implied. Such conflicts were generated by hostility to the consequences of vertical social mobility. Faced with fixed tax assessments, parishes resisted the abstraction of the resources of their wealthier residents because it diminished their tax base. Non-nobles who acquired property and local prominence clashed with their neighbours if they usurped nobility. Better court records give a detailed picture of the cusp of *noblesse* in the fifteenth century, in Burgundy from the 1430s and in Normandy from the 1470s. Verdicts were determined by inquests focusing on the origins and activities of litigants. The questions around which testimony was oriented implied, thought Caron, that 'nobility was an affair of lineage and participation in the prince's campaigns'.

Proving his *noblesse* in 1464 and 1483, Jean des Buats seemed to conform to this model. He stressed that he was of knightly descent, had been on every expedition of the Breton wars, and to Paris, Artois, and Picardy, and produced an ancestor who had survived Agincourt. His neighbours gave a less flattering account: before 1400 Guillaume le Sueur, a *rural* from around Falaise, married into the noble Blouet family. His son inherited his mother's *vavassourie* of les Buaz and assumed the toponym; Jean was the great-grandson. This is an instance of how new nobles 'emerged from the peasantry', as Gallet remarked of the Vannetais, and as Perroy argued for Forez. In Dauphiné and Brittany most promotions occurred during the demographic crises and political conflicts of the fourteenth century, and this surge slackened later. A Vannetais peasant who acquired a fief or a remunerative office, married well, and obtained tax exemption for services stood some chance of promoting himself or his heirs into the *noblesse*. This became increasingly difficult in most areas: later in the period new nobles tended to stem from urban groups.

Hardening legal–fiscal conventions were only haphazardly consistent with an older interface of town and nobility. Urban knights at Toulouse, Dijon, and Flemish cities dated back to the twelfth century. The nobility of the Toulouse patriciate was so well established that *franc-fief* commissions could not extract cash from them (Charles IV stopped trying in 1324), and official resistance could not stop the whole Toulouse bourgeoisie acquiring *noblesse* in the fifteenth century. Flemish bourgeois knights, among whom were many old urban patricians, became fully noble in the fourteenth century. Flanders experienced an unusually large degree of movement in the other direction. The power and economic privileges of their elites made bourgeois status attractive to nobles even after growth ceased in the mid-fourteenth century, and great lords like the Gruuthuyse purchased citizenship at Bruges.

Elsewhere towns developed organic relationships with local nobilities, incorporating nobles as they did so. Périgueux bolstered the established order by investing local grandees with the mayoralty. A local knightly family, the la Roche, entered its notability in the later fourteenth century. They resided in the town's central parishes and described themselves as both nobles and bourgeois, though only the main line clearly preserved *noblesse* and rural property. The core of the Rouen elite lived nobly in the centre parishes long before Louis XI conceded first tax exemption and then *noblesse*. Here as everywhere else the successful reinvested the profits of trade and office in land and noble fiefs. The notables of Rouen, Caudebec, and Dieppe descended from local noble cadets would not necessarily have recognized that their families were in a cycle of alternating bourgeois and noble status.

Downward social movement also generated lawsuits. Poor nobles drifted out of the lifestyle their neighbours and tenants expected. Competition with commoners in economic activity made tax exemption a resented advantage, undermining the community's recognition of their *noblesse*. Jean des Buats incurred his neighbours' hostility by leasing seigneurial rights and trading in pigs. The struggle between the taxpayers of Condé-sur-Noireau and the Banville family was already old when it reached the courts in the 1470s. The Banville claimed descent from an ancient knightly family, the last of whom certified his kinship to Pierre de Banville before the *élus* of Bayeux in May 1479. Pierre and his descendants fought lawsuits over their status in every generation between 1450 and 1520, often winning crucial points. They assumed the Banville arms in 1486, when the *élus* exempted them from taxation. The parishioners could not disprove the blood connection, but the Banville were trapped in low-status marriages and activities incompatible with *noblesse*. Their case crumbled in 1519, when the courts refused to register royal letters naming them *noble et extrait de noble lignée.*[3] The parishioners won because the Banville were poor.

Activities named as derogatory in legal records include membership in the consortia which leased royal rights and the revenues of great lords, most forms of commerce and merchandise, road and river haulage, baking, and tavern-keeping. In 1436 royal commissioners disallowed the Banchereau family's claim to nobility and stripped them of the arms to which they pretended, partly because they held a stall in the *boucherie* at Poitiers. In 1408 the Vivarais witnesses ruled out manual labour (even on one's own lands), leasing and farming other men's rights, merchandise, and usury. These economic negatives shaped their model noble, a landlord living richly off his own property and through the labour of his tenants. If this model extended to the whole of France, this is because it matched the image of the lord, the possessor of a seigneury.

Property and poverty

The seigneury was the vehicle of the wealth, prestige, and power of lords. The homage which marked entry into fiefs (and almost all seigneuries were fiefs) long retained affective elements. For young Burgundian feoffees the ceremony acted as a rite of passage into the *noblesse* as a social milieu. The distribution of property among individuals and families shifted through political and economic contingencies, marriage, inheritance, partition: the life cycle of the noble lineage. The centrality of the seigneury to its holder's identity (expressed in name, arms, battle-cry, choice of burial place) explains the effort lineages made to conserve their patrimony. In the Pays de Caux all noble property went to the eldest son. The cadet might be dumped into a local abbey, or share in the lineage's urban property or lands elsewhere. Pitied as a *bâtard de Caux*, he would have no claim to the Cauchois noble patrimony. Exclusion of cadets was rarely so radical: parents transferred the maternal inheritance to one cadet, conceded a distant estate to another, placed another

[3] Archives Départmentales de la Seine-Maritime, 3 B 1118, dossier de Banville (1503–19).

in the Church, etc. As much as a third of the inheritance might go to the younger brothers to share equally, but the common theme was *preciput*, the concentration of property in the hands of the eldest son.

Discrimination was most intense against women. A bride usually renounced her rights to her patrimony, and *gouvernement noble* deliberately privileged heirs male. Nonetheless, heiresses were nowhere excluded completely, nor was it easy to exclude widows from the property of their late husbands. At any given moment much of the landed wealth of the *noblesse* was in the hands of heiresses and widows, though proportions varied according to local custom. Property was transferred on marriage in the form of dowry, which a bride brought with her into a match, and dower, with which she was invested by her husband. Sentiment and circumstance acted on the benchmarks set by custom, and crystallized in the marriage contract. These arrangements rebounded on heirs when a lineage bid high for a bride, or when family lands fell in value. Dowered kinswomen meant less income for the heir. While a widow often remarried, her first family could never regard this with equanimity. The d'Estouteville resisted the attempts of Marie de la Roche-Guyon (widowed *c.*1470) to leave her sons and remarry until she was rescued by her mother's kin. Custom would have given her usufruct of one-third of her husband's Norman lands, and all his movables and acquisitions. She fought bitterly for eighteen years to extract her rights in dower (set at 3,000 *lt.* of rent) and jointure, eventually getting perhaps a third of what was due.

If women's enjoyment of property threatened to destabilize the male lineage, female inheritance transferred whole estates to other lineages when the heiress married. When there were several daughters or sisters, estates would be dismembered, with the portions usually moving to lineages of equal status. The heiress's lineage might shape identity in crucial ways. Lords leaving only daughters tried to keep their lineage alive by stipulating in the marriage contract the quartering of the bride's arms and the adoption of her patronym. The Burgundian Lourdin de Saligny (d. 1441) left his succession to a grandson who would bear the Saligny name, arms, and cry. The last Harcourt count (d. 1452) tried to favour the nephew who would take his undifferenced arms and name, and the Laval implemented similar arrangements more than once. These 'substitutions' transmitted the name of the heiress's father, of course, but clearly a lineage's identity might be strong enough to disregard an heir's gender.

Local property surveys set out the internal stratification of the *noblesse*. In the Breton see of Vannes there were about 350 landed estates in the late fifteenth century. Four were great lay seigneuries, held by the duke himself and families at the highest level of Breton society. Between twelve and twenty much smaller lordships were comparable in some jurisdictional features. They were large manors covering between a third and a quarter of a parish, centred on defensible *maisons fortes*. The great majority of Vannetais seigneuries, five or six per parish, were small manors held by petty nobles. Their holders could live off their own, and their houses were much grander than peasant dwellings and often defensible. Most lordships at the bottom level were manors leaving no court records, though Bretons certainly expected them to have some residual justice. A parish might have three or four lineages, and those under a noble roof might represent 3–4 per cent of its population.

When in 1389 they contributed to the cost of the marriage of the count's daughter, 115 Boulonnais fief-holders fell into two groups: one composed of barons and tenants of one or several extensive fiefs, the other holding one or several much smaller fiefs. The richer group possessed over half the total landed lay wealth not in the count's own hands, but were outnumbered five to one by petty lords. In the Bourbonnais a 1503 survey found 789 fiefs. The 8.3 per cent worth about 100 *lt.* (roughly the value of a manor) were actual estates still in the hands of the traditional nobility, who also held most fiefs down to a quarter of this value. Here as almost everywhere, fiefs far outnumbered lineages. Only twenty Bourbon lords had more than 200 *lt.* from a single property. In the Vannetais cumulation of manors meant that as many as fifty lineages—perhaps a quarter of local seigneurs—pertained to the relatively comfortable *moyenne noblesse* with revenues averaging ten times those of a lord of *petite noblesse*.

Around Lille in 1475 wealth was concentrated in the hands of the 23 per cent (thirty-two nobles) who collectively enjoyed nearly two-thirds of the revenues of all nobles. About half the local noble fief-holders were relatively comfortable, with income of 100–400 *lt.* A quarter of noble fief-holders declared income below 100 *lt.*, and possessed barely 4 per cent of the income of all fief-holders in the *châtellenie*. A quarter of Boulonnais fief-holders held just one low-value fief. In both areas these were the relatively poor seigneurs, close to a noble *plebs* excluded from these surveys because they held only non-noble property or rents. Around Évreux in 1470, a mere 3 per cent of local nobles could not specify their holding: there was probably little difference between them and others holding only petty fiefs. Nearly half of Bourbonnais fiefs were worth under 10 *lt.*, so nobles had to accumulate fiefs for a comfortable income, and many had no actual manors. In the Vannetais nobles without a manor were the true *noblesse pauvre*, probably more than a third of all local nobles. Those of recent origin tended to cluster in this group: out of 400 nobles in 1470, seventy-five came of families which had gained nobility since 1400, and most were poor and held no manor. Poor Vannetais nobles, with an income of 20 *lt.* or less, could survive modestly but might have chronic problems sustaining the rank they asserted.

Official documents, including these surveys, say more about the stratification of nobles and their property than they do about real income. They systematically minimize the revenue of landholders keen to evade service and fiscal burdens. It is often impossible to reconcile revenues declared in inquests into the lands of a family with known expenditure on building works and marriage gifts. The Norman barony of Courseulles was valued at 250 *lt.* of rent in 1471–2. When seeking compensation for losses, its holder, the Breton captain Guillaume de Rosnivinen, put his Norman revenue at 600 *lt.* The figures refer to the same property, but are distorted in different directions. Charbonnier thought his Auvergnat lords halved their real worth, while René Germain thought his Bourbonnais fief-holders declared only a third of their real resources.

Poor nobles always existed, but when they cast themselves as barely above the level of wealthy peasants, scepticism is in order. Nonetheless, the noble *plebs* was an important group. Possessed of tiny fiefs, collections of rents, or small parcels of property, in service or following an acceptable profession, it amounted to a quarter or more of the *noblesse* of most localities. It comprised cadets of cadets; bastards; individuals ennobling themselves through service or the purchase of noble fiefs; the unlucky in war and the profligate: men and women on the way up and on the way down. Their neighbours would have rejected the nobility of some, but how many, who, and why varied across the realm. Eighteen per cent of a sample taken by Michel Nassiet in the see of Saint-Malo were of contested status around 1480, close to James Woods's estimate of 22 per cent for Bessin nobles of *roturier* origins before 1560. If the status of a fifth of Norman or Breton nobles was dubious, this is lower than some other regions' figures for commoners' acquisition of noble property. Non-nobles held just 2 per cent of seigneuries in the Basse-Auvergne (mid-fourteenth century); a tenth of fiefs in the county of Clermont-en-Beauvaisis (1374); nearly half in a Senlisis *châtellenie* (1374); 30 per cent in Berry (1379–1409); and over a quarter in ducal Burgundy (1474). Non-nobles were 14–18.5 per cent of fief holders in north-east Brittany (*c.* 1480), but only 5 per cent in the Basse-Auvergne (*c.* 1490).

Contemporary surveys understate the numbers of commoners holding noble property, yet also obscure how concentrated their holdings were at the low end by value. The nearly half of Bourbonnais fiefs that were owned by commoners in 1503 were overwhelmingly of paltry revenue. Ninety per cent of fiefs worth under 5 *lt.* were held by commoners. As value rose, the peasants were replaced by priests, clerks, notaries, merchants, and petty officials, with old nobles becoming the majority among holders of fiefs worth above 10 *lt.* In Burgundy, too, the quarter of non-nobles holding fiefs in 1474 held mainly low-value fiefs (notwithstanding a small group of rich nobles of recent origin). Around Lille the third of fief-holders qualified noble accounted for two-thirds of declared income from fiefs, while the 46 per cent of unknown status accounted for less than 20 per cent. The mean income of a noble fief-holder was nearly four times that for one of unspecified status.

Commoners did climb the property ladder into the *noblesse*, but it was not easy. They picked up the scraps: wasted, fragmented, and mortgaged estates needing investment to rehabilitate. Acquisition of a manor with residence and jurisdiction afforded crucial advantages compared to petty fiefs and fragmented estates. This was particularly marked in the south, where those who acquired whole estates benefited from the stress placed there on the status of the property over that of its owner. Around Lyon and Rouen landowning *roturiers* remained on the margins of noble society, poor and vulnerable. New noble families everywhere lacked the circumstantial advantages of their betters, were relatively isolated within the local nobility, lacked the support of noble kin, and were vulnerable to the new legal weapons that royal fiscality gave their neighbours.

Nobles had to meet contemporary expectations of their lifestyle and service, and they needed relative wealth to do so. Failure brought scrutiny by their neighbours and princely officials. This made the cusp of nobility a financial as well as a legal concept, but it was a zone rather than a line, for wealth was only one determinant. The Boulonnais, the Vannetais, the Bourbonnais, and the Lillois all exhibit a substantial gulf between the *noblesse pauvre* in this zone and those of secure status, most of whom were seigneurs and their immediate families. This latter group was itself split into the *petite* and *moyenne noblesse.* Everywhere and always the latter group, small in number, detached itself from the majority of purely local seigneurs and reached up to greater magnates and thence the prince.

Service and the martial ethos of the *noblesse*

The Manceux gentleman Laurens Soyer wooed an heiress with the words 'I am a warrior and have 40 or 50 francs a year from the king, and nothing else in the world, but I have the will to win it and will have it one day.' His ambition was focused on service, into which poor nobles were driven by the plethora of tiny fiefs, *maisons nobles* with little land attached. Consider the Bourbonnais squire Pierre Sélerier, whose property at Tézay might pay a labourer for two months. He might maintain his status as receiver for a rich local squire or knight, or as the household servant of a greater man. In a military retinue he might hope for five *lt.* a month as a bill-man or archer, or ten as an *homme d'armes* in the *arrière ban* (though how would he have afforded the harness?).

Any really valuable office was probably beyond his reach. Absentee seigneurs ran their lordships through servants operating from the noble residence upon which they centred. Communities were linked to their seigneurs by *prévôts, sénéchaux, bayles,* receivers, foresters, sergeants, clerks, and others farming the lord's rights: the true middle class of their communities. In the Bordelais this managerial personnel stemmed mainly from the peasantry: while they often held their positions in fief, only the most important were noble. In contrast, four-fifths of officials of great Vannetais seigneuries sampled for 1450–80 were noble, though of poor or recent lineages. The real difference may have been Breton liberality in recognizing *noblesse.* The wages of top seigneurial officials in Brittany might match the income from a small manor, but it was the perquisites that made even minor office so remunerative. Few Vannetais petty lords got into the *ordonnance* or great households, but local public office–judicial, fiscal, administrative—was largely in their hands. There were positions for as many as a third of them. Avranchin peasants thought even minor royal offices would pay enough to live nobly. In Normandy cumulation meant that there were far more posts, seigneurial and royal, than officials, and many were not (yet) noble: fewer than half the royal officials at Évreux held fiefs within the *bailliage* in 1470. They came from rural stock or small towns, but from the richer strata, and service to a great lord amplified opportunities of social advancement. A man who kept a tavern near Mont-Saint-Michel was evidently noble to one witness because he had governed the Avranchin property of the d'Estouteville. Whether what was important here was the post's local power and prominence, or the sociability with great lords which it implied, it was clearly not simply the income it generated. Just as technocrats of non-noble origin met with magnates on a surprisingly even footing within the princely entourage, so too might service to a lesser magnate efface social distinctions.

Administration, finance, and above all the law were vital to the fortunes of petty and poor nobles, and crucial routes of social advance. This is where French historians have searched, often ingeniously, around the edges of medieval conventions for the origins of the great divide between robe and sword. *Noblesse de robe* was not yet recognized anywhere, but contemporaries occasionally claimed to be nobles *par science,* and officials exploited confusion over whether their privileges stemmed from their post or their personal *noblesse.* Autrand showed how late fourteenth-century lawyers before the Parlement of Paris evolved a concept of notability in character sketches of their clients. They described nobles in terms of their status and ancestry, blameless life, and service to the king, but also drew parallel portraits of bourgeois as holders of positions at the summit of the commons, with prominent family, blamelessly exercising their professional activity or royal office.

By refracting military service into general royal service, lawyers tried to assimilate public office to it. This is one root of *noblesse de robe,* but the rhetorical device demonstrates the real primacy accorded arms. Accounts of nobles' careers sparkled with the names of famous *chefs de guerre*, battles, sieges, expeditions, etc. Of seventeen factual claims made by Jean Barbin defending his *noblesse* in Poitou around 1470, eight concerned the military careers of his predecessors. His father had been at the sieges of Chinon and Tours, and held a stretch of the Loire against the English in 1421. His brother was killed on the coronation campaign of 1429. In 1493 a witness described 'the harness and cuirass' in the house of the late Guillaume du Fay, 'and all the other equipment necessary to those who follow arms and the hosts of princes'.[4] The ability to *porter harnois* or *chevaucher* was synonymous with the end of youth, signifying in grants of property or pardon the conventional beginning to a career. It implied political consciousness: when, for instance, the young noble in northern France had to choose to join Charles VII, or remain and fight for Henry of Lancaster.

After lineage itself, the salience of arms in the definition of the noble is unmistakable. Other forms of service were honourable but secondary. Young Jean Burnouf was at five successive sieges during the French reconquest of Normandy and was captured by the enemy garrison of Saint-Sauveur-le-Vicomte. Later he was in the Granville garrison, and appeared at successive noble musters. Witnesses stressed these activities, only mentioning in passing his career as *homme de vocation de justice.* Such litigants' *noblesse* was questionable, and testimony reflects (and disguises) social ascent through judicial, administrative, and financial office. Yet when they talked of service, contemporaries had nothing like *noblesse de robe* in mind. They meant war.

If knighthood originated as a military *métier*, the social exaltation of knightly vassals to the point where they fused with the Carolingian aristocracy was also a militarization of the nobility. On this conventional logic, around 1300 the nobility was a military class. The proportion of nobles who were knights declined precipitately in the fourteenth century, and while this coincided with a serious erosion of the revenues of many nobles, the retreat of dubbing is not clearly linked to any real diminution of lineages' wealth or status. As Contamine noted, debate on the parallel phenomenon in England stresses evasion of administrative burdens and service obligations. In France

[4] Archives Départmentales de la Seine-Maritime, 3 B 1123, dossier du Fay (1493).

knighthood became rarer within the *noblesse*, but this continued rather than aborted its rise in relative social status. Lesser men who became knights were often the most prominent service nobles with established reputations, especially captains with extensive military experience.

The rarification of knighthood has also been characterized as a demilitarization of the *noblesse*. For John Bell Henneman, 'the French army in the early fourteenth century still consisted mainly of people who owed customary military service'. He used the term 'military class' to avoid the problem of the social origins of troops, assuming that 'many nobles did not serve regularly'. Marc Bloch's knights and vassals gradually lost their defining military functions and became merely a gentry of birth by the late fifteenth century. Contamine's massive study of French royal military institutions (1970) is a history of the professionalization of French armies. However, the question of whether the French nobility was a military class in accordance with its own self-image is distinct from how French kings made war. The Hundred Years War changed the character of French royal armies in fundamental ways, without this undermining the nobility's martial identity.

In the first half of the fourteenth century nobles, towns, and rural commons were mobilized by the crown through the *arrière ban*, an ancient and general summons. However, difficulties in maintaining huge armies in the field, and the ineffectiveness of large communal contingents, led kings to dispense with the services of most commoners. By the 1350s the *arrière ban* had metamorphosed into the *semonce des nobles*. Royal armies became more rather than less noble, even as they shrank in size and kings hired mercenaries who might be neither noble nor French. Within a generation Charles V made paid companies under effective control the backbone of his armies, but supplemented them with general or regional mobilizations of the nobility. The wars of the 1410s and 1420s were fought with magnate retinues and forces mobilized by customary summonses, and old problems recurred: nominally royal companies became *routiers* and *écorcheurs*, a disorderly soldiery penetrated by aristocratic faction. Charles VII rediscovered his grandfather's solution, creating the royal *ordonnance* in the 1440s.

In aggregating small independent followings into large, controllable, regularly paid standing companies of heavy cavalry, the crown used practical and political criteria; but also social and ideological ones, for the captains, lieutenants, and *hommes d'armes*, were mostly noblemen frequenting arms—just as under Charles V. Yet only a minority of nobles were incorporated, and the notion that kings could unleash an effective noble army through feudal and customary means survived increasing de facto reliance on the *ordonnance*. Its expense was an incentive to make the obligations inherent in status and tenure effective, especially since noble wealth was not reachable through direct taxation. Hence the proliferation of regional surveys of noble property later in the period. Those obliged to serve were nobles, fief-holders, royal officials, and those accustomed to follow the wars: distinct but overlapping categories.

Musters were usually annual, but more frequent in emergencies. The officials who organized them had lists of those liable to summons, and knew their residences and why and how they were obliged. Those not serving in person, including the elderly and unwell, women, minors, and clergymen, provided substitutes. In 1470, in the *bailliage* of Évreux, three-quarters of respondents served in person. This figure rises to over 86 per cent if persons sending sons, brothers, or close kin are added. Only 6 per cent sent proxies without offering explanations like debility, gender, or clerical orders, a group which was more likely to hold communally with others, and to admit that they were commoners. The two crucial groups left out of these calculations were the defaulters and the exempted. Most of the latter were excused from current military service. Of those exempted in the Caux 40 per cent were serving in the *ordonnance* and 20 per cent were in household service with the king or a great magnate; 20 per cent obtained exemption by certifying their presence at a muster elsewhere. Around Évreux nearly 28 per cent of those summoned defaulted, much higher than in the Caux: the muster seems to have been redacted before many defaulters could make their excuses or certify appearance elsewhere. Seven men held land around Évreux itself, but were named as resident in the Caux: only one defaulted there. If given time a high proportion of defaulters would indeed certify legitimate excuse.

These figures, particularly that for the personal service of nobles, indicate that the *noblesse* of Upper Normandy was still highly militarized in 1470. In Brittany, too, it remained notoriously martial. The greatest lay lords in the Vannetais were still in the second half of the fifteenth century military chiefs, they still built and controlled defensible castles, and their lordships were still organized for war. The *moyenne noblesse* could still house men and horses in numbers, and were often *chefs de guerre.* 'Professional' soldiers belonged to these higher strata. Few Vannetais petty nobles entered the Breton duke's *ordonnance* companies: their military experience was mainly in the *arrière ban*, but two-thirds attended 'assiduously'.

The effectiveness of customary summonses is contested, but this is irrelevant to their role in sustaining the military ethos of the nobility. They were a standard military tool throughout the period, and consistent response to them produced impressive career histories. Those who served assumed that the martial experience they gained affirmed their *noblesse.* The profession of arms was not yet defined by membership of a standing army, and few nobles would have lacked military experience. This was true even of a *noblesse bourgeoise*: Dutour reconstructed the careers of thirty-nine Dijon nobles in the fourteenth and early fifteenth centuries. He classed ten as essentially financiers, eight as merchants, and five as lawyers. However, sixteen had largely military careers, had the best contacts with the ducal court, and tended to be absent from local economic activity.

The armies of Louis XI differed from those of Philip VI, but these changes had not evicted nobles from a central role. Professionalization (however defined) left nobles, especially the higher strata, their monopoly of command. Magnate households retained their military capabilities, and indeed war within the realm belonged to magnates as well as the king. Many conflicts racked France in the fourteenth and fifteenth centuries. Some of these were feuds characterized by retaliatory killings in successive generations, and yet others little more than a formal state of hostility between lineages, a publicly recognized relationship characterized by insult, symbolic violence, and brawling. But where the parties had the resources, full-scale campaigns might result. In the 1460s bands from twenty to eighty strong clashed over a Hospitaller *commanderie* in the Auvergne. The counts of Armagnac and Foix waged war recurrently over seventy years, and mobilized the Pyrenean aristocracy behind them. The key difference between 'private' wars is not of principle, but of the extent to which the king and others opted to become involved.

Although the crown's assertion of a monopoly of war within the realm was an important moment, it came late (under Charles VII), and never applied to all noble violence. War between noblemen was not a challenge to the crown but a noble privilege regulated by custom. Kings began to move against it under Louis IX, but their approach was ameliorative rather than prohibitionist. Philip IV banned it when he was himself at war, not wanting his nobles distracted from his own enterprises. From the 1290s royal justice began to set limits by targeting *port d'armes, chevauchée*, ambush. Also crucial was the extension across the realm and across social strata of royal safeguard, and of judicial registration of peace agreements. Violation now brought the courts into play, and cases exploded in number after 1300. Resort to ever more effective royal justice allowed communities to prevent violence from getting out of hand, and losers to contain defeats. Historians have tended to conclude that the crown was progressively constricting 'private' war. Even if this was the effect, conflicts in which officials did not intervene are obscure, and it is not clear where the initiative for rising official activism lay, nor what proportion of conflicts ran up against it. Interventions recorded by the fourteenth-century Parlement Criminel usually followed incidents involving senior royal servants. When the king struck at violence against his officials wearing his livery or arms, he was defending his lordship: any extension to the sovereignty of his 'state' was incidental.

It was a logic lesser nobles understood and shared. The imperative of protecting the *familia* extended to those under one's roof, officials, valets, and other servants. When the crown penalized acts against persons under its safeguard, or breaches of truces brokered in its courts, the underlying assumptions were equally conventional for lords. The role of royal government distracts attention from settlement processes that were more important in limiting violence. Even when arbitrations were registered in the courts, they betokened the weakness of such institutions. From parish level up, the peacemaking undertaken by clerics, officials, and above all nobles was their Christian duty and social role—and success enhanced their honour. When parties to disputes involved their social superiors in arbitration, they did so because of these individuals' leadership roles. Part of the equation was the capacity of lords to enforce the agreements they brokered. In 1372 feuding inhabitants of Fauquembergues in Picardy swore 'in the hands' of Jean de Bournonville, lord of Rinxent, to suspend violence among them. The knight may have been initially neutral, but regarded breaches of the truce by one man as 'in contempt' of his own honour: when threats failed, he killed the offender.[5]

Tension between noble and commoner featured in conflicts between towns and local lords, and was latent in the relationship of lord and tenant. Constraint was essential to seigneurial exploitation, and violence certainly featured: the killing of the insolent farrier or cowherd by the mild-mannered nobleman was a commonplace of pardon tales. That the victim might be stigmatized as seditious implies broad awareness of hostility between noble and commoner. Yet in return for deference and material dues peasants expected leadership, protection, justice, and police from their lords, not at an abstract geopolitical level but in the conflicts of everyday life. Service and social links enabled commoners to call on nobles for maintenance in their quarrels. During a dispute in the 1460s over control of a parish school at Vedrines in Picardy rival schoolmasters solicited aid from noblemen upon whom they had been dependent. The usurper was beaten up by a gang led by a local noble bastard, a professional soldier. He was feasted with a fat goose by the rival, who was himself subsequently butchered by the noble patrons of the victim.

Honour was the conventional spur to violence, usually the implicit or explicit justification for violence given in pardon tales. Its explanatory power extended to narratives of the king's own wars. At the end of 1349 Geoffroi de Charny negotiated the betrayal of Calais with an Italian mercenary serving the English. Double-crossed, his force was routed and he was captured. Eighteen months later, expensively ransomed and back in harness, he seized the Italian in a night raid, beheaded him, and displayed his quartered corpse on the walls of Saint-Omer. Charny was Jean II's captain-general in Picardy, but this was not public war for a truce was in force at the time: he observed the niceties by abandoning the castle after seizing his man.

The logic of honour and the reflexes of inter-noble violence infested the forms within which the king's war was conducted. And this was not a social evil but part of the virtue of the noble, valued by Charny as the ardour which was a basic requirement of the young knight. From his perspective, the complex of behaviours and

[5] B. Schnerb, *Enguerrand de Bournonville et les siens: un lignage noble du Boulonnais aux XIVe et XVe siècles* (Paris 1997), 169.

attitudes which made up chivalrous culture was essential for the *noblesse*'s utility to the public good. Maurice Keen thought chivalry the characteristic form of noble piety, and attributed to its idealistic components some responsibility for the difficulties contemporaries had in recognizing disorderly soldiers as a social problem, and hence for the pervasiveness of warfare. The continuing strength of chivalrous ideas was more than a cultural habit. If princes and captains valued ardour and impetuosity, this was partly because actual fighting was dynamic. Victory went to those ready to throw themselves into and follow a combat, often highly mobile, centred on the banners, battle-cries, and persons of their leaders. Discipline could never be identified with restraint. So too with largesse: if chivalrous reputation helped muster men behind a captain, only generosity would keep them there, and that required cash. As Bertrand Schnerb observed of Enguerrand de Bournonville, warlords could not be particular about the sources of their winnings of war. 'Rapacity', too, was 'functional'.

Some have detected in the cultural flowering at the Burgundian Valois court novel ideas about nobility's relationship to virtue. Charity Canon Willard thought vernacular translations of classical authors propagated the notion that virtue was the only justification for *noblesse*. In fact, these texts simply put a mild humanist gloss on a topos going back to the twelfth century and much reworked by well-known fourteenth-century French authors. The 'debate' over whether virtue or gentle birth made for true nobility was a sham: as Ellery Schalk pointed out, no one would argue against virtue. It was really a vehicle for moralistic prescription and appeals in the name of the public good. Keen saw its revival by the author of the *Songe du vergier*, Alain Chartier and Christine de Pisan as a polemical literary response to the fourteenth-century crisis. Cast as a failure of the *noblesse* itself, this generated endless nostrums against vainglorious living and calls to abandon the habits of disorder.

Into the sixteenth century, thought Schalk, the nobility was defined by contemporaries in terms of its martial calling: 'nobility was indeed a profession or function—it was something you did—and to be noble you had to fight'. The nature of the 'Virtue' identified by late medieval writers as the essence of *noblesse* was indeed military. The record is saturated with the expectation that a nobleman would have served in arms. Protests that scholarship has privileged the military role of the late medieval nobility over its social reality founder on this fact. For peasants watching their bread being fed to the horse of a threadbare *routier*, or the townsman giving bed and board for months at a time to unwelcome guests from the king's *ordonnance*, the nobility's social reality and its military role were one and the same.

Household, friends, and servants

'There is no fishing but in the sea, no gift but that of a king', said Jean I le Meingre. He made his career as a courtier of Philip VI, becoming John II's marshal in 1356. His avarice earned him the sobriquet Boucicaut, a wicker fishing basket—a pejorative reference to his snout in the trough of royal largesse. The extraordinary scale of the rewards available to top princely servants is a theme of social as well as anecdotal significance. In 1475, unlike the Vannetais and the Bourbonnais, the ten richest nobles of the Lille area were not really its traditional elite. The richest of all had risen from local but modest origins. Two families had been bourgeois in the fourteenth century and two more, though rich old nobles, were incomers to the Lillois. What these five had in common with the five who did come from local magnate houses was strong links to the Burgundian dukes: serving at an exalted level, they had received commensurate reward.

Across the period spectacular examples of parvenus acquiring noble property often illustrate the advance of the bourgeoisie or the decline of the old nobility, but their central feature is usually princely service. In Burgundy in the 1470s recent nobles who were rich had all risen through service. Yet such service was the preserve of the *noblesse*, mainly its upper strata. Barely 4 per cent of all nobles in the Breton sees of Dol and Saint-Malo were magnate or princely commensals, or in the ducal *ordonnance*, but they were a much higher proportion of the area's *moyenne noblesse*, to which over 70 per cent of them belonged. Of the forty nobles in great households, nineteen served the duke, but two great families (Laval and Rohan) employed between them just as many.

Magnates did not retain followers only through their households. In recruiting military contingents, they used customary summonses of vassals, but their utility was declining. *Lettres de retenue* by which a lord obtained service in return for pensions or lump sums can be instanced for fourteenth-century French kings, dukes of Brittany, the duke of Orléans, and the count of Foix. Contemporaries assumed that these retainers would offer the same service as vassals. Yet such instruments hardly touched most of France, though underlying notions of alliance and service certainly structured nobles' political loyalties. French kings required their *ordonnance* troops to swear that they would not 'repute themselves' any other man's servant (including their 'natural' lord). This implies that vaguer, more affective bonds were really operative, perhaps simply personal histories of contact and favour. References to the 'gens' of particular lords might mean kinsmen, commensals, *ordonnance hommes d'armes*, and officials, but equally followers for whom there is no evidence of pension or other specific bond. Great lords looked to have as many nobles around them as possible on important occasions, such as visits to princes or merely their first visit to an estate. The nobles attending them were often rewarded, and such expressions of solidarity were sufficiently meaningful for names to be noted, by others as well as the lord in question. Yet surviving lists are not reducible to the servants, pensioners, and allies of the lord, but opened out into neighbours and sympathizers.

The multiplicity, vagueness, and obscurity of operative links makes it hard to reconstruct the vertical and horizontal ties that structured provincial nobilities. Moreover, saving those closest to them, magnates were unlikely to get exclusive service and hardly expected it. Berthin de Silly began the 1460s under Louis XI's admiral Jean de Montauban in the Cherbourg garrison, where his father had served Charles VII's admiral Jean de Bueil. At the same time he rose in the d'Estouteville household to become (allegedly) *maître d'hôtel*. From here he jumped to the household of René d'Alençon, count of Perche, and thence to the household and favour of Louis XI in 1468. These transfers of service were not necessarily transfers of loyalty, and (except for his departure from d'Estouteville service) were expected to benefit the erstwhile patron. Individuals built careers by moving between the service of different lords, who were quite capable of shaping and exploiting the web of service links which resulted. What magnates had to fear most, after all, was isolation.

Great courtier politicians had their offices in the royal household, while their own commensals participated in their masters' political action and in its rewards. All magnate households were also military retinues, but the *ordonnance* too exemplified the social structures of the French *noblesse* from which it was drawn. Able captains of modest origins were poles of attraction on a par with magnates, for royal subventions gave them noble retinues on a scale which would have beggared their betters. The obligations of the table and the hall supplemented those of the camp, and the model of good lordship extended to intervention in debt, lawsuit, ransom, and other difficulties. Captains interweaved their companies with the jurisdictional and patronage aspects of their other royal offices, enhancing their authority in every sphere and hence their usefulness to their master.

Kings and princes maximized their noble commensals by rotating them through court on, say, a quarterly basis (see Chapter 7). For them, numbers mattered more than cost because they needed to generalize their contacts with vast regional nobilities. The duke and duchess of Orléans had more than 150 persons in their combined households in the early 1460s. Dozens of these would have been noble: the count of Maine had between thirty and forty knights and squires in his household in the 1440s. Magnates neither needed nor could afford such universal reach, but some—like Gilles de Raiz—nonetheless maintained entourages in the hundreds. The more modest retinues of the *moyenne noblesse* were comparable in essential features. Servants were salaried, clothed, fed, and housed as part of the ordinary maintenance of the household, the greatest routine expense in any noble budget. Burgundian knights were typically accompanied by at least one squire, more if they could afford it or if they 'followed the wars'. More difficult than numbers is servants' status, a vital yardstick. The composition of a lord's household is a crucial index of his or her importance.

All noble households were political institutions to the varying degrees of the power of the lord or lady upon whom they centred. Yet this was a consequence of the social world within which nobles lived. The king's household was like that of any other noble in that its life was a vehicle of honour and prestige. Nassiet stressed the conviviality in which nobles lived: wine, drinking, and eating were important. Eating was a communal affair and keeping *bon table* was a key aspect of the conspicuous consumption that was central to noble display. In the arrangements made when marriages failed, or when the partners had to separate temporarily for other reasons, domestic expenditure might be detailed down to the last bushel of chickpeas: the lifestyle appropriate to the *estat* of the parties had to be maintained. Similar formal agreements might be reached when control of sense and property failed. When the elderly *homme d'armes* Jacques Mouchet gave all his harness, plus property worth 120 *lt.*, to the Hôtel-Dieu of Rouen on his retirement there in 1463, he stipulated that he would always dine at the table of the master of the house. At the opposite end of the scale the duke of Burgundy's servants reported to their master on the doings of neighbouring princes, down to how the soused trout had been prepared and the ceremonial style with which they were taken.

Noble values have shaped modern stereotypes of masculinity, in that ardour, courage, and physical prowess were crucial. Yet courtly culture had its civilizing, even feminizing elements, and the urbanity required of the young courtier made the successful nobleman a lover as well as a fighter. The 'power' this gave to the lady was conventionally passive, and coexisted with coarseness and quotidian brutality. A young noblewoman unlucky at cards was told by her host that 'you have only your cunt left to play with'. The incident formed part of a pardon tale designed to blacken her reputation, given that she was 'protected' and married against the will of her mother and the bishop of Le Mans. The wardships and marriages of heiresses formed part of the stock of princely patronage and so were traded within princely followings. Suitors might resort to direct action (*rapt*) in pursuit of a worthwhile and vulnerable bride, and this was plausibly alleged in cases involving women of such high-born families as Amboise, de Thouars, and Luxembourg-Saint-Pol. Many noble feuds were traced to offences against women, a trope of seduction which is not so far-fetched given the material interests involved. Yet the vulnerability of women in a male-dominated and violent society is not the whole story. The domestic arena in particular gave to noblewomen large possibilities for initiative. The household as an arena of sociability underpinned the noblewoman's recognized role in brokering marriages, peacemaking, intercession, and religious devotion, while managing the domestic economy merged seamlessly into management of the broader estate.

The noble household was a crucial social institution. It was the principal means whereby the nobility reproduced its own mode of life, key to the projection of collective and individual interests, even within the parish. For even petty seigneurs the household was more than a residence, but also the local focus of social life and property management. In such a context sociability shaded through micro-politics into (if the household was important enough) the brokerage of major political issues. Whose marriage or career prospects the lord or lady advanced, whose causes they took up, whose quarrels they pacified, whom they lent to or borrowed from, were hardly distinct from whom they chose to hunt, play cards, hear mass, or dance with. Larger magnate and princely households centred in on the *familia* of the lord, and extended out through kin, friends, and well-wishers to orchestrate the patterns of inter-noble dependence across whole regions. A prince's household officials played a more or less formal role in the governance of the principality and the politics of the kingdom. Those who ran the kingdom as *baillis*, *sénéchaux*, captains, and *prévôts* of *bonnes villes* were royal commensals. Peter Lewis's image of the king's court as a vast nuclear pile catches the radiation of power and policy, and its attractions and dangers.

Conclusion

The rulers of medieval France were overwhelmingly nobles. Non-nobles who participated in government—even at modest levels or in towns—stood a good chance of elevating themselves or their heirs. The local domination of the nobility was a reflexive logic: anyone of real importance in an area was taken for noble. Charles VII's wars swept Simonnet Ferrant from the Gatinais into Lower Normandy, where he made a career in d'Estouteville service. From here he entered the bodyguard of Louis XI, who returned him to Avranches as petty official and local political enforcer for a shaky royal regime. Louis's Breton enemies killed him in 1468. The next generation of local nobles knew that he had lived nobly and married into a local noble family, and remembered him as a valiant man skilful with a lance, and a governor of Avranches. He had surely been noble. Actually, he was probably low-born, but the link between notability and *noblesse* was basic. This is why it was so useful a concept for Parlement lawyers trying to promote their clients.

Jean de Bueil's observation that 'a man with a bascinet on his head is a noble, and fit to fight a king' is an oddly egalitarian comment to come from a count of Sancerre and successful courtier-officer. But he was also an experienced knight who thought arms the root of all lordship. His comment dovetails with Geoffroi de Charny's meritocratic slogan 'He who does more is worth more'. Warfare and violence were central to noble identity and mythology. War was both a collective behaviour and a stage on which individual worth and self-consciousness could be displayed and honour gained. Hence service, and above all fighting, was the one really legitimate social ladder. This underlies a paradox: the French nobility was organized as a social class in a rigid and hierarchical fashion, but could exhibit noble egalitarianism and promote social disorder.

Service is the key to the main changes in the structure of the nobility through the late Middle Ages as, rather later, to the robe–sword division. Clearer criteria of noble status stemmed from a dialectic between noble defence of fiscal and legal privilege, and pressure from politically organized taxpayers. This hardened the lower boundary of *noblesse* throughout the period. In contrast, the *noblesse* had no upper social boundary at all, for the king was the highest-ranking nobleman. He could hope to exercise personal lordship between the Loire and the Somme, while elsewhere princes stood at the apex of regional nobilities. Their wealth and power have made princes and magnates the best-documented section of the nobility, but Contamine put the titled *haute noblesse* at just 1 per cent of it. Their doings are the stuff of high politics more than social history, but historians now stress the role of princes, their courts and states, in shaping the rest of the nobility.

Indeed, the nobility is becoming the object of renewed interest just when the princely state is regaining its centrality in discussion of medieval society. This may obscure how far the *noblesse* was the real master of princely states: not because nobles were the enemies of princes, but by virtue of being their servants. They staffed most posts at most levels in most princely institutions. The network of great and not-so-great households which made up noble society functioned as a web of power parallel to the prince's state, and just as vitally connected to his court and household. In understanding the horizontal and vertical ties which constituted the *noblesse* as a class and defined its political loyalties and divisions, the pressing need remains an investigation of lordship. In 1970 Guy Fourquin deplored the conflation of lordship with seigneury as tending to confuse property not just with status but also with social relationships. The abandonment of feudal models should not lead a monocausal concept like vassalage to be replaced with another, the princely state. Our focus must broaden from princes to the lives, loyalties, interests, and purposes of the lesser noble retainers of regional magnates.

Conclusion

David Potter

How did Frenchmen view their world by the end of the Middle Ages? For the mass of the population it was a world stalked by the threat of a return to war and famine, in which the powers of evil represented by ever more dangerous activities of sorcerers could only be combated by the powers of the clergy. The Church, though, as it had been throughout the Middle Ages, was compromised by political corruption and worldliness; hence the opening up of spiritual life in the fifteenth century to a vibrant lay piety that was to pave the way for Protestant and Catholic reform in the following century. As was seen in Chapter 8, the nobility was a vast and highly differentiated social order; most noblemen were preoccupied by the restoration of their estates, but the militarily active held to a mental landscape whose main contours were mapped still by the dictates of that slippery notion chivalry. After the ruthless violence of the civil wars, these might appear hollow, and yet they continued to exercise their compulsion in social norms and military conduct, and the battlefields of Italy beckoned as a new field for such endeavours.

Naturally, the realm of systematic thought was limited by the traditions of intellectual discourse and by limited literacy. It is fair to note that during the fourteenth and fifteenth centuries a sophisticated tradition of discourse and thought on the nature of power had grown up in France, much of it drawing on chronicle and history for its inspiration. There was no consensus in this. Legists pressed the king's imperial jurisdiction; the innumerable Mirrors for Princes produced for the Valois kings sought to inculcate in them age-old virtues. The work of the legist Evrart de Trémaugon (*Le songe du vergier*, 1376–8) and of Philippe de Mézières's *Le songe du vieil pelerin* (*c.*1389), in its third book one of the most extended Mirrors of the age, the great philosophical works of Oresme and Gerson, the political writings of Juvénal des Ursins, all testify to a degree of caution about the untrammelled exercise of power but also a reverence for the religious charisma of the crown as head of the body politic. Naturally, the circulation of such ideas was limited given the technological problems of book production and distribution, and in any case we must question how far such ideas could interact with 'public opinion', the 'public voice and fame' of 'what most people commonly said' that a priest at Cahors mentioned in court towards the end of the fourteenth century. While, in the time of Jeanne d'Arc, Jean Batiffol of Bialon believed in the 'mark' of true kings, Guillaume le Juponnier at Orléans in 1384, faced by taxes, said, 'do you think they have what they have lawfully? They tax me time after time and think they can take whatever they like. What right do they think they have to take what I earn by the sweat of my labour? I would rather all kings were dead than that my son should lose anything.'

The second half of the fifteenth century, on the threshold of printing, is paradoxically by no means so varied and intensive as the late fourteenth in its production of systematic analysis yet, and if we look at three individuals from the last two decades of the century, a king, a politician, and a soldier-administrator, we can identify certain traditional themes and new pressures. The most important of these was a consciousness that it was the crown which stood between the kingdom and the chaos that had dominated the first half of the century.

The king was seen to stand at the end of a long line of spiritually sanctioned rulers, whose credentials were on display in the publicly approved *Grandes chroniques de France.* Chief among these was St Louis, who had drawn up, in the *Enseignements* for his successor, a text profoundly imbued with the ideas of the nascent Mirror for Princes tradition. Half of it is concerned with the religious duties of a king: 'My dear son, take care to be good in all things so it is clear that you acknowledge the gifts and honours that Our Lord has made to you so that, if it please Our Lord that you succeed to this kingdom, you may be worthy to receive the holy unction by which that king of France is anointed.' But Louis administered practical advice also: his son was to return all things taken unjustly from his subjects, honour the clergy and the Pope, advance the princes of the blood, maintain justice, control the actions of local officials and of his household, and spend revenues wisely. It is interesting to compare this with another testament by a king but at the end of this period. A consciousness of dynastic and historical continuity is also profoundly characteristic of the *Rosier des guerres*, a work now widely agreed after much uncertainty to have been dictated in 1481–2 by Louis XI to Pierre Choisnet, his physician, for the instruction of his son Charles VIII. It was first printed, if defectively, in 1523 and should be read in conjunction with Louis's *Instructions* drawn up formally for the dauphin in September 1482 and registered in the courts. The abbreviated chronicle of France that is attached to it forms an integral part of the composition and the argument. The work is obviously remarkable as an insight into the thinking of a late medieval king of France and is partly a practical guide and partly a manifesto in general terms on common obligation: 'None may doubt the merit of death in defence of the common good. One must fight for one's country.' 'All good people must at need spare nothing but give up all their goods for the defence of their country.' Royal objectives in terms of 'conserving and extending' the kingdom are present, again with considerable tradition behind them going back to the fourteenth-century insistence that the royal domain be maintained intact. Louis was to re-emphasize the point in the formal *Instructions* he drew up for his son on his deathbed: 'We have lost nothing of the crown but have augmented and increased it by great lands and lordships.' So too in the *Rosier*: 'The noble kings of France have always worked to widen and enlarge their kingdom, punish rebels and all those who could harm them, destroy enemies of the faith and succour the church of Rome' (the latter indeed was a point much laboured by the king in his 1478 Instructions for his ambassador to Rome). In the *Rosier* Louis is also explicit on the true job of a ruler along lines mapped out at least since Gilles of Rome's widely read *De regimine principum* (1277–9) addressed to Philip the Fair: 'to defend the common good . . . and maintain justice and peace between their subjects' and to 'strive for the common good which is always more desirable than the private'. Gilles and his contemporaries had accepted the idea that the king who respected natural law was above positive law. Louis XI, though, is more reserved:

> A king is good and noble who replaces bad law by good and takes care not to break laws useful for the people. When kings do not observe the law . . . they make their people serfs and lose their name of king, for none should be called

kings who do not reign over free men. For men free of nature love their lords but serfs, like slaves, hate their masters.

Curiously enough Louis makes the science of war (what he called the 'knowledge of chivalry'), distilled through the writings of Vegetius but adding a great deal of insight into his own sense of insecurity throughout his reign, one of his main preoccupations in chapters 4–6:

This knowledge of chivalry is especially important for the king to know, for though the fighting of battles and the defence of the common good belongs to knights and those whom the king places in command, it is the king's job especially to know about such matters . . . art and wisdom are worth more than power . . . or great numbers in an army . . . the king should not risk battles . . . battle is the most perilous thing in the world.

The importance of the *Rosier* lies in showing how a ruler of such devious subtlety as Louis XI shaped his view of the *métier du roi* in profoundly traditional and moralistic terms.

Was Louis a hypocrite? Two other texts of the same period are worth juxtaposing with the *Rosier*. The most obvious is the *Mémoires* of Philippe de Commynes, if only because the vividness of that narrative has tended to shape the historical perception of Louis. Commynes, won over by Louis from Burgundy in 1472, composed his work initially in 1489–91 as material for a history of his master to be written by Angelo Cato, archbishop of Vienne (the work was printed in 1524, well after his death and not entitled *Mémoires* until the first serious edition of 1552). Commynes, who had to be very careful in the way he expressed his ideas on politics, especially in view of the difficulties he experienced after Louis XI's death, was both writing a history of his times and conveying an appreciation of statecraft which was largely unencumbered by the Mirror for Princes tradition. He produced an extraordinary text written by a true politician whose unusual career enabled him to step outside convention. In his work we hear little or nothing of the themes so dear to the great traditions of French political thought: the religious charisma of the crown, the organic idea of the monarch as the head of the body politic (present both in Mézières and Juvenal) or of the king as the image of God on earth. It comes as a shock to read in Commynes's dedication that kings 'are but men like us'. Of his predecessors, Joinville had written a hagiography of Louis IX, and Christine de Pisan yet another Mirror for Princes in her *Life of Charles V*. But though, like them, he used the device of his constant and privileged access to the king, Commynes was able to reflect on political motivation, fear, suspicion, and the role of personal pride in princely relations. Above all, he gives the first convincing psychological portrait of a French king, with all his constant and febrile activity, shrewdness, impulsiveness, and cruelty.

The political world for Commynes, whether through his own observation or recounting the words of his master, King Louis, was one of perpetual suspicion and lack of faith. Indeed, as portrayed by Commynes, Louis XI is the great example of fear used to intelligent advantage. The relish with which he described Louis's stratagems for outwitting his enemies, winning over new servants from them, ironic or not, conveys a vision of politics which in some ways anticipates the insights of Machiavelli and should be compared with what we know of Louis XI's own viewpoint in the *Rosier*. Commynes shows that he is thoroughly imbued with the late medieval preoccupation with the problems of counsel. A king must be well-read in history, as we have seen Louis XI certainly was in the *Rosier*, in order to have at his disposal a range of experience, and like Louis he should be powerfully inquisitive—'God never designed the office of a king to be executed by beasts'—and Louis's brother Charles is held up to ridicule as just such a figure. He must be able to make his own decisions and not be led by the nose by councillors: 'I have always found that proud and stately princes who will hear but few, are more likely to be imposed on than those who are open and accessible.' It is no use relying on councillors alone; kings must 'cull and select their ministers and employ them frankly and without complaint'. He must have 'judgement and . . . cunning management of his affairs', qualities which Charles the Bold, for all his bravery and resources, lacked. He must know when and how to deceive—the art of 'dissimulation'—as did Louis XI amply and which Commynes implies without criticism is practised universally. Commynes's Louis is profoundly cautious, especially about battle, 'for he thought he was not well liked by his subjects, especially the grands'. Indeed, it has been suggested by Jacques Krynen that Commynes illustrates a gap opening up between the tropes of the warrior king and the wise king. But in other ways he was rash, and freely admitted that he made enemies by his busy tongue, though supremely able to rescue himself from the consequences of his actions. Commynes's Louis is not an entirely

Machiavellian figure, however. His personal cruelty comes with a price in the form of fear of eternal damnation 'so before he died he himself was in greater torment and more terrible apprehension than those whom he had imprisoned'. Ultimately, Commynes judges by the 'utility' of an action; yes, King Louis burdened his subjects with heavy taxes and in taking from the poor to give to the rich caused problems, but he spent the money wisely rather than hoarded it.

Towards the very end of the fifteenth century, probably around 1492–3, a nobleman of some influence in royal service, probably the military commander Robert de Balsac (whose parallel work *Le nef des princes et des batailles* was printed in 1502), wrote a completely practical guide for the young king Charles VIII on how to gain control of the governmental machinery that he was about to assume. His treatise is hardly a great piece of literary composition but is notable for its complete avoidance of theory and legal precedent and its insistence on the necessity to control the system by well-chosen appointees. There is the traditional emphasis on the prince as a successful head of household: 'the prince must first be master and well obeyed and keep order in his household if he wishes to be obeyed and feared outside and in the country'. The approach also employs all the traditional tropes of government by good counsel, though in an utterly practical way. The king must choose his advisers carefully, and avoid being deceived; Balsac even suggests that the king put forward what he knows to be completely undesirable plans 'to find out what sort of men they are, if they are sufficient and truthful or flatterers and ignorant'. It is essential that councillors be given liberty to speak without fearing the king's anger, otherwise they will not speak the truth, but the king must consider whether those who speak ill of others are backbiters and flatterers. Yes, he must be frank and show his mind on occasion, but 'too much familiarity in a prince engenders great disdain and disobedience to him', a point made by Machiavelli. He must be open, welcoming, and generous to his servants, avoid tyranny but punish misdemeanours rigorously, treat old servants of the crown with courtesy as an incentive to the younger. Louis XI, too, had been obsessed in his *Instructions* of 1482 with making sure his successor did not repeat his mistake of dismissing his father's councillors and urging him to seek the advice of those who had been loyal to the dynasty over several reigns. Like Louis XI in the *Rosier*, Balsac shows a clear understanding that power rests upon military force.

'The finest treasures that a prince can have are well-mounted and armed men-at-arms . . . without them he cannot do nothing, dominate or reign . . . force allows the prince to live in security and be obeyed.' There is nothing about mechanisms for the control of tyranny. The Estates General is treated with caution; the princes and towns are to be summoned but seen separately 'not in the manner of Estates', which customarily seek to 'reform and correct' a prince. The grands are to be controlled by managing them.

There seems no reason to doubt that the main building blocks of France as a 'royal state' were in place by the end of the fifteenth century. The institutions necessary for this were in some cases venerable through age, but a tension still remained at the heart of the public realm between generally accepted nostrums of obligation to the king and the practicalities of exercising power in a highly diverse country difficult to govern. The notion of the kingdom as a collective enterprise of princes was still alive, and the threat this posed to royal power was still a living memory. The exaltation of monarchical authority which developed in the first half of the sixteenth century and even more so in the seventeenth never really dealt with this. The France of the Ancien Régime remained a society in which the 'absolute power' of sovereigns was tempered by the fact that this power could only be exercised through a society of privileges, primarily noble privileges. The infringement of such privileges always engendered instability, and indeed eventually brought the royal state crashing down.

Further reading

ABSHF	*Annuaire-bulletin de la Société de l'Histoire de France*
AN	*Annales de Normandie*
BEC	*Bibliothèque de l'École des Chartes*
Bull. SH Paris	*Bulletin de la Société de l'Histoire de Paris*
EHR	*English Historical Review*
JIH	*Journal of Interdisciplinary History*
J. Med. H.	*Journal of Medieval History*
JS	*Journal des Savants*
JWCI	*Journal of the Warburg and Courtauld Institutes*
RH	*Revue Historique*
SHF	*Société de l'Histoire de France*
TAPS	*Transactions of the American Philosophical Society*
TRHS	*Transactions of the Royal Historical Society*

Introduction

Studies of later medieval France in general are relatively rare in English and mostly out of print. Peter Lewis's *Later Medieval France: The Polity* (London, 1968) remains the most subtle study in English of political institutions. Otherwise there is only G. Duby, *France in the Middle Ages, 987–1460* (Oxford, 1991), which is naturally rather cursory on the later periods, and A. Tilley's *Medieval France: A Companion to French Studies* (1964). There are some collections of essays that are valuable, most notably P. S. Lewis (ed.), *The Recovery of France in the Fifteenth Century* (London, 1971); J. R. L. Highfield and R. Jeffs (ed.), *The Crown and Local Communities in England and France in the Fifteenth Century* (Gloucester, 1981) and C. Allmand (ed.), *Power, Culture and Religion in France c.1350–c.1550* (Woodbridge, 1989). Books which cover culture and society are J. Evans, *Life in Medieval France*, rev. edn. (London, 1957), Barbara Tuchman's impressionistic *A Distant Mirror: The Calamitous Fourteenth Century* (London, 1979) and E. Le Roy Ladurie's *Montaillou: Cathars and Catholics in a French Village, 1274–1324* (London, 1978). Aspects of the Hundred Years War are naturally more extensively covered in English (see below, on Chapter 4).

Studies in French are obviously more extensive. Among general works, we have J. Favier, *La France médiévale* (Paris, 1983), covering the period down to 1328; C. Gauvard, *La France au Moyen Âge, du Ve au XVe siècle* (Paris, 1996); M. Bourin-Derruau, *Temps d'équilibres, temps de ruptures, XIIIe siècle* (Paris, 1990); M. Mollat, *Genèse médiévale de la France moderne, XIVe–XVe siècle* (Paris, 1977); A. Demurger, *Temps de crises, temps d'espoirs, XIVe–XVe siècle*

(Paris, 1990). Jean Favier has edited a *Dictionnaire de la France médiévale* (Paris, 1993). There are also some important collections of essays including B. Chevalier and P. Contamine (eds.), *La France de la fin du XVe siècle—Renouveau et apogée* (Paris, 1985) and the collected essays of R. H. Bautier, *Sur l'histoire économique de la France médiévale* and *Recherches sur l'histoire de la France médiévale* (Variorum, Aldershot, 1991), which cover the period down to the early fourteenth century. M.-T. Caron in *La société en France à la fin du Moyen Âge* (Paris, 1977) has published a collection of documents in the PUF series Documents d'histoire. C. Raynaud, *La violence au Moyen Âge: XIIIe–XVe siècle* (Paris, 1990) is also of general interest.

For this introduction, studies which cover broad themes are C. Beaune, *Naissance de la nation France* (Paris, 1985), trans. as *The Birth of an Ideology: Myths and Symbols in Late Medieval France* by S. H. Huston and F. L. Cheyette (Berkeley, 1991); R. Fawtier, 'Comment, au début du XIVe siècle, un roi de France pouvait-il se représenter son royaume', *Comptes Rendus de l'Académie des Inscriptions et Belles-Lettres* (1959), 117–23; B. Guenée, 'Espace et état dans la France du bas Moyen Âge', *Annales*, 23 (1968), 744–58; id., 'État et nation en France au Moyen Âge' *RH* 237 (1967), 17–30; id., 'Les limites', in M. François (ed.), *La France et les français* (Paris, 1972), 50–69; id., 'Des limites féodales aux frontières politiques', in P. Nora (ed.), *Lieux de mémoire*, II: *La nation*, vol. ii (Paris, 1984), 11–33.

For national sentiment, there is a general survey by P. Contamine, 'Mourir pour la patrie, Xe–XXe siècle', in P. Nora (ed.), *Lieux de mémoire*, II: *La nation*, vol. iii (Paris, 1986), 11–43. N. Grévy-Pons, 'Propagande et sentiment national pendant le règne de Charles VI: l'exemple de Jean de Montreuil', *Francia*, 8 (1980), 127–45; N. Pons, 'La propagande de guerre française avant l'apparition de Jeanne d'Arc', *JS* (Apr.–June 1982), 191–214. The writings of Peter Lewis remain valuable, reprinted in his *Essays in Later Medieval French History* (London, 1985), particularly 'War Propaganda and Historiography in Fifteenth-Century France and England', but also 'France in the Fifteenth Century: Society and Sovereignty'; 'The Centre, the Periphery and the Problem of Power Distribution in Later Medieval France'; and 'Decayed and Non-feudalism in Later Medieval France'. See also id., 'A Note on Nationalism in Fifteenth-Century France', *JWCI* (1964), 317–40; S. H. Cuttler, *The Law of Treason and Treason Trials in Later Medieval France* (Cambridge, 1981).

On royal symbolism and ceremony: L. M. Bryant, 'The Medieval Entry Ceremony at Paris', in J. M. Bak (ed.), *Coronations* (Berkeley, 1990); R. Jackson, *Vive le roi! A History of the French Coronation from Charles V to Charles X* (Chapel Hill, NC, 1984); M. Bloch, *Les rois thaumaturges: étude sur le caractère surnaturel attribué à la puissance royale particulièrement en France et en Angleterre* (Paris, 1924), trans. as *The Royal Touch* (London, 1973); P. Contamine, 'L'oriflamme de Saint-Denis aux XIVe et XVe siècles: étude de la symbolique religieuse et royale', *Annales de l'Est* (1973), 179–244; M. François, 'Les rois de France et les traditions de Saint-Denis à la fin du XVe siècle', *Mélanges dédiés à la mémoire de Félix Gret*, vol. i (Paris, 1946), 367–82; R. Giesey, *The Royal Funeral Ceremony in Renaissance France* (Geneva, 1960).

On royal iconography, see C. R. Sherman, *The Portraits of Charles V of France (1338–1380)* (New York, 1969), and on royal visual propaganda, the useful series of studies by G. B. Blumenshine, 'Monarchy and Symbol in Later Medieval France: The Tree of Jesse Window at Evreux', *Fifteenth-Century Studies*, 9 (1984), 19–57; 'Popular Piety and the Valois Dynasty: The St. Anne Window at Evreux and Louis XI', *Majestas*, 2 (1994), 17–39; 'Patronage, Piety and Power at Evreux: Valois Propaganda in Later Medieval France', *AN* 52 (2002), 334–43.

The political world of France (Chapter 1)

Given the recent preoccupations of French historians, it is not surprising that historians of the French political world are frequently Anglophone. The only book that gives an overview of almost the whole period is E. M. Hallam and J. Everard, *Capetian France 987–1328*, 2nd edn. (Harlow, 2001). Also useful is R. Cazelles, *De la fin du règne de Philippe Auguste à la mort de Charles V (1223–1380): nouvelle histoire de Paris* (Paris, 1972). The clearest surveys of French government are contained in a series of studies of individual kings. On administration of all sorts, J. W. Baldwin, *The Government of Philip Augustus: Foundations of French Royal Power in the Middle Ages* (Berkeley and Los Angeles, 1986) is of crucial importance. G. Sivéry, *Louis VIII* (Paris, 1995) and J. Richard, *Saint Louis* (Paris, 1983) both have useful information; on the finances of Louis IX's first crusade, W. C. Jordan, *Louis IX and the Challenge of the Crusade: A Study in Rulership* (Princeton, 1979) is extremely enlightening. J. R. Strayer, *The Reign of Philip the Fair* (Princeton, 1980) is more useful on the nuts and bolts of finance and administration than J. Favier, *Philippe le Bel* (Paris, 1978). For the later period, there are P. Lehugeur, *Philippe le Long, roi de France 1316–22: le mécanisme du gouvernement* (Paris, 1931) and R. Cazelles, *La société politique et la crise de la royauté sous Philippe de Valois* (Paris, 1958). J. R. Strayer and C. H. Taylor, *Studies in Early French Taxation* (Cambridge, Mass., 1939) established the main facts. J. B. Henneman, *Royal Taxation in Fourteenth-Century France: The Development of War Financing, 1322–1356* (Princeton, 1971) carried the story on. J. Le Patourel, 'The King and the Princes in Fourteenth-Century France', in J. Hale, R. Highfield, and B. Smalley (eds.), *Europe in the Later Middle Ages* (London 1965) is still the best introduction to the principalities. For narrative on the constant problems with Flanders, see D. Nicholas, *Medieval Flanders* (London, 1992). The troubles over Gascony are clearly analysed in M. Vale, *The Angevin Legacy and the Hundred Years*

War 1250–1340 (Oxford, 1990). On the apanages, C. T. Wood, *The French Apanages and the Capetian Monarchy 1224–1328* (Cambridge, Mass., 1966) remains useful.

On law, there is an absence of good, up-to-date work. The anthropological insights that have given so much dynamism to the study of French law of the eleventh and early twelfth centuries are thought to be of less relevance to the later period. Law is consequently studied mainly, in the books mentioned above, as a facet of the increasing power of the crown. For a broader picture, it is necessary to revert either to rather old works or to more modern ones devoted to particular themes, usually on a European canvas. In the first category there are: Y. Bongert, *Recherches sur les cours laïques du Xe au XIIIe siècles* (Paris, 1949); F. Olivier-Martin, *Histoire du droit français des origines à la revolution* (Paris, 1948); and R. Aubenas, *Cours d'histoire du droit privé* (Aix-en-Provence, 1956–62). In the second category come E. M. Peters, *Torture* (New York, 1985) and A. Murray, *Suicide in the Middle Ages, i: The Violent Against Themselves* (Oxford, 1998), esp. 180–97. The sterling work of F. P. K. Akehurst in providing English translations and comment on *The Coutumes de Beauvaisis of Philippe le Beaumanoir* (Philadelphia, 1992) and *The Établissements de St Louis: Thirteenth-Century Law Texts from Tours, Orléans and Paris* (Philadelphia, 1996) has made comment on local customs much easier. On royal law-making, see G. Langmuir, ' "Judei nostri" and Capetian legislation', *Traditio*, 16 (1960). On sovereignty, J. Strayer, *On the Medieval Origins of the Modern State* (Princeton, 1970).

On warfare and military matters, there is a useful introduction to the earlier part of the period in J. France, *Western Warfare in the Age of the Crusades, 1000–1300* (London, 1999); for the later period, P. Contamine, *La guerre au Moyen Âge*, 4th edn. (Paris, 1994). For a case study in the problems of mounting a war at some distance from Paris, Vale, *The Angevin Legacy*, 175–226. On the cost of St Louis's first crusade, see Jordan, *Louis IX and the Challenge of the Crusade.* On Philip VI's attempt to mount a crusade, C. Tyerman, 'Philip VI and the recovery of the Holy Land', *EHR* 100 (1985), 25–52. On the Jews and the crusade, W. C. Jordan, *The French Monarchy and the Jews* (Philadelphia, 1989). On the economic problems of the early fourteenth century that made financing of war much more difficult, see W. C. Jordan, *The Great Famine* (Princeton, 1998).

On policies and the royal servants who carried them out, see Baldwin, *The Government of Philip Augustus*; Jordan, *Louis IX and the Challenge of the Crusade*; Strayer, *The Reign of Philip the Fair*; Henneman, *Royal Taxation in Fourteenth-Century France*; J. Favier, 'Les légistes et le gouvernement de Philippe le Bel', *JS* (1969); J. Strayer, *Les gens de justice du Languedoc sous Philippe le Bel* (Toulouse, 1970); J. Favier, *Un conseiller de Philippe le Bel: Enguerran de Marigny* (Paris, 1963); F. Pegues, *The Lawyers of the Last*

Capetians (Princeton, 1962); E. Lalou, 'La chancellerie royale à la fin du règne de Philippe IV le Bel', in M. Bent and A. Wathey (eds.), *Fauvel Studies: Allegory, Chronicle, Music, and Image in Paris, Bibliothèque Nationale de France, MS Français 146* (Oxford, 1998).

On ideology, J. le Goff, *Saint Louis* (Paris, 1996); C. Beaune, *Naissance de la nation France* (Paris, 1985); and J. Krynen, *L'empire du roi: idées et croyances politiques en France, XIIIe–XV siècles* (Paris, 1993) are three recent studies that, between them, pick up the main aspects. Comment continues on M. Bloch's famous *Les rois thaumaturges* (Strasbourg, 1924). In particular, see F. Barlow, 'The King's Evil', in *EHR* 95 (1980), 3–27, and P. Buc, 'David's Adultery with Bathsheba and the Healing Power of the Capetian Kings', *Viator*, 24 (1993). On courts, see M. Vale, *The Princely Court* (Oxford, 2002).

The economy and society of France in the later Middle Ages (Chapters 2 and 5)

Studies are numerous but rarely very recent because research workers, at least in France, are nowadays turning their attention to the history of mentalities.

A book often quoted as a synthesis of the subject is G. Bois, *Crise du féodalisme: économie rurale et démographie en Normandie orientale du début du 14e siècle au milieu du 16e siécle* (Paris, 1976) trans. as *The Crisis of Feudalism: Economy and Society in Eastern Normandy c. 1300–1350* (Cambridge, 1984), but it is too theoretical as is his *Grande depression médiévale, XIVe–XVe siècles* (Paris, 2000). J. Heers, *L'Occident aux XIVe et XVe siècles: aspects économiques et sociaux* (Paris, 1990) tends to emphasize Italy. Better is E. Carpentier and M. Le Mené, *La France du XIe au XVe siècle: Population, société, économie* (Paris, 1996). P. S. Lewis (ed.), *The Recovery of France in the Fifteenth Century* is useful. It is also convenient to refer to the appropriate chapters in the thematic collections: G. Duby and others, *Histoire de la France rurale*, vols. i and ii (Paris, 1975); G. Duby and others, *Histoire de la France urbaine*, vol. ii (Paris, 1980); J. Dupâquier and others, *Histoire de la population française* vol. i (Paris, 1988).

There are chapters devoted to late medieval France in general studies such as *The Cambridge Economic History of Europe*, i: *Agrarian Life of the Middle Ages* (1966); ii: *Trade and Industry in the Middle Ages* (1987); iii: *Economic Organization and Policies in the Middle Ages* (1963). See also W. G. Naphy, *The Black Death and the Plague, 1345–1725* (2001); P. Musgrave, *The Early Modern European Economy* (1999); K. F. Kiple and K. C. Ornelas, *The Cambridge World History of Food* (Cambridge, 2000).

For deeper studies, regional monographs must be used, especially those based on state doctoral theses. Among them we can point out those of R. Boutruche, *La crise d'une société: seigneurs et paysans du Bordelais pendant la Guerre de Cent Ans* (Paris, 1947); P. Wolff, *Commerces et marchands de*

Toulouse (vers 1350–vers 1450) (Paris, 1954); G. Fourquin, *Les campagnes de la région parisienne à la fin du Moyen Âge, du milieu du XIIIe siècle au début du XVIe siècle* (Paris, 1964); and P. Charbonnier, *Une autre France: la seigneurie rurale en Basse Auvergne du XIVe au XVIe siècle* (Clermont-Ferrand, 1980).

On Jacques Cœur, se M. Mollat, *Jacques Cœur, ou, L'esprit de l'entreprise* (Paris, 1988) and J. Heers, *Jacques Cœur* (Paris, 1977).

The crown and the provinces in the fourteenth century (Chapter 3)

P. S. Lewis, *Later Medieval France* a sophisticated and subtle analysis of power, remains the only good detailed modern general treatment in English of fourteenth- and fifteenth-century France. Two important works by Raymond Cazelles, *La société politique et la crise de la royauté sous Philippe de Valois* (Paris, 1958) and *Société politique, noblesse et couronne sous Jean le Bon et Charles V* (Paris, 1982), pay great attention to relations between the crown and provinces, with particular reference to the personal groupings vying for power at the centre. Briefer accounts, with full bibliographies, can be found in the chapters by Michael Jones and Françoise Autrand in M. Jones (ed.), *The New Cambridge Medieval History*, vi: *c.1300–c.1415* (Cambridge, 2000). Two complementary articles provide essential reference points: J. Le Patourel, 'The King and the Princes in Fourteenth-Century France', in J. Hale, R. Highfield, and B. Smalley (eds.), *Europe in the Late Middle Ages* (London, 1964) and A. Leguai, 'Les "états" princiers en France à la fin du Moyen Âge', *Annali della fondazione italiana per la storia amministrativa*, 4 (1967). C. T. Wood, *The French Apanages and the Capetian Monarchy 1224–1378* (Cambridge, Mass., 1966) is a valuable synthesis. Considerable work has been done on many individual principalities: for Burgundy to 1361, see J. Richard, *Les ducs de Bourgogne et la formation du duché du XIe au XIVe siècle* (Paris, 1954). Richard Vaughan's splendid biographies *Philip the Bold: The Formation of the Burgundian State* (London, 1962) and *John the Fearless: The Growth of Burgundian Power* (London, 1966) deal with the first two Valois dukes, while W. Blockmans and W. Prevenier, *The Promised Lands: The Low Countries Under Burgundian Rule, 1369–1530* (Philadelphia, 1999) is wide-ranging and perceptive. For the other great principalities, M. Jones, *Ducal Brittany 1364–1399* (Oxford, 1970), *The Creation of Brittany: A Late Medieval State* (London, 1988), and *Between France and England: Power, Politics and Society in Late Medieval Brittany* (Aldershot, 2003); R. Lacour, *Le gouvernement de l'apanage de Jean, duc de Berry 1360–1416* (Paris, 1934); A. Leguai, *De la seigneurie à l'état: le Bourbonnais pendant la Guerre de Cent Ans* (Moulins, 1969); and O. Mattéoni, *Servir le prince: les officiers des ducs de Bourbon à la fin du Moyen Âge (1356–1523)* (Paris, 1998) contain important material. For those in the Midi, C. Higounet, *Le Comté de Comminges de ses origines à son annexion à la couronne*, 2 vols. (Toulouse, 1949) was a pioneering work, and

P. Tucoo-Chala, *Gaston Fébus et la vicomté de Béarn (1343–1391)* (Bordeaux, 1960) discusses the most flamboyant prince of his generation. Some idea of the range of Angevin interests is revealed in N. Coulet and J.-M. Matz (eds.), *La noblesse dans les territoires angevins à la fin du Moyen Âge*, (Paris, 2000). The earliest Estates General and provincial assemblies are usefully surveyed in J. R. Major, *Representative Government in Early Modern France* (New Haven, 1980), while P. Contamine, 'Les fortifications urbaines en France à la fin du Moyen Âge: aspects financières et économiques', *RH* 260 (1978), 23–47, summarizes much recent work on town finances and administrative developments under the pressures of war. John, duke of Normandy's relations with his father are reassessed in J. Tricard, 'Jean, duc de Normandie et héritier de France, un double échec?', *AN* 29 (1979), 23–44.

France and the Hundred Years War (Chapter 4)

The work of E. Perroy *The Hundred Years War* (London, 1951) remains the best single-volume narrative of the war. In recent years Jonathan Sumption has begun a new multi-volume account, of which *The Hundred Years War: Trial by Battle* (London, 1990) and *The Hundred Years War: Trial by Fire* (London, 1999) have so far appeared. The illustrated study by K. A. Fowler, *The Age of Plantagenet and Valois* (London, 1967), now, sadly, out of print, covers a wide range of themes, and is particularly strong on French military organization. C. T. Allmand, *The Hundred Years War: England and France at War* (Cambridge, 1988) raises important issues on the impact of the war on civilians, as well as providing a broader treatment and a useful guide to further reading. There are some thematic essay collections on various aspects, such as K. A. Fowler (ed.), *The Hundred Years War* (London, 1971) and A. Curry and M. Hughes (eds.), *Arms, Armies and Fortifications of the Hundred Years War* (Stroud, 1994). C. T. Allmand also edited a useful collection of documents in *Society at War: The Experience of England and France During the Hundred Years War*, 2nd edn (Woodbridge, 1998). H. S. Lucas, *The Low Countries and the Hundred Years War, 1326–1347* (Ann Arbor, 1929, repr. Phildelphia, 1976) is useful on the international ramifications, while C. Rogers, *War Cruel and Sharp: English Strategy Under Edward III, 1327–1360* (Woodbridge, 2000) reconsiders the earlier phase of the conflict.

There are also some important studies of the political background, first of all the two works by Cazelles *La société politique et la crise de la royauté sous Philippe de Valois* (Paris, 1958) and *Société politique, noblesse et couronne sous Jean le Bon et Charles V* (Geneva, 1982), and, for the civil war of the early fifteenth century, R. C. Famiglietti, *Royal Intrigue: Crisis at the Court of Charles VI 1392–1420* (New York, 1986) and J. Henneman, *Olivier de Clisson and Political Society in France Under Charles V and Charles VI* (Philadelphia, 1996). The reign of Charles VII is well served by the biography of the king by Malcolm Vale, *Charles VII* (London, 1974), and by R. Little, *The Parlement of Poitiers: War, Government and Politics in France 1418–1436* (London, 1984), which places Joan of Arc firmly within the contemporary political context. On military organization, nothing can surpass P. Contamine's magisterial study *Guerre, état et société à la fin du Moyen Âge* (Paris, 1972). On national identity, the best work is C. Beaune, *Naissance de la nation France* (Paris, 1985), trans. as *The Birth of an Ideology: Myths and Symbols in Late Medieval France* by S. H. Huston and F. L. Cheyette (Berkeley, 1991). John Henneman's two volumes on taxation in France are central to understanding the impact of the war on royal government: *Royal Taxation in Fourteenth-Century France: The Development of War Financing, 1322–1356* (Princeton, 1971) and *Royal Taxation in Fourteenth-Century France: The Captivity and Ransom of John II, 1356–1370* (Philadelphia, 1976).

Valuable regional studies in English are M. C. E. Jones, *Ducal Brittany, 1364–99* (Oxford, 1976); C. T. Allmand, *Lancastrian Normandy* 1415–1450 (Oxford, 1983); M. G. A. Vale, *English Gascony 1399–1453* (Oxford, 1970); and G. Thompson, *Paris and Its People Under English Rule: The Anglo-Burgundian Regime 1420–1436* (Oxford, 1991). For works on the impact of the war, see N. Wright, *Knights and Peasants: The Hundred Years War in the French Countryside* (Woodbridge, 1998) and G. Bois, *The Crisis of Feudalism* (see under Chapters 2 and 5). Two important studies in French are R. Boutruche, *La crise d'une société: seigneurs et paysans du Bordelais pendant la Guerre de Cent Ans* (Paris, 1947) and P. Desportes, *Reims et les Remois aux XIII et XIV siècles* (Paris, 1979).

The crown and the provinces in the fifteenth century (Chapter 6)

For brief introductions to the period the reader may refer to chapters by M. Vale and B. Chevalier in C. Allmand (ed.), *The New Cambridge Medieval History*, vii: *c.1415–c.1500* (Cambridge, 1998). Biographies of kings remain a valuable source of information on the relations between crown and province, in particular R. Famiglietti, *Royal Intrigue: Crisis at the Court of Charles VI 1392–1420* (New York, 1986) and M. Vale, *Charles VII* (London, 1970). Two books which move outwards from the crown to its subjects are P. S. Lewis, *Later Medieval France: The Polity* (London, 1968) and D. L. Potter, *A History of France, 1460–1560: The Emergence of a Nation State* (London, 1995). Three other general collections of essays deserve particular mention: P. S. Lewis (ed.), *The Recovery of France in the Fifteenth Century* (London, 1971); id. (ed.), *Essays in Later Medieval French History* (London, 1985) and B. Guenée, *Politique et histoire au Moyen Âge* (Paris, 1981). See also B. Guenée, *Between Church and State: The Lives of Four French Prelates in the Late Middle Ages*, trans. A. Goldhammer (Chicago, 1991); S. Cuttler, *The Law of Treason and Treason Trials in Late Medieval France* (Cambridge, 1981).

The English-language reader is fortunate to have several studies of fifteenth-century French provinces. Richard Vaughan's history of the Valois dukes of Burgundy *Philip the Good: The Formation of the Burgundian State* (London, 1962); *John the Fearless: The Growth of Burgundian Power* (London, 1966); *Philip the Good: The Apogee of Burgundy* (London, 1970), *Charles the Bold: The Last Valois Duke of Burgundy* (London, 1973) has now been republished by the Boydell Press, but see also W. Blockmans and W. Prevenier, *The Promised Lands: The Low Countries Under Burgundian Rule, 1369–1530* (Pennsylvania, 1999). Three studies are usefully taken together: D. L. Potter, *War and Government in the French Provinces: Picardy 1470–1560* (Cambridge, 1993); R. Harris, *Valois Guyenne: A Study of Politics, Government and Society in Late Medieval France* (Woodbridge, 1994); and G. Prosser, 'After the Reduction: Re-structuring Norman Political Society and the *Bien Publique*, 1450–65', Ph. D. thesis (University College London, 1996). On many Breton matters, see M. Jones, *The Creation of Brittany: A Late Medieval State* (London, 1988). Examples and summaries of recent French research on principalities and noble affinities include M.-T. Caron, *Noblesse et pouvoir royal en France (XIIIe–XVIe siècles)* (Paris, 1994); J. Kerhervé, *L'état breton aux XIVe et XVe siècles: les ducs, l'argent et les hommes*, 2 vols. (Paris, 1987); and O. Mattéoni, *Servir le prince: les officiers des ducs de Bourbon à la fin du Moyen Âge (1356–1523)* (Paris, 1998). See also J. Gazzaniga, 'La politique bénéficiale du cardinal Pierre de Foix l'ancien (milieu du XVe siècle)', *Revue de Pau et du Béarn*, no. 11 (1983), 11–27; repr. in id., *L'église de France à la fin du Moyen Âge: pouvoirs et institutions* (Goldbach, 1995); A. Leguai, *De la seigneurie à l'état: le Bourbonnais pendant la Guerre de Cent Ans* (Moulins, 1969); J. Krynen, 'La rebellion du Bien public (1465)', in M.-T. Fögen (ed.), *Ordnung und Aufruhr im Mittelalter* (Frankfurt, 1995).

Essays in English on provincial French towns in the fifteenth century are to be found in J. Highfield and R. Jeffs (eds.), *The Crown and Local Communities in England and France in the Fifteenth Century* (Gloucester, 1981) and C. Allmand (ed.), *War, Government and Power in Late Medieval France* (Liverpool, 2000). There is also interesting comment on relations between the monarchy and towns in R. Little, *The Parlement of Poitiers: War, Government and Politics in France, 1418–36* (London, 1984). The two most valuable general works are in French: B. Chevalier's survey *Les bonnes villes de France du XIVe au XVIe siècle* (Paris, 1982) and the collected essays of A. Rigaudière, *Gouverner la ville au Moyen Âge* (Paris, 1993).

It would be fair to say Anglo-Saxon scholarship has made a particular impact on the history of the estates in late medieval France. For differing approaches, see P. S. Lewis, 'The Failure of the French Medieval Estates', in id. (ed.), *The Recovery of France in the Fifteenth Century*, with further comment in his *Later Medieval France* and *Essays in later Medieval French History*; and

J. R. Major, *Representative Institutions in Renaissance France, 1421–1559* (Madison, 1960) and *Representative Government in Early Modern France* (New Haven, 1980); and *The Monarchy, the Estates and the Aristocracy in Renaissance France* (London, 1988). There is also a short regional study, J. M. Tyrell, *A History of the Estates in Poitou* (The Hague, 1968). For more recent insight into the Estates General, see N. Bulst, *Die französischen Generalstände von 1468 und 1484. Prosopograpische Untersuchungen zu den Delegierten* (Sigmaringen, 1992).

The king and his government under the Valois (Chapter 7)

For a general overview: F. Autrand, *Pouvoir et société en France, XIVe–XVe siècles* (Paris, 1974); P. S. Lewis, *Later Medieval France*. The historiography of the subject is usefully summarized by B. Guenée, 'Les tendances actuelles de l'histoire politique du Moyen Âge français' *Actes du 100e Congrès national des sociétés savantes* (Paris, 1975), vol. i, 'Philologique et historique', 45–70, and Guenée, 'L'histoire de l'état en France à la fin du Moyen Âge', *RH* 232 (1964), 331–60. For basic structures: B. Guenée, 'La géographie administrative de la France à la fin du Moyen Âge: élections et bailliages', *Le Moyen Âge*, 67 (1961), 293–323.

On the ideology of power: J. Krynen, *L'idéal du prince et du pouvoir royal en France à la fin du Moyen Âge (1380–1440): étude de la littérature politique du temps* (Paris, 1981); id., *L'empire du roi: idées et croyances politiques en France XIIIe–XIVe siècle* (Paris, 1993); id., 'Genèse de l'état et histoire des idées politiques en France à la fin du Moyen Âge', in *Culture et idéologie dans la genèse de l'état moderne: actes de la table ronde organisée par le CNRS et l'École Française de Rome, Rome, 6–17 octobre 1984* (Rome, 1985); id., ' "Le mort saisit le vif": genèse médiévale du principe d'instantanéité de la succession royale française', *JS* (1984), 187–221. For specialized studies: R. Born, 'The Perfect Prince: A Study in Thirteenth- and Fourteenth-Century Ideals', *Speculum*, 3 (1928), 470–504; D. Byrne, 'Rex imago Dei: Charles V of France and the *Livre des propriétés des choses*', *JMedH*, 7 (1981), 97–113; C. Gauvard, 'Christine de Pisan, a-t-elle eu une pensée politique? A propos d'ouvrages récentes', *RH* 97 (1973), 417–29; P. Arabeyre, 'La France et son gouvernement au milieu du XVe siècle d'après Bernard de Rosier', *BEC* 150/2 (1992), 245–86; S. M. Babbitt, 'Oresme's *Livre de politiques* and the France of Charles V', *TAPS* 75/1 (1985); J. Barbey, *La fonction royale, essence et légitimité d'après le 'Tractatus' de Jean de Terre-Vermeille* (Paris, 1981); D. M. Bell, *L'idéal éthique de la royauté au Moyen-Âge* (Paris, 1962). The idea of 'Reform' is acutely discussed by R. Cazelles, 'Une exigence de l'opinion publique depuis Saint-Louis: la réformation du royaume', *ABSHF* (1962–3), 91–9, and P. Contamine, 'Le vocabulaire politique en France à la fin du Moyen Âge: l'idée de réformation', in J. P.Genet, and B. Vincent (eds.), *État et église dans la genèse de l'état moderne* (Madrid, 1986), 145–56. For other aspects of political culture, see R. Cazelles, 'Les mouvements révolutionnaires du milieu du XIVe siècle et le cycle de l'action politique', *RH* 228 (1962) 279–312; P. S. Lewis, 'Jean Juvénal des Ursins and the Common Literary Attitude Towards Tyranny in Fifteenth-Century France', in his *Essays in Later Medieval French History* (London, 1985), 169–88.

On the role of officials: F. Autrand, 'Offices et officiers royaux en France sous Charles VI', *RH* 242 (1969), 285–338; A. Demurger, 'Guerre civile et changements de personnel administratif dans le royaume de France de 1400 à 1418: l'exemple des baillis et sénéchaux', *Francia*, 6 (1978), 151–298; C. Gauvard, 'Les offices royaux et l'opinion publique en France à la fin du Moyen Âge', *Actes de XIVe colloque historique franco-allemande* (Munich, 1980), 583–93; S. Luce, 'Le principe électif, les traductions d'Aristote et les parvenus au xive siècle', in his *La France pendant la Guerre de Cent Ans* (Paris, 1890), 179–202.

On administrative elites in general: B. Chevalier, *Tours, ville royale* (Paris, 1972); M. Harsgor, 'Les maîtres d'un royaume', in B. Chevalier and P. Contamine (eds.), *La France de la fin du XVe siècle: renouveau et apogée* (Paris, 1985); G. Ouy, 'Paris, l'un des principaux foyers de l'humanisme en Europe au début du xve siècle', *Bull. SH Paris*, années 94–5 (1967–8), 71–98; Ouy, 'L'humanisme et les mutations politiques et sociales en France aux XIVe et XVe siècles', *Colloque internationale de Tours (XIVe stage): l'humanisme français au début de la Renaissance* (Paris, 1973); A. de Reilhac, *Jean de Reilhac: secrétaire, maître des comptes, général des finances et ambassadeur des rois Charles VII, Louis XI et Charles VIII*, 2 vols. (Paris, 1886–7); A. Coville, *Gontier et Pierre Col et l'humanisme en France au temps de Charles VI* (Paris, 1934); B. Guenée, *Between Church and State: The Lives of Four French Prelates in the Late Middle Ages* (Chicago, 1991).

On central institutions, the Parlement is covered by F. Autrand, *Naissance d'un grand corps d'état: les gens du Parlement de Paris, 1345–1454* (Paris, 1981); E. A. R. Brown and R. C. Famiglietti, *The Lit de Justice: Semantics and Ceremonial and the Parlement of Paris, 1300–1600* (Sigmaringen, 1994); R. C. Famiglietti, 'The Role of the Parlement of Paris in the Ratification and Registration of Acts During the Reign of Charles V', *J. Med. H.* 9 (1983), 217–25. An older but still useful study is E. Maugis, *Histoire du Parlement de Paris*, 3 vols. (Paris, 1913–16, repr. Geneva, 1997). For the judicial activities of the crown: C. Gauvard, *De Grâce especial: crime, état et société en France à la fin du Moyen Âge*, 2 vols. (Paris, 1991); id., 'Grâce et exécution capitale, les deux visages de la justice royale française à la fin du Moyen Âge', *BEC* 153/2 (1995), 275–90; S. Cuttler, *The Law of Treason and Treason Trials in Later Medieval France* (Cambridge, 1981).

On the royal court: M. Vale, *The Princely Court: Medieval Courts and*

Culture in North-West Europe, 1270–1380 (Oxford, 2001); F. Autrand, 'De l'enfer au purgatoire: la cour à travers quelques textes français du milieu du XIVe à la fin du XVe siècles', in P. Contamine (ed.), *État et aristocraties . . . XIIe–XVIIe siècle* (Paris, 1989); B. Guenée, 'Paris et la cour du roi de France au XIVe siècle', in M. Bourin (ed.), *Villes, bonnes villes, cités et capitales: études d'histoire urbaine offertes à Bernard Chevalier*, (Tours, 1989), 259–65; id., *Un meurtre, une société: l'assassinat du duc d'Orléans 23 novembre 1407* (Paris, 1992); R. C. Gibbons, 'The Queen as Social Mannequin: Consumerism and Expenditure at the Court of Isabeau of Bavaria, 1391–1422', *J. Med. H.* 26 (2000), 371–95.

On the council: P.-R. Gaussin, 'Les conseillers de Charles VII (1418–1461)', *Francia*, 10 (1982), 67–130; id., 'Les conseillers de Louis XI (1461–1483)', in Chevalier and Contamine (eds.), *La France de la fin du XVe siècle*, 105–34; M. Harsgor, *Recherches sur le personnel du conseil du roi sous Charles VIII et Louis XII (1483–1515)*, thèse d'état, Paris IV, 1972 (Lille, 1980) An older work: N. Valois, *Le conseil du roi aux XIVe, XVe et XVIe siècles* (Paris, 1888).

On finance, the number of studies is vast but the following have been used: P. Contamine and O. Mattéoni (eds.), *La France des principautés: les chambres des comptes aux XIVe et XVe siècles* (Paris, 1996); G. Dupont-Ferrier, *Études sur les institutions financières de la France à la fin du Moyen Âge*, 2 vols. (Paris, 1930–3); id., *Nouvelle série d'études* (Paris, 1936); J. B. Henneman, *Royal Taxation in Fourteenth Century France: The Development of War Financing, 1322–1356* (Princeton, 1971); id., *Royal Taxation in Fourteenth Century France: The Captivity and Ransom of John II, 1356–1370* (Philadelphia, 1976); H. Jassemin, *La Chambre des Comptes de Paris au XVe siècle* (Paris, 1933); H. A. Miskimin, *Money, Prices and Foreign Exchange in Fourteenth-Century France* (New Haven, 1963); id., *Money and Power in Fifteenth-Century France* (New Haven, 1984); M. Rey, *Le domaine du roi et les finances extraordinaires sous Charles VI 1388–1413* (Paris, 1963); id., *Les finances royales sous Charles VI: les causes du déficit 1388–1413* (Paris, 1965); M. Wolfe, *The Fiscal System of Renaissance France (New Haven, 1972).*

Studies of rulers and politics: R. Cazelles, *La société politique et la crise de la royauté sous Philippe de Valois*; id., *Société politique, noblesse et couronne sous Jean le Bon et Charles V* (Geneva, 1982); R. Delachenal, *Histoire de Charles V*, 5 vols. (Paris, 1909–31); F. Autrand, *Charles V, le sage* (Paris, 1994); id., *Charles VI: la folie du roi* (Paris, 1986); J. B. Henneman, *Olivier de Clisson and Political Society in France Under Charles V and Charles VI* (Philadelphia, 1996). For politics in the reign of Charles VI, we have M. Nordberg, *Les ducs et la royauté: études sur la rivalité des ducs d'Orléans et de Bourgogne 1392–1407* (Uppsala, 1964); R. Famiglietti, *Royal Intrigue: Crisis and the Court of Charles VI (1392–1420)* (New York, 1986); R. C. Gibbons, 'Isabeau of Bavaria, Queen of France (1385–1422): The Creation of an Historical Villainess', *TRHS*,

6th ser., 6 (1996), 51–73. One of the most stimulating studies of politics and culture of the early fifteenth century, with wide implications, is Guenée, *Un meurtre, une société.* A. Coville, *Les cabochiens et l'ordonnance de 1413* (Paris, 1888), though old, is still useful, as is id., *Jean Petit: la question du tyrannicide au commencement du XVe siècle* (Paris, 1932). The period from 1420 is less well served by new studies of central politics. Among the classic works we have G. Du Fresne de Beaucourt, *Histoire de Charles VII*, 6 vols. (Paris, 1881–2) and E. Cosneau, *Le connétable de Richemont (Artur de Bretagne) (1393–1458)* (Paris, 1886). Modern studies include M. Vale, *Charles VII* (London, 1974) and P. R. Gaussin, *Louis XI* (Paris, 1972). One of the best modern studies of a political figure is J. Blanchard, *Commynes l'Européen: l'invention du politique* (Geneva, 1996).

The later medieval French *noblesse* (Chapter 8)

The foremost scholar of the late medieval *noblesse* is Philippe Contamine. His conspectus *La noblesse au royaume de France de Philippe le Bel à Louis XII* (Paris, 1996) summarizes a large body of research on regional nobilities, filtered through his own research. It should be the first port of call for further reading, and its bibliography is sufficient to explore the subject in depth. So rooted in the sources is this excellent introduction to the subject that my efforts to bypass it in this account have sometimes been quite pointless: I would wish in particular to acknowledge that the figures for non-noble property-holding draws on his review, with the addition of estimates by Michel Nassiet, James Woods, and myself.

The pillars of this chapter were regional studies: Marie-Therèse Caron's fine book *La noblesse dans le duché de Bourgogne, 1315–1477* (Lille, 1987) and her article on the Lillois, 'Enquête sur la noblesse du bailliage d'Arras à l'époque de Charles le Téméraire', *Revue du Nord*, 310/87 (1995), 407–26; Jean Gallet's *La seigneurie Bretonne, 1450–1680: L'exemple du Vannetais* (Paris, 1983); Robert Boutruche, *La crise d'une société, seigneurs et paysans du Bordelais pendant la Guerre de Cent Ans* (Paris, 1947); R. Germain, *Les campagnes bourbonnaises à la fin du Moyen Âge* (Clermont-Ferrand, 1987) and his article 'Seigneurie et noblesse en Bourbonnais d'après un dénombrement du ban en 1503', in *Seigneurs et seigneuries au Moyen Âge* (Paris, 1995).

In addition I used J.-M. Constant, *Nobles et paysans en Beauce aux XVIe et XVII siècles* (Lille, 1981); J. Rogozinski, *Power, Caste and Law: Social Conflict in 14th Century Montpellier* (Cambridge, Mass., 1982); J. Wood, *The Nobility of the Election of Bayeux, 1463–1666: Continuity Through Change* (Princeton, 1980); E. Perroy, Social Mobility Among the French *Noblesse* in the Later Middle Ages', *Past and Present*, 21 (1962), 25–38. On urban nobilities, see T. Dutour, *Les élites urbains au Moyen Âge*, (Paris, 1997). I also used Philippe Wolff's 'La noblesse toulousaine: essai sur son histoire médievale', in

P. Contamine (ed.), *La noblesse au Moyen Âge, XIe–XVe siècles: essais à la mémoire de Robert Boutruche* (Paris, 1976); A. Higounet-Nadal, *Familles patriciennes de Périgueux à la fin du Moyen Âge* (Paris, 1983); Marie-Thérèse Lorcin, *Les campagnes de la région lyonnaise aux XIVe et XVe siècle* (Lyon, 1974). The details on Dijon nobles were taken from T. Dutour, 'La noblesse dijonnaise dans la seconde moitié du XIVe siècle (1350–1410)', in P. Contamine, T. Dutour, and B. Schnerb (eds.), *Commerce, finances et société (XI-XVIe siècles): recueil de travaux d'histoire médiévale offert à M. le Professeur Henri Dubois* (Paris, 1993). Remarks on Flanders were drawn from David Nicholas's work, especially *Town and Countryside: Social, Economic and Political Tensions in 14th Century Flanders* (Bruges, 1971).

There is surprisingly little on the cusp of *noblesse* and the official definitions of nobility which emerge out of it: J. Mourier, 'Nobilitas, qui est? Un procès à Tain-l'Hermitage en 1408', *BEC* 142 (1984), 255–69; G. Giordanengo, 'Les roturiers possesseurs de fiefs nobles en Dauphiné aux XIVe et XVe siècles', *Cahiers d'Histoire*, 40 (1970), 319–34. Autrand discusses ennoblement in 'L'image de la noblesse en France à la fin du Moyen Âge: tradition et nouveauté', *Comptes Rendus de l'Académie des Inscriptions et Belles Lettres* (1979), 340–54. My Poitevin examples were taken from R. Favreau, 'La preuve de noblesse en Poitou au XVe siècles d'après les textes', *Bullétin de la Société des Antiquaires de l'Ouest et des Musées de Poitiers*, ser. 4, 5/3 (1960), 618–22. Caron gives some Burgundian examples, and the Norman instances were all from manuscript sources in the *dossiers particuliers* of the Cour des Aides now preserved at Rouen. Jean-Richard Bloch's book on ennoblement is always cited but is now outdated. Although they do not necessarily translate well into the earlier period, the most sophisticated discussions focus on the sixteenth century and later. Arlette Jouanna's thesis has been particularly influential: *L'idée de race en France au XVIe siècle (1498–1614)* (Lille 1976).

There was no space to detail the downward drift in the proportion of nobles who were knighted in the fourteenth and fifteenth century. Contamine's review of this important subject is indispensable: 'Points de vue sur la chevalerie en France à la fin du Moyen Âge', *Francia*, 4 (1976), 254–85. Significant in itself, the subject opens out into a discussion of noble income in the catastrophes of the fourteenth and fifteenth centuries, for a brief overview of which, see Contamine, 'La seigneurie en France à la fin du Moyen Âge: quelques problèmes généraux', in *Seigneurs et seigneuries au Moyen Âge* (Paris, 1995). The debate goes back to Marc Bloch's *Les Caractères originaux de l'histoire rurale française* (Paris, 1964). Particularly important contributions were Guy Bois, *Crise du féodalisme: économie rurale et démographie en Normandie orientale du début du 14e siècle au milieu du 16e siècle* (Paris, 1976); Boutruche, *La dévastation des campagnes pendant la guerre de Cent Ans et la reconstruction agricole de la France* (Paris, 1947); Wood, 'Noblesse et crise de revenus seigneuriaux en France aux XIVe et XVe siècles', in *La Noblesse au Moyen Âge, XIe–XVe siècles: essais à la mémoire de Robert Boutruche* (Paris, 1976). P. Charbonnier, 'La crise de la seigneurie á la fin du Moyen Âge vue de l'autre France', in *Seigneurs et seigneuries au Moyen Âge* (Paris, 1995).

The discussion on noble poverty was strongly informed by Michel Nassiet's *Noblesse et pauvreté: la petite noblesse en Bretagne, XVe–XVIIIe siècles* (Rennes, 1993), and by discussions with Professor Nassiet in May 2002. On women, see M.-T. Caron, 'Mariage et mésalliance: la difficulté d'être femme dans la société nobiliaire', in M. Rouche and J. Heuclin (eds.), *La femme au Moyen Âge* (Maubeuge, 1990), a useful collection.

There is a vast bibliography on chivalry. The lively debate on the relationship between noblesse, chivalry, and warfare can be followed in M. Keen, *Chivalry* (New Haven, 1984) and id., 'Some Late Medieval Ideas about Nobility', in his *Nobles, Knights and Men-at-Arms in the Middle Ages* (London, 1986); Ellery Schalk, *From Valor to Pedigree: Ideas of Nobility in France in the 16th and 17th Century* (Princeton, 1986). On warfare itself it is hard to avoid Contamine's massive *Guerre, état et société à la fin du Moyen Âge: études sur les armées du roi de France, 1337–1494* (Paris, 1972), but see also J. B. Henneman, 'The Military Class and the French Monarchy in the Late Middle Ages', *American Historical Review*, 83 (1978), 946–65; R. W. Kaeuper, *War, Justice and Public Order* (Oxford, 1988); id., *Chivalry and Violence in Medieval Europe* (Oxford, 1999). I also plundered Bertrand Schnerb's wonderful *Enguerrand de Bournonville et les siens: un lignage noble du Bourbonnais aux XIVe et XVe siècles* (Paris, 1997).

One argument of this chapter is that the *noblesse* was the political class par excellence, so politics cannot be removed from any account of it. Treatments of late medieval French politics tend to centre on the monarchical or princely state, and the assumption that this is a valid approach to the nobility itself has hardly been challenged. The best introduction is still P. S. Lewis, *Later Medieval France: The Polity* (London, 1968). For noble self-organization, see J. R. Major, ' "Bastard Feudalism" and the Kiss: Changing Social Mores in Late Medieval and Early Modern France', *JIH* 17 (1987), 509–35; G. Prosser, ' "Decayed Feudalism" and "Royal Clientèles": Royal Office and Magnate Service in the 15th Century', in C. Allmand (ed.), *War Government and Power in Late Medieval France* (Liverpool, 2000); P. Charbonnier, *Guillaume de Murol: un petit seigneur auvergnat au début du XVe siècle* (Clermont-Ferrand, 1973).

Some primary sources used

Contemporary writings

Bonet (Bovet), Honoré, *The Tree of Battles*, ed. G. W. Coopland (Liverpool, 1949).

Charny, Geoffroy de, *The Book of Chivalry*, ed. R. W. Kaeuper and E. Kennedy (Philadelphia, 1996).

Chartier, A, *Le curial*, ed. F. Heuckenkamp (Halle, 1988; repr. Geneva, 1974).

—— *Le quadrilogue invectif*, ed. E. Droz, rev. edn. (Paris, 1950); 15th-century Eng. trans. ed. M. S. Blayney, Early English Text Society, no. 270 (1974).

Deschamps, E., *Œuvres complètes*, ed. marquis de Queux de Saint-Hilaire and G. Raynaud, 11 vols. (Paris, 1878–1904).

Gerson, J., *Œuvres complètes*, ed. P. Glorieux, 10 vols. (Paris, 1960–73).

Juvénal des Ursins, J., *Écrits politiques*, ed. P. S. Lewis, 2 vols. (Paris, 1978–85).

Meschinot, J., *Les lunettes des princes*, ed. C. Martineau-Genieys (Geneva, 1972).

Mézières, P. de, *Le songe du veil pelerin*, ed. G. W. Coopland, 2 vols. (Cambridge, 1969).

Montreuil, J. de, *L'œuvre historique et polémique*, in his *Opera*, ed. N. Grévy, E. Ornato, and G. Ouy, 2 vols. (Turin, 1963–75).

—— '*Le Tragicum argumentum de miserabili statu regni Franciae de François de Montebelluna (1357)*', ed. A. Vernet, *ABSHF* (1962–3), 101–63.

Pisan, C. de, *Le livre des fais et bonnes meurs du sage roy charles V*, ed. D. Solente, 2 vols. (Paris, 1936–40).

—— *Le livre du corps de policie*, ed. R. H. Lucas (Geneva, 1967); trans. K. L. Forham as *The Book of the Body Politic* (Cambridge, 1994).

—— *The Book of Deeds of Arms and Chivalry*, ed. S. and C. Willard (University Park, Pa., 1999).

Pons, N. (ed.), *'L'honneur de la couronne de France': quatre libelles contre les Anglais (vers 1418–vers 1429)* (Paris, 1990).

Le rosier des guerres, ed. M. Diamantberger (Paris, 1925).

Le songe du vergier, ed. M. Schnerb-Lièvre, 2 vols. (Paris, 1982).

'Le songe véritable, pamphlet politique d'un Parisien du XVe siècle', ed. H. Moranvillé, *Mémoires de la Société de l'Histoire de Paris et de l'Île-de-France*, 17 (1890), 217–438.

Royal Acts (ordonnances and letters)

Cazelles, R., 'Lettres closes, lettres "de par le roy" de Philippe de Valois', *ABSHF 1956–7* (1958), 61–225.

Coville, A. (ed.), *L'ordonnance cabochienne (26–27 mai 1413)* (Paris, 1891).

Delisle, J. (ed.), *Mandements et actes divers de Charles V (1364–1380) recueillis dans les collections de la Bibliothèque Nationale* (Paris, 1874).

Ordonnances des rois de France de la troisième race, 22 vols., ed. E. L. de Laurière and D. Secousse (Paris, 1723–1849).

Registres du Trésor des Chartes, iii: règne de Philippe de Valois, ed. J. Viard and A. Vallet, 3 vols. (Paris, 1978–84).

Vaesen, J. (ed.), *Lettres de Louis XI, roi de France*, 11 vols. (Paris, 1883–1909).

Collections of documents

Douet d'Arcq, L., *Choix de pièces inédites relatives au règne de Charles VI*, 2 vols. (Paris, 1863–4).

—— *Comptes de l'Hôtel des Rois de France aux XIVe et XVe siècles* (Paris, 1865).

—— *Nouveau recueil des comptes de l'Argenterie des Rois de France* (Paris, 1884).

Secousse, D., *Mémoire pour servir à l'histoire de Charles II, roi de Navarre et comte d'Evreux, surnommé le Mauvais*, 2 vols. (Paris, 1755–8).

Contemporary histories and chronicles, including modern commentaries

Basin, T., *Histoire de Charles VII*, ed. and trans. C. Samaran, 2 vols. (Paris, 1933–44).

—— *Histoire de Louis XI*, ed. and trans. C. Samaran, 3 vols. (Paris, 1963–72).

Baye, N. de, *Journal de Nicolas de Baye, greffier du Parlement de Paris, 1400–1417*, ed. A. Tuetey, 2 vols. (Paris, 1885–8).

Boucquey, D., 'Enguerran de Monstrelet, historien trop longtemps oublié', *Publications du Centre Européen des Études Bourguignons*, 31 (1991), 113–25.

Chabaud, F., 'Les "Mémoires" de Philippe de Commynes: un "Miroir aux princes"?', *Francia*, 19 (1992), 95–114.

Chartier, J., *Chronique de Charles VII, roi de France*, ed. V. de Viriville, 3 vols. (Paris, 1858).

Chastelain, G., *Œuvres*, ed. Baron Kervyn de Lettenhove, 8 vols. (Brussels, 1863–8).

La Chronique de bon duc Loys de Bourbon, ed. A. M. Chazaud (Paris, 1876).

Chronique des quatre premiers Valois (1327–1393), ed. S. Luce (Paris, 1862).

Chronique des règnes de Jean II et de Charles V, ed. R. Delachenal, 4 vols. (Paris, 1910–20).

Commynes, Philippe de, *Mémoires*, ed. J. Calmette, 3 vols. (Paris, 1964–5); trans. A. R. Scoble as *The Memoirs of Philip de Commines*, 2 vols. (London, 1855–6).

Contamine, P., 'Un traité' politique inédit de la fin du XVe siècle', *ABSHF 1983–4* (1986), 139–71.

Dufournet, J., *La vie de Philippe de Commynes* (Paris, 1969).

Fauquembergue, C. de, *Journal de Clément de Fauquembergue*, ed. A. Tuetey, 3 vols, (Paris, 1903–15).

Froissart, J., *Chroniques*, ed. K. de Lettenhove, 26 vols. (Brussels, 1867–79); trans. T. Johnes, 12 vols. (London, 1808), 2 vols. edn London 1859.

Les grandes chroniques de France, ed. J. Viard, 10 vols. (Paris, 1920–53).

Grévy-Pons, N., 'Qui est l'auteur de la chronique latine du règne de Charles VI dite du religieux de Saint-Denis?', *BEC* 134 (1976), 85–102.

Guenée, B., 'Documents insérés et documents abrégés dans la chronique du religieux de Saint-Denis', *BEC* 152/2 (1994), 375–428.

—— *Un roi et son historien: vingt études sur le règne de Charles VI et la Chronique du religieux de Saint-Denis* (Paris, 2000).

—— 'Tragédie et histoire chez le religieux de Saint-Denis', *BEC* 150/2 (1992), 223–45.

Journal d'un bourgeois de Paris (1405–49), ed. A. Tuetey (Paris, 1881), trans. as *A Parisian Journal, 1405–1449*, ed. J. Shirley (Oxford, 1968).

Juvenal des Ursins, J., *Histoire de Charles VI*, ed. J.-F. Michaud and J.-J. Poujoulat, Nouvelle Collection des Mémoires, vol. ii (Paris, 1857).

Monstrelet, E. de, *Chroniques*, ed. L. Douet d'Arcq, 6 vols. (Paris, 1857–62); trans. T. Johnes, 2 vols. (London, 1840).

Le religieux de Saint-Denis, *Chronique de Charles VI*, ed. and trans. L. P. Bellaguet, 6 vols. (Paris, 1839–52).

Venette, J. de, *The Chronicle of Jean de Venette*, ed. R. A. Newhall, trans. J. Birdsall (New York, 1953).

Chronology

1180 Accession of Philip II Augustus, 19 September (crowned November 1179)

1200 Treaty of Péronne, January; treaty of Le Gonlet, 22 May

1202 Appeal to Philip by Hugh de Lusignan against King John

1204 Philip's conquest of Normandy

1208 Declaration of the first Albigensian Crusade by Pope Innocent III, 10 March

1214 Battle of Bouvines, 27 July

1218 Death of Simon de Montfort at the siege of Toulouse, 25 June; Prince Louis (VIII) takes over the crusade in Toulouse, December

1223 Death of Philip II and accession of Louis VIII, 14 July

1226 Death of Louis VIII and accession of Louis IX (aged 12), 8 November; regency of Blanche of Castille (1226–34, 1248–52)

1229 Treaty of Paris, the submission of Raymond VII of Toulouse, 12 April

1248 First crusade of Louis IX starts, June

1254 Return of Louis IX from crusade, and captivity, 7 September; great ordinance of Louis IX, December

1259 Peace of Paris; Henry III pays homage to Louis IX for the duchy of Aquitaine (Gascony)

1270 Second crusade of Louis IX; his death, 25 August; accession of Philip III, le Hardi

1271 Death of Alphonse of Poitiers without direct heir, 21 August

1278 Execution of Pierre de la Brosse

1283 Aragonese crusade

1285 Death of Philip III and accession of Philip IV, le Bel, 5 October

1293 Edward I summoned to his court by Philip IV, 27 October

1294 Annexation of Gascony by Philip IV, 19 May

1297 Devaluation of French coinage

1302 Battle of Courtrai, Flemish victory, 11 July

1303 Nogaret's denunciation of Boniface VIII, March; great reform ordinance, March; restoration of Gascony to Edward I (treaty of Paris), 20 May; attack on Boniface VIII at Anagni, 7 September

1305	First minting of the silver *gros*, May; peace of Athis-sur-Orge with the Flemish, 23 June
1306	Jews expelled
1307	Arrest of the Templars, October
1310	Lyon occupied (confirmed 1312)
1312	Suppression of the Templars, April; treaty of Pontoise, annexation of Lille and Douai by Philip IV
1314	Leagues of nobles; death of Philip IV and accession of Louis X, 29 November
1314–17	Tempest, dearth, and famine
1315	Hanging of Enguerrand de Marigny, chamberlain to Philip IV, 30 April
1316	Severe famine; death of Louis X, 5 June, regency of Philippe, count of Poitiers; John I born 5 November, died 19 November; accession of Philip V, le Long, 19 November
1320	The 'Pastoureaux' movement
1321–2	Slaughter of the Jews and lepers
1322	Death of Philip V and accession of Charles IV, le Bel, 2/3 January
1324–5	War of Saint Sardos
1328	Death of Charles IV, 1 February; regency and accession of Philip VI, 2 April; battle of Cassel and defeat of Flemish rebels, 29 May
1337	Beginning of Hundred Years War
1339	First meeting of the estates of Normandy
1341	Battle of Sluys, 24 June; War of Succession in Brittany; introduction of the salt tax (*gabelle*)
1346	Battle of Crécy, 26 August
1347	Edward III takes Calais, August; royal law on the conservation of woodlands
1348–50	Black Death
1349	France acquires the Dauphiné, 31 March; Montpellier acquired
1350	Death of Philip VI and accession of John II, le Bon, 22 August; execution of Constable Raoul de Brienne, count of Eu, 18 November
1351	Royal law aiming to limit the consequences of the Black Death
1354	Murder of Charles d'Espagne, constable of France, by Charles

II of Navarre, 8 January; estates of Languedoil at Paris, 30 November–28 December

1355 First English *chevauchée* in Languedoc

1356 Arrest of Charles of Navarre and execution of Harcourt, 5 April; battle of Poitiers and capture of John II, 19 September

1357 Opening of the estates, Paris, 5 February; ordinance of the estates, 3 March; *réformateurs-généraux*, 8 March; truce of Bordeaux for two years between France and England, 9 April; escape of the King of Navarre, 9 November

1358 Meeting of the estates at Paris, February; murder of the marshals, 22 February; meeting of the estates at Compiègne, 1 May; the Jacquerie in the Beauvaisis and elsewhere, 28 May–10 June; murder of Étienne Marcel, *prévôt des marchans* of Paris, 27 July; the dauphin Charles re-enters Paris, August

1359 End of Anglo-French truce, April; treaty of London rejected by the dauphin, May (and by the estates, 25 June); treaty of Pontoise between regent and Navarre, August; Lancaster's *chevauchée* in Artois and Picardy, October; Edward III's siege of Reims, December

1360 *Chevauchée* of Edward III in Burgundy and Île-de-France, January–April; treaty of Brétigny confirmed 8 May (modified, Calais, 24 Oct.; release of John II); ordinance of Compiègne, promulgating sound money in the form of the 'franc', 5 Dec.; permanent taxes, *aides* and *gabelle*; routiers (the Tard-Venus) take Pont-Saint-Esprit

1361 Death of Philippe de Rouvre, last Capetian duke of Burgundy, 21 November; new rupture between John II and Charles of Navarre; return of the Black Death

1362 Defeat of the royal army by the routiers at Brignais, April

1363 Estates of Languedoil at Amiens: authorization of the *fouage*, December; John II returns to captivity in England, December

1364 Death of John II at London, accession of Charles V, le Sage, 18 April; battle of Cocherel (defeat of Navarre by du Guesclin), 16 May; battle of Auray (defeat of Charles de Blois), 29 September

1369 Philip the Bold, duke of Burgundy, marries Marguerite, heiress of Flanders, 13 June; estates approve the reception of Gascon appeals; war with England resumes

1370 *Chevauchée* of Robert Knowles

1373 *Chevauchée* of John of Gaunt; war in Brittany

1374	Ordinances on the majority of kings, regency, apanages, army, coinage, and taxes, August
1375	Famine; Anglo-French truce agreed at Bruges, July
1377	War with England resumes
1378–82	Anti-tax risings in Languedoc, the Tuchin movement
1380	*Chevauchée* of Buckingham; death of Charles V and accession of Charles VI (aged 12), 16 September
1382	Revolt of the Harelle at Rouen, 24 February; Maillotin rebellion in Paris, 1 March; battle of Roosebeke, 27 November
1384	Death of Louis de Male, count of Flanders, 30 January
1387	Death of Charles II of Navarre, 1 January
1388	Charles VI assumes power, 3 November
1392	Charles VI suffers first bout of insanity, 5 August
1396	Richard II of England marries Isabella of France (aged 6), 12 March; battle of Nicopolis, 25 September
1399	Death of John IV, duke of Brittany
1401	Outbreak of Burgundian–Orléanist violence
1404	Death of Philip the Bold, duke of Burgundy, 26/7 April
1407	Murder of Louis, duke of Orléans, 23 November
1408	Return of John the Fearless to Paris, 28 February
1410	League of Gien marks formation of the Armagnac party, 15 April
1411	Start of Burgundian–Armagnac wars
1413	Cabochien movement in Paris, April–August; Cabochien ordinance, 26–7 May; Armagnac control of Paris, August
1415	Henry V captures Harfleur, 18 September; battle of Agincourt, 25 October
1416	Death of John, duke of Berry, 15 June
1417	Start of the English invasion of Normandy, June; Burgundian government at Troyes, November
1418	Burgundian control of Paris, 29 May; massacre of Armagnacs and others, June; English start siege of Rouen, June; creation of the Armagnac Parlement of Poitiers, 21 September (to 1436)
1419	Capitulation of Rouen, 2 January; English entry, 19 January; murder of John the Fearless, duke of Burgundy, at Montereau-fault-Yonne, 10 September
1420	Creation of Lyon fairs, 9 February; treaty of Troyes, 2 May; creation of the Parlement of Toulouse

1421	Battle of Baugé, 22 May
1421–2	Very high prices due to monetary crisis and linked to dearth
1422	Death of Henry V, 31 August; death of Charles VI and accessions of Charles VII, le Victorieux, and Henry II (VI) of Lancaster, 21 October
1423	Battle of Crévant, near Auxerre, July
1424	Battle of Verneuil, 17 August
1428	Estates General at Chinon; Battle of the Herrings at Janville (Beauce), 12–13 February; start of siege of Orléans, 12 October
1429	Meeting of Charles VII and Jeanne d'Arc, 8 March; relief of Orléans by Jeanne, 8 May; capture of Jargeau, 12 June; capture of Beaugency, 15 June; battle of Patay, 18 June; coronation of Charles VII at Reims, 17 July; failure before Paris, 8 September
1430	Last campaign of Jeanne d'Arc, April–May; her capture at Compiègne, 23 May
1431	Trial, February–March, and execution, 30 May, of Jeanne d'Arc at Rouen
1435	Treaty of Arras with Burgundy, 21 September
1436	Recovery of Paris by Charles VII, 13 April
1438	Famine; Pragmatic Sanction of Bourges, 7 July
1439	Estates General of Orléans, 25 September; ordinance of Orléans, 2 November; Jacques Cœur *argentier* to the king
1440	Revolt of the Praguerie, February–July
1441	Capture of Pontoise from the English, 29 September
1442	Conference of the princes at Nevers, failure of new League, February–March
1444	Truce of Tours with the English, 28 May
1445	Ordinances on military reform, *compagnies de l'ordonnance*, 29 January–16 May
1447	Legislation to allow lords to let long-uncultivated land despite the rights of old tenants
1448	Creation of the *francs-archers*
1449	English seizure of Fougères, end of the truce, 24/5 March; French recovery of Rouen, 29 October
1449–53	Military recovery of Normandy and Guyenne
1450	Battle of Formigny, 15 April; recovery of Caen, 24 June
1451	30 June, French recovery of Bordeaux, 30 June, and of Bayonne, 21 August; arrest of Jacques Coeur, 31 July

1452	English recovery of Bordeaux, 22 October
1453	Battle of Castillon, 17 July; final recovery of Bordeaux, end of English Gascony, 19 October
1456	The dauphin Louis begins five-year stay in lands of Philip the Good
1458	Jean II, duke of Alençon, convicted of treason, 10 October
1461	Death of Charles VII, accession of Louis XI, 22 July
1462	Creation of the Parlement of Bordeaux
1463	Repurchase of the Somme towns by Louis XI; creation of a fourth fair at Lyon on the same date as that of Geneva, 8 March
1465	League and War of the Public Weal, April–October; battle of Montlhéry, 16 July; treaty of Conflans, 5 October
1466	Creation of silk manufacture at Lyon, then transferred to Tours
1468	Treaty of Péronne, 14 October; Estates General at Tours
1472	Death of Charles of France, brother of Louis XI, 28 May; siege of Beauvais by Charles the Bold raised, 10 July
1473	Murder of Jean V of Armagnac at Lectoure, 5 March
1475	Military coalition of Edward IV and Charles the Bold comes to nothing; truce of Picquigny, 29 August; execution for treason of Louis of Luxembourg, count of Saint-Pol, 19 December
1476	Defeat of Charles the Bold at Grandson, 2 March; battle of Morat, 22 June
1477	Death of Charles the Bold, last Valois duke of Burgundy, at the battle of Nancy, 5 January; execution of Jacques d'Armagnac, duke of Nemours, 4 August
1479	Battle of Guinegatte, August
1480	Death of René of Anjou, count of Provence and titular king of Naples, Sicily, and Jerusalem at Aix, 10 July
1481	Death of Charles, count of Maine, royal annexation of Provence, 25 Jan.
1481–3	Harsh taxation
1482	Severe starvation; Louis XI's attempts to create a maritime company and legislation to allow nobles to trade
1483	Death of Louis XI and accession of Charles VIII (aged 13), 30 August; 'regency' of his sister Anne, dame de Beaujeu
1484	Estates General opens at Tours, 15 January

1484–5 Guerre Folle

1488 Death of Francis II, last Montfort duke of Brittany; battle of Saint-Aubin du Cormier, 28 July; treaty of Sablé with Brittany, 20 August

1491 Charles VIII's marriage to Anne of Brittany, 6 December

1492 English invasion; treaty of Étaples (Charles agrees to pay pension to Henry VII), 3 November

1493 Treaty of Barcelona (Charles VIII abandons Cerdagne and Roussillon to Ferdinand and Isabella), 19 January; treaty of Senlis with Maximilian and Archduke Philip (Charles VIII abandons Artois, Franche-Comté, Charolais to Habsburgs), 23 May

1494 Charles VIII invades Italy and claims Naples, August

1495 Charles created emperor of Constantinople by Pope Alexander VI, January; solemn entry into Naples, 12 May; battle of Fornovo, 6 July

1498 Death of Charles VIII and accession of Louis XII, 7 April

1499 Louis XII's marriage to Anne of Brittany, 9 January

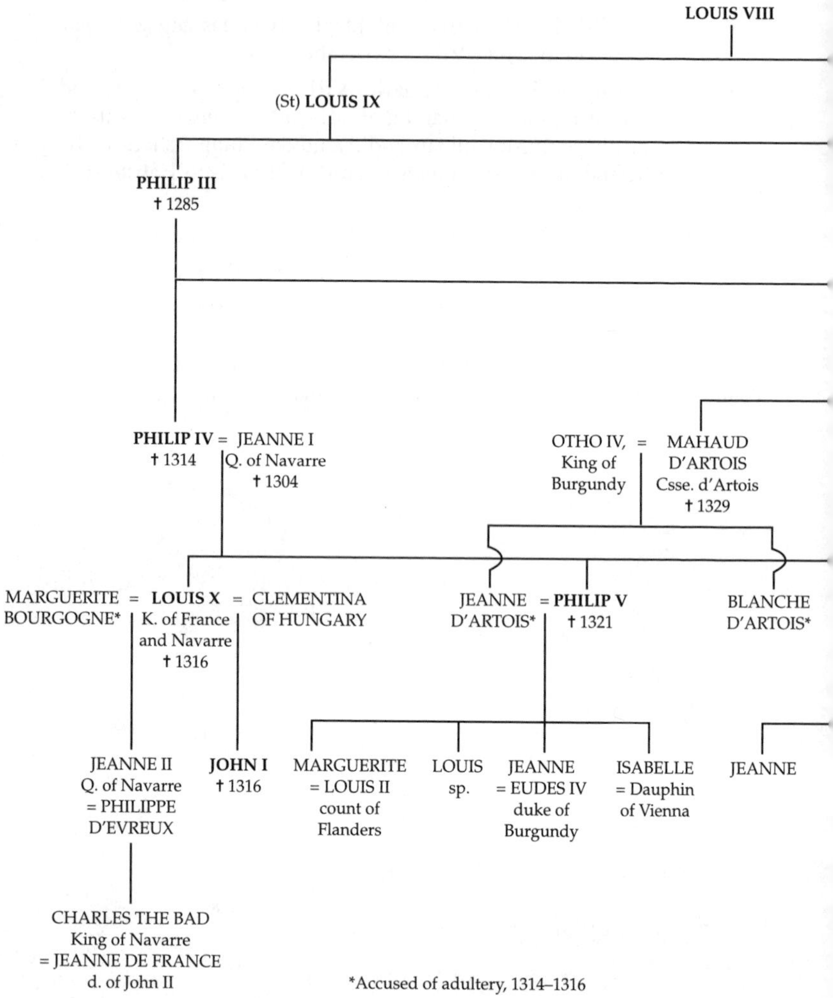

1 The royal succession 1316–1328.

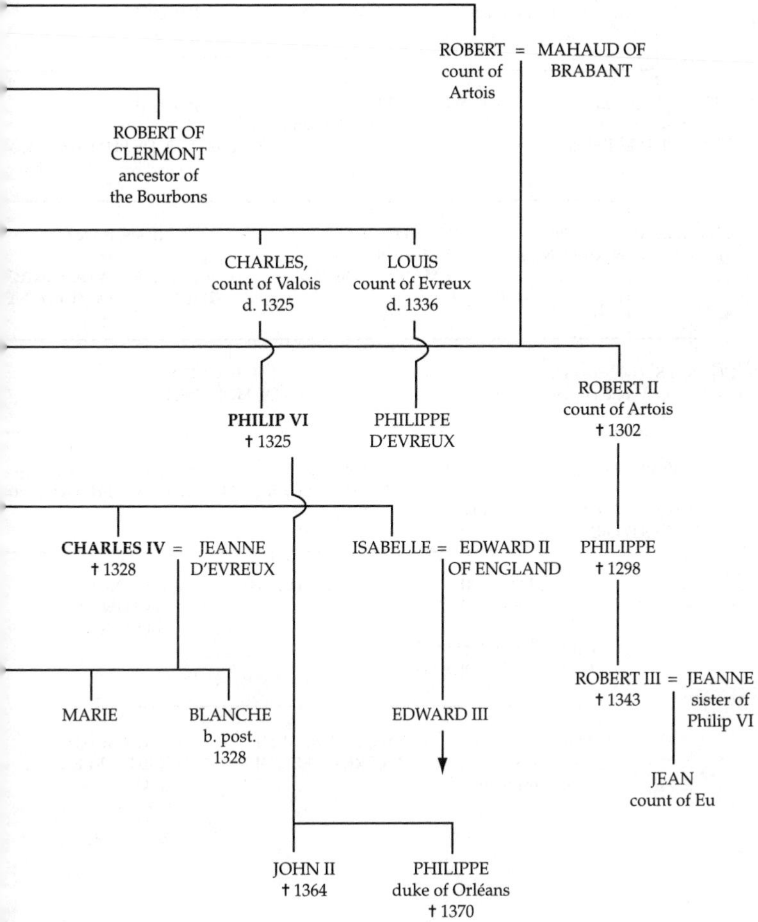
ROBERT count of Artois = MAHAUD OF BRABANT
ROBERT OF CLERMONT ancestor of the Bourbons
CHARLES, count of Valois d. 1325
LOUIS count of Evreux d. 1336
PHILIP VI † 1325
PHILIPPE D'EVREUX
ROBERT II count of Artois † 1302
CHARLES IV † 1328 = JEANNE D'EVREUX
ISABELLE = EDWARD II OF ENGLAND
PHILIPPE † 1298
MARIE
BLANCHE b. post. 1328
EDWARD III
ROBERT III † 1343 = JEANNE sister of Philip VI
JEAN count of Eu
JOHN II † 1364
PHILIPPE duke of Orléans † 1370

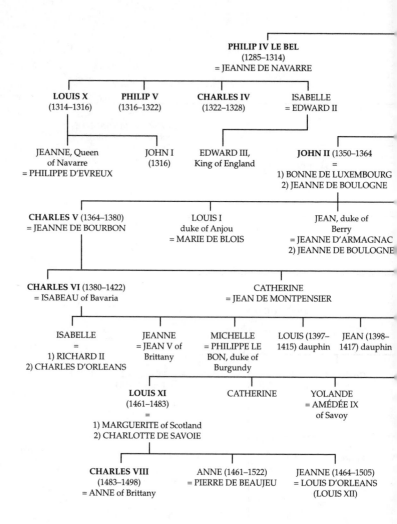

- **PHILIP IV LE BEL** (1285–1314) = JEANNE DE NAVARRE
  - **LOUIS X** (1314–1316)
    - JEANNE, Queen of Navarre = PHILIPPE D'EVREUX
    - JOHN I (1316)
  - **PHILIP V** (1316–1322)
  - **CHARLES IV** (1322–1328)
  - ISABELLE = EDWARD II
    - EDWARD III, King of England
- **JOHN II** (1350–1364 = 1) BONNE DE LUXEMBOURG 2) JEANNE DE BOULOGNE
  - **CHARLES V** (1364–1380) = JEANNE DE BOURBON
    - **CHARLES VI** (1380–1422) = ISABEAU of Bavaria
      - ISABELLE = 1) RICHARD II 2) CHARLES D'ORLEANS
      - JEANNE = JEAN V of Brittany
      - MICHELLE = PHILIPPE LE BON, duke of Burgundy
      - LOUIS (1397–1415) dauphin
      - JEAN (1398–1417) dauphin
        - **LOUIS XI** (1461–1483) = 1) MARGUERITE of Scotland 2) CHARLOTTE DE SAVOIE
          - **CHARLES VIII** (1483–1498) = ANNE of Brittany
          - ANNE (1461–1522) = PIERRE DE BEAUJEU
          - JEANNE (1464–1505) = LOUIS D'ORLEANS (LOUIS XII)
        - CATHERINE
        - YOLANDE = AMÉDÉE IX of Savoy
    - CATHERINE = JEAN DE MONTPENSIER
  - LOUIS I duke of Anjou = MARIE DE BLOIS
  - JEAN, duke of Berry = JEANNE D'ARMAGNAC 2) JEANNE DE BOULOGNE

2 Capetians and Valois.

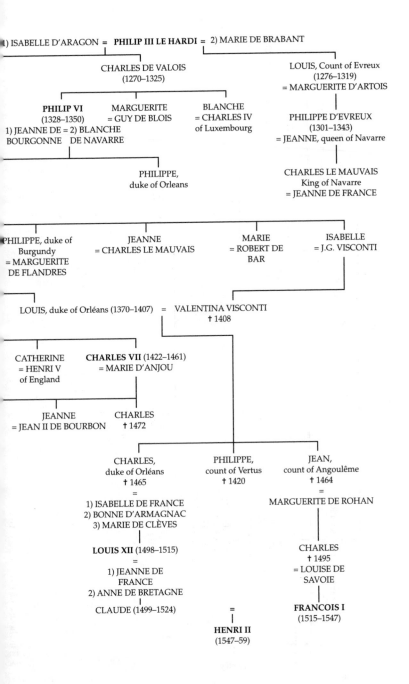

1) ISABELLE D'ARAGON = **PHILIP III LE HARDI** = 2) MARIE DE BRABANT

CHARLES DE VALOIS
(1270–1325)

LOUIS, Count of Evreux
(1276–1319)
= MARGUERITE D'ARTOIS

PHILIP VI
(1328–1350)
1) JEANNE DE BOURGONNE = 2) BLANCHE DE NAVARRE

MARGUERITE
= GUY DE BLOIS

BLANCHE
= CHARLES IV
of Luxembourg

PHILIPPE D'EVREUX
(1301–1343)
= JEANNE, queen of Navarre

PHILIPPE,
duke of Orleans

CHARLES LE MAUVAIS
King of Navarre
= JEANNE DE FRANCE

PHILIPPE, duke of Burgundy
= MARGUERITE DE FLANDRES

JEANNE
= CHARLES LE MAUVAIS

MARIE
= ROBERT DE BAR

ISABELLE
= J.G. VISCONTI

LOUIS, duke of Orléans (1370–1407) = VALENTINA VISCONTI
† 1408

CATHERINE
= HENRI V
of England

CHARLES VII (1422–1461)
= MARIE D'ANJOU

JEANNE
= JEAN II DE BOURBON

CHARLES
† 1472

CHARLES,
duke of Orléans
† 1465
=
1) ISABELLE DE FRANCE
2) BONNE D'ARMAGNAC
3) MARIE DE CLÈVES

PHILIPPE,
count of Vertus
† 1420

JEAN,
count of Angoulême
† 1464
=
MARGUERITE DE ROHAN

LOUIS XII (1498–1515)
=
1) JEANNE DE FRANCE
2) ANNE DE BRETAGNE

CHARLES
† 1495
= LOUISE DE SAVOIE

CLAUDE (1499–1524) = **FRANCOIS I** (1515–1547)

HENRI II
(1547–59)

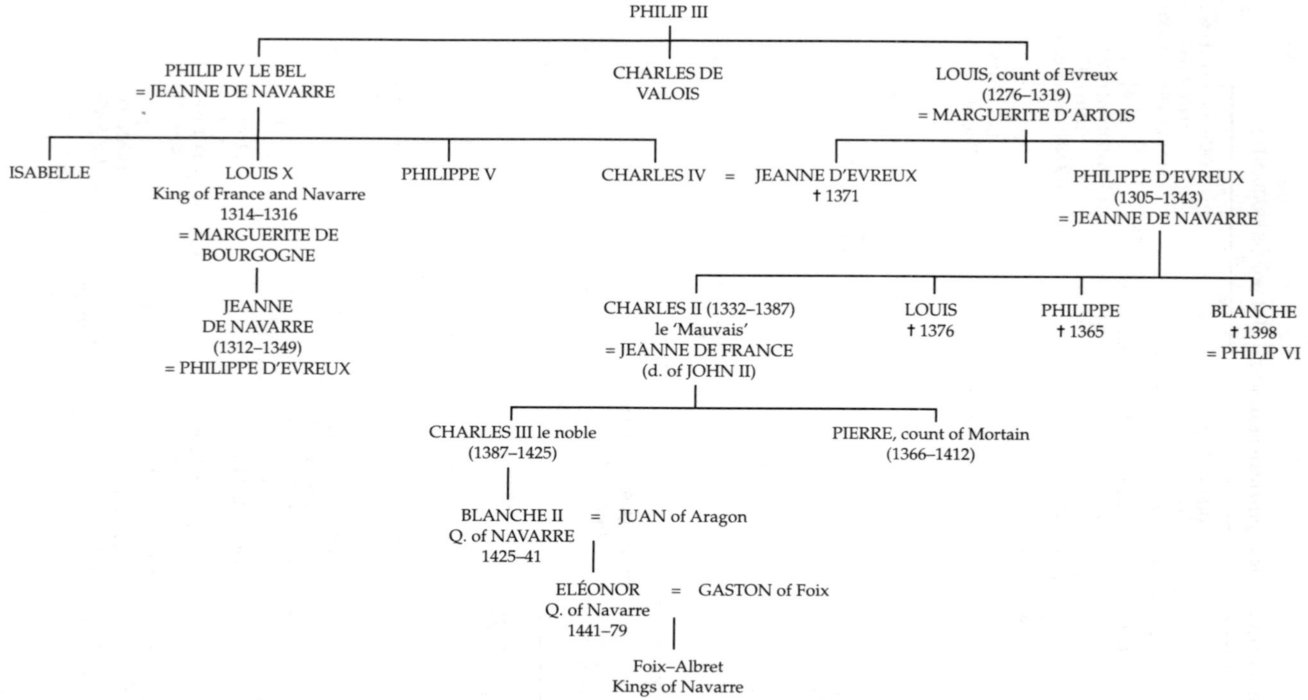

3 The house of Evreux-Navarre.

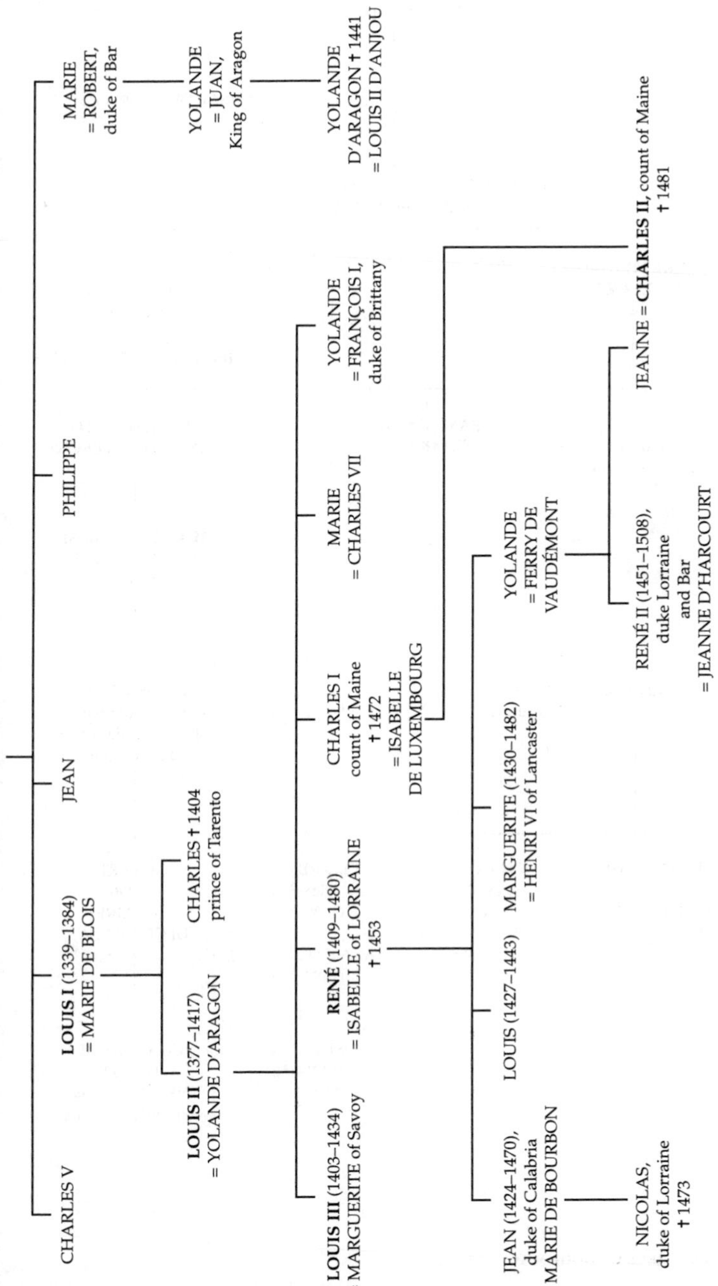

4 The house of Anjou-Provence.

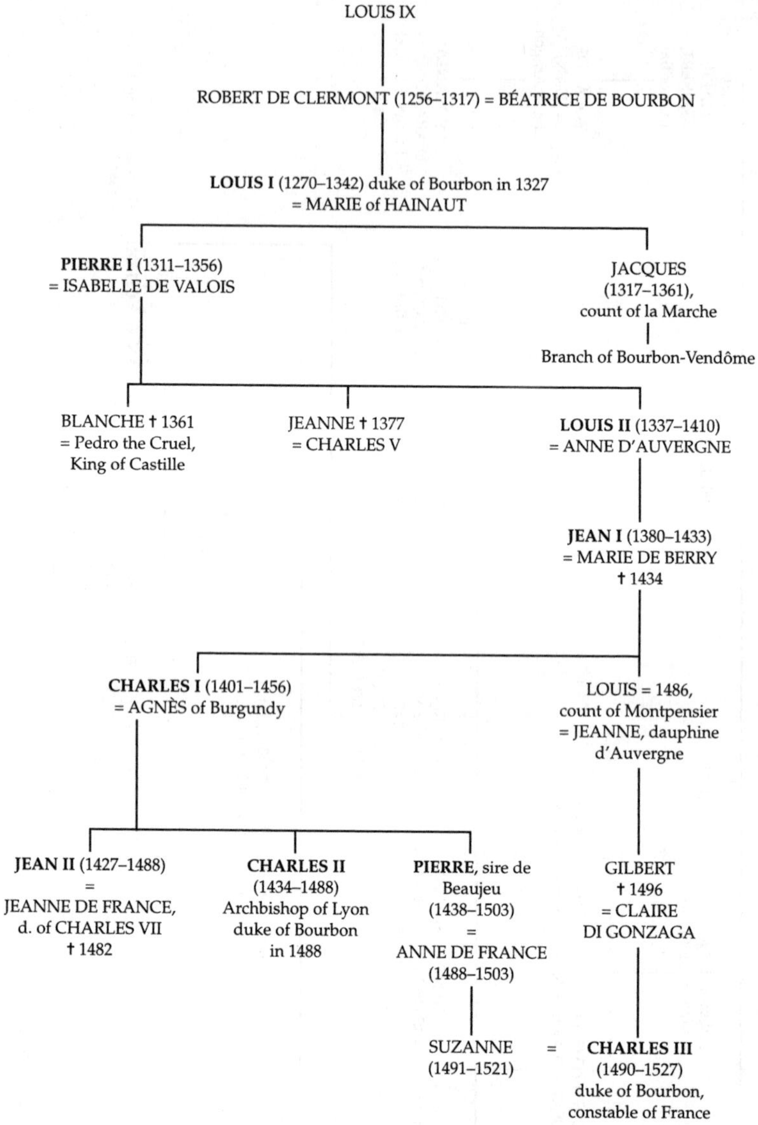
LOUIS IX
ROBERT DE CLERMONT (1256–1317) = BÉATRICE DE BOURBON
LOUIS I (1270–1342) duke of Bourbon in 1327
= MARIE of HAINAUT
PIERRE I (1311–1356)
= ISABELLE DE VALOIS
JACQUES
(1317–1361),
count of la Marche
Branch of Bourbon-Vendôme
BLANCHE † 1361
= Pedro the Cruel,
King of Castille
JEANNE † 1377
= CHARLES V
LOUIS II (1337–1410)
= ANNE D'AUVERGNE
JEAN I (1380–1433)
= MARIE DE BERRY
† 1434
CHARLES I (1401–1456)
= AGNÈS of Burgundy
LOUIS = 1486,
count of Montpensier
= JEANNE, dauphine
d'Auvergne
JEAN II (1427–1488)
=
JEANNE DE FRANCE,
d. of CHARLES VII
† 1482
CHARLES II
(1434–1488)
Archbishop of Lyon
duke of Bourbon
in 1488
PIERRE, sire de
Beaujeu
(1438–1503)
=
ANNE DE FRANCE
(1488–1503)
GILBERT
† 1496
= CLAIRE
DI GONZAGA
SUZANNE
(1491–1521)
=
CHARLES III
(1490–1527)
duke of Bourbon,
constable of France

5 The dukes of Bourbon.

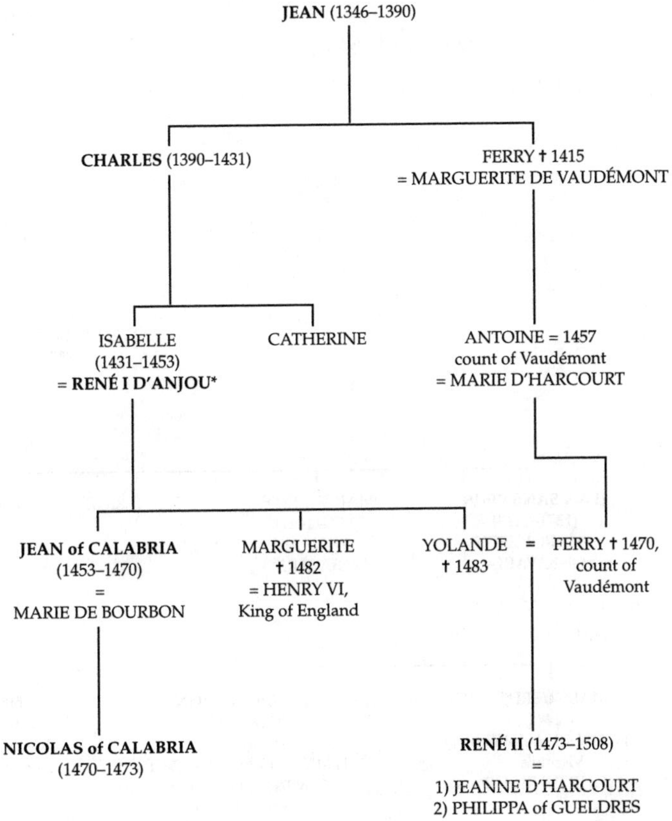

*Duke of Lorraine in his wife's right
(see also Table 4)

6 The dukes of Lorraine.

- JEAN LE BON
  - 2) **PHILIPPE LE HARDI** = (1342–1404)
    - **JEAN SANS PEUR** (1371–1419) = MARGUERITE OF BAVARIA
      - MARGUERITE = 1442
        1) = LOUIS, dauphin of Viennois
        2) = ARTHUR DE RICHEMONT
      - **PHILIPPE LE BON** (1396–1467) =
        1) MICHELLE DE FRANCE
        2) BONNE D'ARTOIS (widow of his uncle Philippe of Rethel)
        3) ISABELLE of PORTUGAL
        - **CHARLES LE TEMERAIRE** (1433–1477) = 1) CATHERINE DE FRANCE 2) ISABELLE DE BOURBON 3) MARGARET OF YORK
          - MARIE of Burgundy (1457–1482)
            - PHILIPPE LE BEAU d. 1506 = Juana of Castile
              - Emperor Charles V
      - ANNE † 1432 = JOHN, duke of Bedford
    - MARGUERITE (1374–1441) = WILLIAM OF BAVARIA
    - CATHERINE
    - BONNE

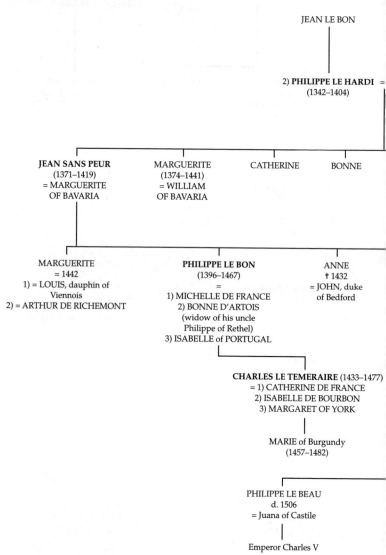

7 The Valois house of Burgundy.

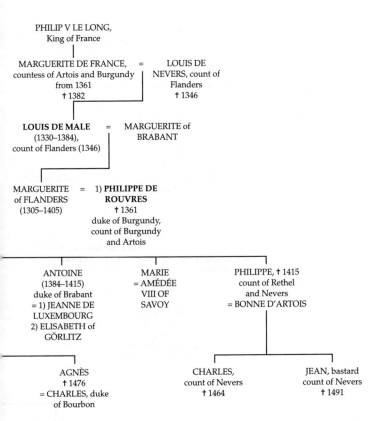

PHILIP V LE LONG,
King of France

MARGUERITE DE FRANCE,
countess of Artois and Burgundy
from 1361
† 1382
=
LOUIS DE
NEVERS, count of
Flanders
† 1346

LOUIS DE MALE
(1330–1384),
count of Flanders (1346)
=
MARGUERITE of
BRABANT

MARGUERITE
of FLANDERS
(1305–1405)
=
1) **PHILIPPE DE
ROUVRES**
† 1361
duke of Burgundy,
count of Burgundy
and Artois

ANTOINE
(1384–1415)
duke of Brabant
= 1) JEANNE DE
LUXEMBOURG
2) ELISABETH of
GÖRLITZ

MARIE
= AMÉDÉE
VIII OF
SAVOY

PHILIPPE, † 1415
count of Rethel
and Nevers
= BONNE D'ARTOIS

AGNÈS
† 1476
= CHARLES, duke
of Bourbon

CHARLES,
count of Nevers
† 1464

JEAN, bastard
count of Nevers
† 1491

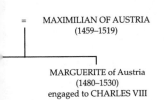

= MAXIMILIAN OF AUSTRIA
(1459–1519)

MARGUERITE of Austria
(1480–1530)
engaged to CHARLES VIII

MARIE DE SÉGUR-COMBORN = 1) **ARTHUR II**
vicomtesse de Limoges (1305–1312)

JEAN III
(1312–1341)

JEANNE D'AVAUGOUR-PENTHIÈVRE = GUY
† 1331

JEANNE DE PENTHIÈVRE = **CHARLES DE BLOIS**
† 1384 (1341–1364)

MARGUERITE DE CLISSON = 5 children including
JEAN DE PENTHIÈVRE
† 1404

several children including
OLIVIER DE PENTHIÈVRE
† 1433
= ISABELLE of Burgundy,
d. of JOHN THE FEARLESS

FRANÇOIS I
(1442–1450)
= 1) YOLANDE D'ANJOU
2) ISABEAU of Scotland

MARGUERITE
= FRANÇOIS II

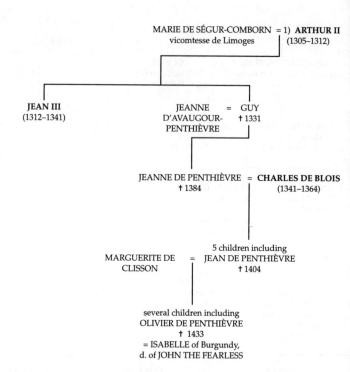

8 The dukes of Brittany.

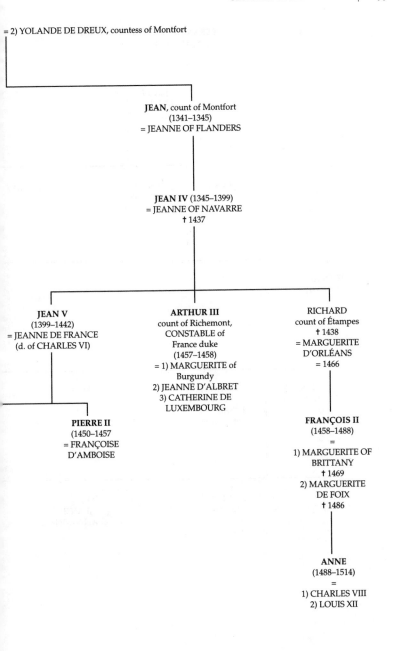

= 2) YOLANDE DE DREUX, countess of Montfort

JEAN, count of Montfort
(1341–1345)
= JEANNE OF FLANDERS

JEAN IV (1345–1399)
= JEANNE OF NAVARRE
† 1437

JEAN V
(1399–1442)
= JEANNE DE FRANCE
(d. of CHARLES VI)

ARTHUR III
count of Richemont,
CONSTABLE of
France duke
(1457–1458)
= 1) MARGUERITE of
Burgundy
2) JEANNE D'ALBRET
3) CATHERINE DE
LUXEMBOURG

RICHARD
count of Étampes
† 1438
= MARGUERITE
D'ORLÉANS
= 1466

PIERRE II
(1450–1457
= FRANÇOISE
D'AMBOISE

FRANÇOIS II
(1458–1488)
=
1) MARGUERITE OF
BRITTANY
† 1469
2) MARGUERITE
DE FOIX
† 1486

ANNE
(1488–1514)
=
1) CHARLES VIII
2) LOUIS XII

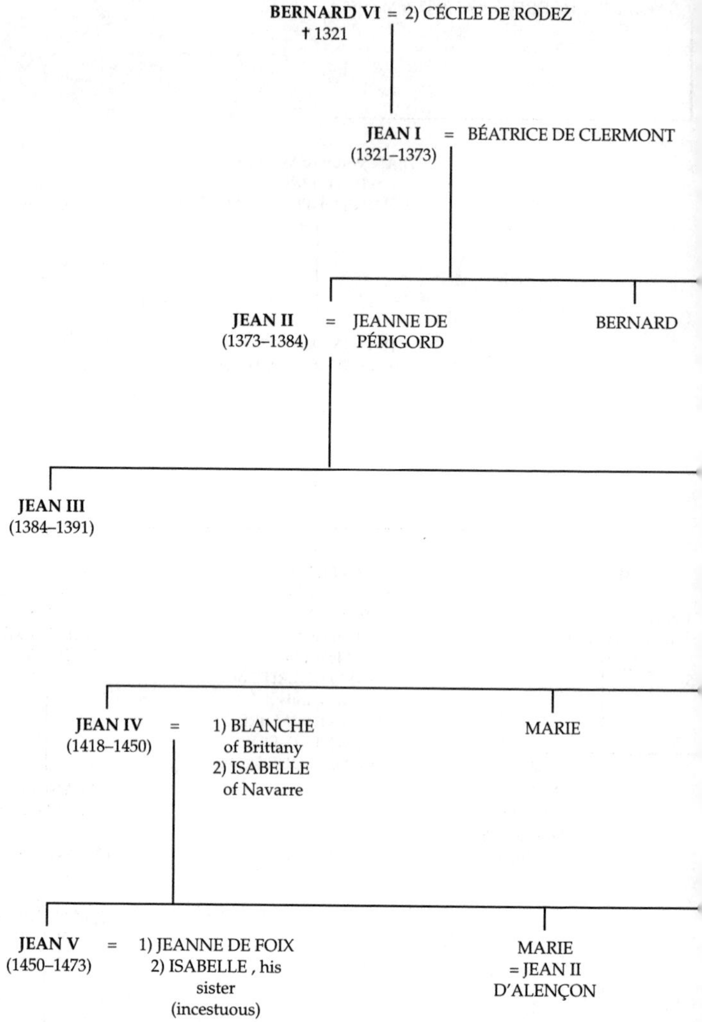

9 The house of Armagnac-Nemours.

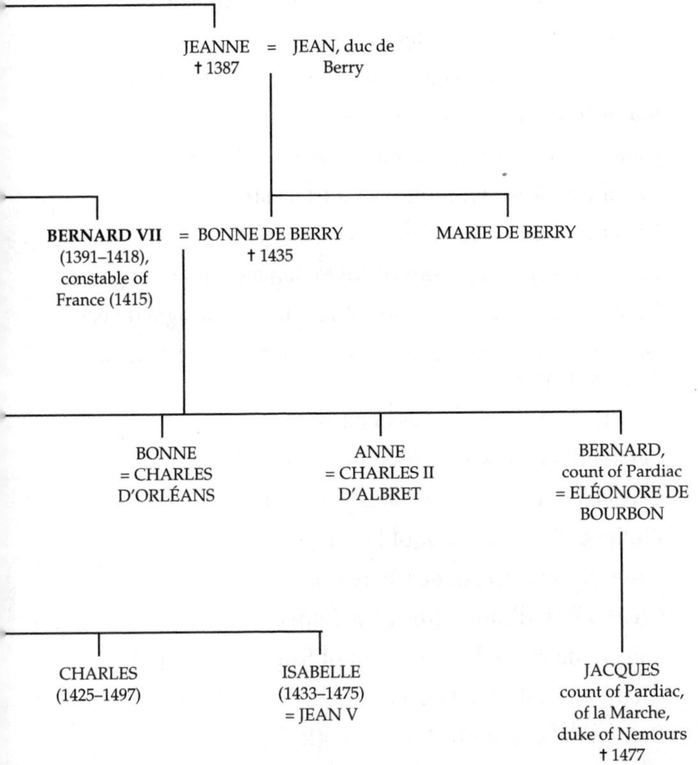
JEANNE
† 1387
= JEAN, duc de Berry
BERNARD VII
(1391–1418),
constable of
France (1415)
= BONNE DE BERRY
† 1435
MARIE DE BERRY
BONNE
= CHARLES
D'ORLÉANS
ANNE
= CHARLES II
D'ALBRET
BERNARD,
count of Pardiac
= ELÉONORE DE
BOURBON
CHARLES
(1425–1497)
ISABELLE
(1433–1475)
= JEAN V
JACQUES
count of Pardiac,
of la Marche,
duke of Nemours
† 1477

Chief office-holders of France

Constables

1191	Dreux IV de Mello, sr. de Saint-Prise (d. 1218)
1218	Matthieu II, seigneur de Montmorency (d. 1230)
1231	Amaury VI, count of Montfort-l'Amaury (d. 1241)
1241?	Humbert V, sire de Beaujeu
1249	Gilles, dit le Brun, seigneur de Trasignies (alive 1271)
1287	Raoul II de Clermont, sr. de Néelle (k. 1302)
1302	Gaucher de Chastillon, count of Porcien (d. 1329)
By 1336	Raoul I de Brienne, count of Eu (d. 1344/5)
1346?	Raoul II de Brienne, count of Eu (ex. 1350)
1351	Charles d'Espagne, count of Angoulême (k. 1354)
1354	Jacques I de Bourbon, count of La Marche (resigned 1356)
1356	Gauthier VI de Brienne, count of Brienne and duke of Athens (k. 1356)
1356	Robert, sr. de Fiennes (resigned 1370)
1370	Bertrand du Guesclin, count of Longueville (d. 1380)
1380	Olivier IV, sr. de Clisson (dismissed 1392)
1392	Philippe d'Artois, count of Eu (d. 1397)
1397	Louis de Sancerre, sr. de Charenton (d. 1402)
1402	Charles I, sr. d'Albret (dismissed 1411)
1411	Valeran de Luxembourg, count of Saint-Pol (d. 1413)
1413	Charles I, sr. d'Albret (k. 1415)
1415	Bernard VII, count of Armagnac (k. 1418)
1418	Charles I, duke of Lorraine (d. 1424)
1424	Jean Stuart of Albany (k. 1424)
1425	Artus III de Montfort, count of Richemont, duke of Brittany (d. 1458)
1465	Louis de Luxembourg, count of Saint-Pol (ex. 1475)
1483	Jean II, duke of Bourbon (d. 1488)
1515	Charles III, duke of Bourbon (dismissed 1523)

Chancellors under the Valois kings

1328	Matthieu Ferrand, canon of Saint-Quentin (dismissed)
1329	Jean de Marigny, bishop-count of Beauvais (dismissed)
1329	Guillaume de Sainte-Maure, dean of Tours, canon of Saint-Quentin (d. 1334)
1334	Pierre Rogier, bishop of Arras, archbishop of Rouen, cardinal (Pope Clement VI)
1334	Guy Baudet, bishop of Langres (d. 1338)
1338	Étienne de Vissac, sr. d'Arlenc (resigned 1339)
1339	Guillaume Flotte, chevalier, sr de Revel (resigned 1347)
1347	Firmin Cocquerel, bishop of Noyon (d. 1349)
1349	Pierre de la Forest, cardinal, bishop of Tournai (dismissed 1357)
1357	Gilles Aycelin, bishop of Thérouanne
1361	Jean de Dormans, bishop-count of Beauvais (resigned 1371)
1371	Guillaume, chevalier, sr. de Dormans (d. 1373)
1373	Pierre d'Orgemont, sr. de Mery (resigned 1380)
1380	Miles de Dormans, bishop of Beauvais (resigned 1383)
1383	Pierre, sr. de Giac, chevalier (dismissed 1388)
1388	Arnaud de Corbie, chevalier, sr. de Jaigny (dismissed 1398)
1398	Nicolas du Bosc, bishop of Bayeux (resigned 1400)
1400	Arnaud de Corbie (dismissed 1405)
1405	Jean de Montagu, archbishop of Sens (dismissed 1409)
1413	Eustache de Laistre, chevalier, sr. d'Escury (Burg) (dismissed August)
1413	Henri Le Corgne, dit de Marle, chevalier, sr. de Versigny (Armagnac) (k. 1418)
1418	Eustache de Laistre (d. 1420)
1420	Jean Le Clerc, sr. de la Motte (Burgundian)
1418	Robert le Maçon, sr. de Treves (Armagnac)
1421	Martin Gouges, bishop of Chartres and Clermont (dismissed 1425) (Dauphinist)
1425	Renaud de Chartres, cardinal archbishop of Reims (for Charles VII) (d. 1445)
1424	Louis de Luxembourg, bishop of Thérouanne (for Henry VI) (resigned 1535)
1435	Thomas Hoo (for Henry VI) (resigned 1449)

1445	Guillaume Juvénal des Ursins, chevalier, baron de Traynel (dismissed 1461)
1461	Pierre de Morvilliers, chevalier, sr. de Clary (dismissed 1465)
1465	Guillaume Juvénal des Ursins (d. 1472)
1472	Pierre d'Oriolle, sr. de Loiré (dismissed 1483)
1483	Guillaume, sr. de Rochefort (d. 1492)
1492	Adam Fumée, sr. des Roches garde des sceaux (d. 1494)
1495	Robert Briçonnet, archbishop of Reims
1497	Guy de Rochefort, chevalier, sr de Pleuvaut (d. 1507)

Admirals

1422	Louis de Culant
1437	André de Laval, sr. de Lohéac
1439	Prégent de Coetivy
1450	Jean du Bueil, comte de Sancerre
1461	Jean, sr. de Montauban (1461 Guillaume de Cazenave, vice-admiral)
1466	Louis, bâtard de Bourbon, count of Roussillon (Odet d'Aydie, admiral of Guyenne)
1487	Louis Malet, sr. de Graville
1517	Guillaume Gouffier, sr. de Bonnivet

Grands maîtres de l'hôtel

1408	Jean de Montaigu
1409	Guichard Dauphin, sr. de Jaligny
1412	Louis de Bourbon, count of Vendôme
1418, 1425	Thibault, sr. de Neufchâtel
1449	Tanneguy du Châtel
1449	Charles de Culant
1451	Jacques de Chabannes, sr. de La Palice
1456	Raoul de Gaucourt
1463	Antoine de Croy
1465	Charles de Melun, sr. de Nantouillet
1467	Antoine de Chabannes, count of Dammartin
1484	Guy XIV de Laval

1502 Charles II d'Amboise, sr. de Chaumont
1511 Jacques II de Chabannes, sr. de La Palice

Glossary

bailli Representative of the kings' justice in the regions (by the fifteenth century usually nobles) whose jurisdiction was in the appeal of the *parlements.* From 1413 *baillis* were allowed to delegate their legal role to experts (*lieutenants-généraux, civils,* etc.) and from 1493 compelled to do so. They retained their military role (for instance, in the summons of the *arrière-ban*). Also administrative officials of seigneurs in lordships

bailliage Jurisdiction of the chief local representative of royal justice (in northern regions)

ban, arrière-ban The summoning of the nobility to military service under their feudal obligations. The troops serving in this capacity are customarily referred to as the *arrière-ban*

Chambre des Comptes The chief audit court of the monarchy, roughly equivalent to the English Exchequer of Audit. Many princes also had *chambres des comptes*

châtellenie Territorial lordship centred on a fortified castle, in which the *seigneur châtelain* held high, middle, and low justice and within which there was a single legal custom. The *châtelain* became more clearly distinguished from other seigneurs in the course of the thirteenth century. An ordinance of 1578 finally prescribed a fair, market, *prévôté,* and church as the appurtenances of a *châtellenie*

curé A *prêtre,* priest, the main local representative of the parish clergy (in England, the rector or vicar, but note, in France a 'vicaire' was roughly what would be called a curate in England)

échevin City magistrate sometimes translated as 'alderman', usually in northern France, who with the *maire* exercised the government of chartered towns. In other regions *échevins* had other titles such as *capitoul* (Toulouse), *jurat* (Bordeaux), *pair* (La Rochelle), *consul* (in the towns of Guienne, and also Tournai in the north), and *gouverneur* (in some northern towns: Compiègne, Beauvais, etc.)

écorcheur A band of free soldiers and brigands from *c.*1435 who wrought the worst ravages in the wake of military campaigns

élu Royal official charged with the collection of taxes in an area called an *élection.* They were conceived by the Estates General of the 1350s as local notables to be 'elected' in order to oversee the collection of taxes at a time of reform. By the end of the fourteenth century, however, they had become *officiers du roi* and essentially responsible to the crown. Usually, in those territories where taxes continued to be voted by the estates, there were no *élus*

fermier A farmer in the English sense is usually a *censier*. A *fermier* holds one of a wide range of concessions, many for the collection of dues or taxes on a profitable basis

greffier Initially the privately employed clerk of a judge but increasingly regulated by royal laws from the fourteenth century. The first use of the name was for the *greffier* of the Parlement and the title proliferated from the late fifteenth century

marmouset A royal favourite; a term brought into currency by Michelet, based on a remark of Froissart's at the time of the attack on the constable de Clisson in 1392 (*Chronicles*, trans. Johnes, ii. 523; see also F. Autrand, *Charles VI*, 191). Initially grotesques, by extension *marmousets* were favourites or, in the parlance of the time, 'Mahomets'

métier Craft and sometimes craft guild

mouvance The scope of feudal allegiance owed to a superior (i.e. all the king's vassals are in the *mouvance du roi* and owe homage to him)

ordonnance Formation of *compagnies de l'ordonnance*, heavy cavalry maintained permanently under the royal ordinance of 1445, ultimately consisting of one-third *gens d'armes* (men-at-arms), generally nobles, and two-thirds archers

Parlement Not, of course, a Parliament in the English sense except that of jurisdiction. The Parlement of Paris (and subsequently provincial *parlements*) were supreme appeal courts and chambers for registering and disseminating royal legislation

pays (lit. 'country', derived from late Latin *pagus*, hence *pagenses*, country people; by extension, pagans) A coherent territory, smaller than the modern idea of a province, which generated real identification

prévôt (lit. 'provost') Local royal official whose authority was subordinate to that of the *baillis royaux*; the *prévôts* exercised first-instance justice in the royal demesne. Their equivalents in Normandy were the *vicomtes* and in Provence the *viguiers*. Also seigneurial officials. In Paris the *prévôt du roi* was in effect the royal governor. The *prévôt des marchands* at Paris held the role roughly of mayor

routier Band of mercenary soldiers whose name derived from the word *route* (Lat. *rupta*, troop or band), usually applied to the worst brigands

roturier Term applied to all those without privilege of personal or hereditary nobility, a commoner

sénéchaussée Jurisdiction of a local representative of royal justice in southern

France, equivalent to the *bailliage* in the north (though in some northern areas such as Boulonnais there were *sénéchaussées*)

sergent (Lat. *serviens*, Eng., serjeant) Generally a servant, in origin used to designate a gentleman following a knight banneret but by the fourteenth century the term had become restricted to court ushers (who nevertheless retained military attire). *Sergents à pied* generally delivered court summonses, those *à cheval* arrested malefactors

tabellion Broadly, a court archivist. By the fifteenth century, while *notaires* were responsible for drawing up the drafts (*minutes*) of legal acts, the *tabellions* filed them and produced necessary copies

Map section

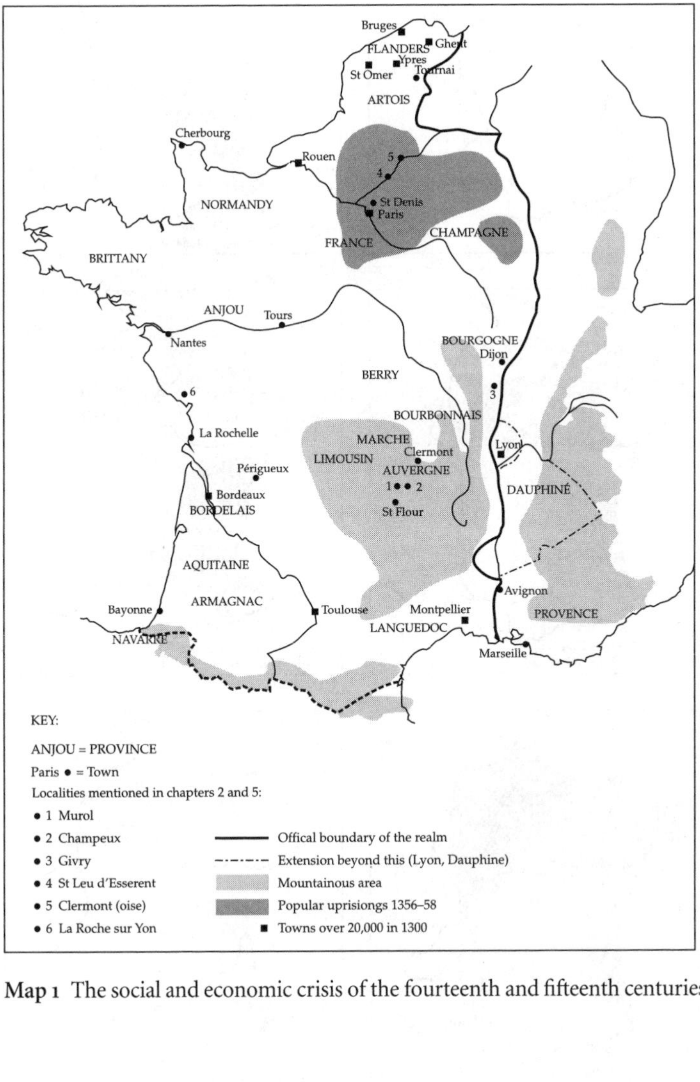

Map 1 The social and economic crisis of the fourteenth and fifteenth centuries.

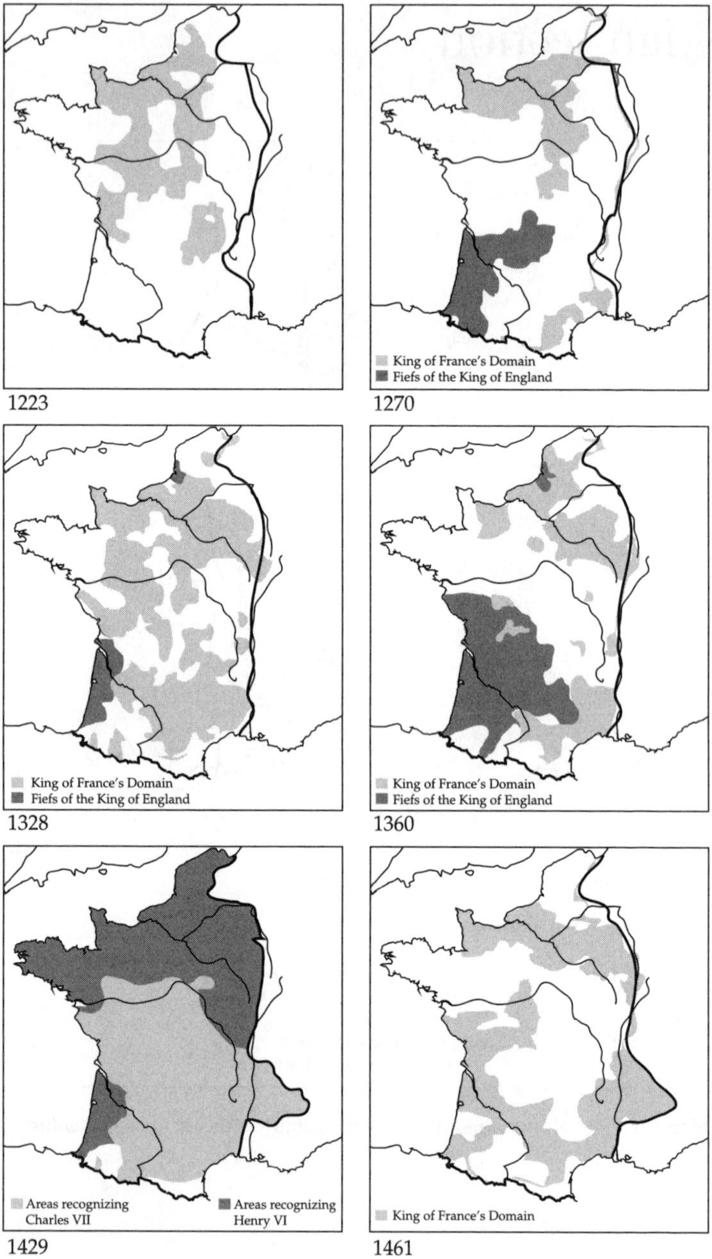

Map 2 The development of the royal domain.

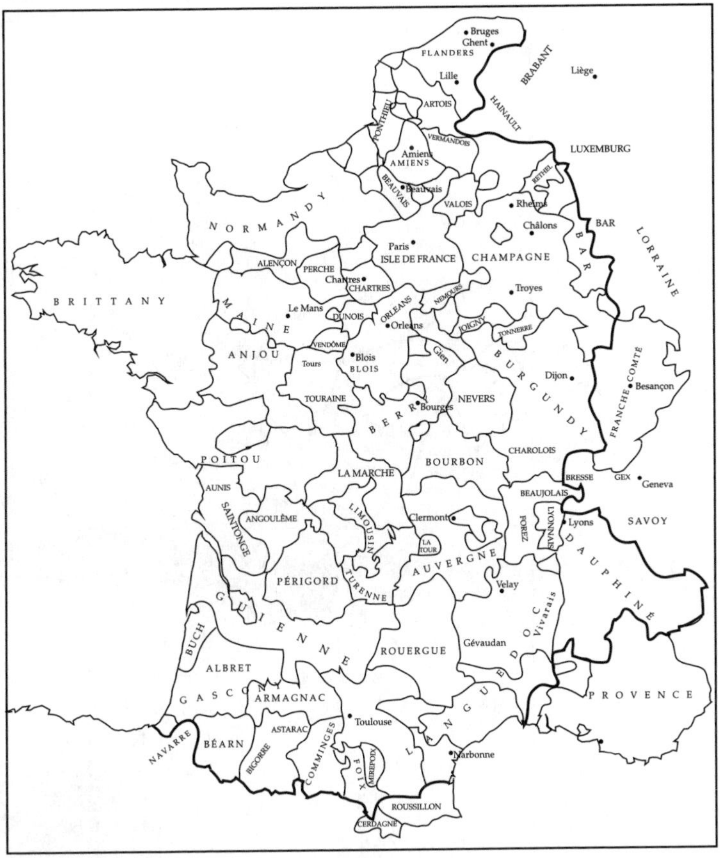

Map 3 The principal fiefs and apanages of medieval France.

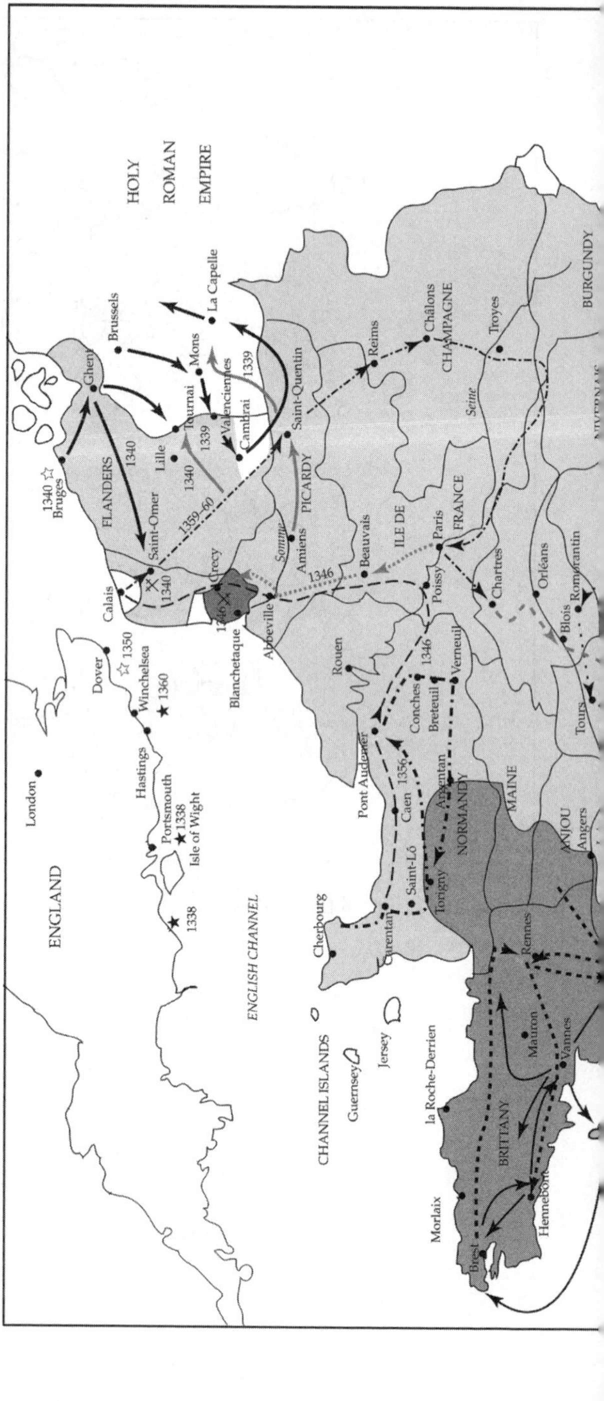
HOLY
ROMAN
EMPIRE
ENGLAND
London
Dover
Winchelsea
Hastings
Portsmouth
Isle of Wight
1338
1350
1360
ENGLISH CHANNEL
CHANNEL ISLANDS
Guernsey
Jersey
Calais
1340 Bruges
Ghent
Brussels
FLANDERS
Saint-Omer
Lille
Tournai
Mons
Valenciennes
Cambrai
La Capelle
Saint-Quentin
1339
1340
1359–60
Crecy
1346
Blanchetaque
Abbeville
Somme
Amiens
PICARDY
Beauvais
ILE DE
FRANCE
Paris
Poissy
Reims
Châlons
CHAMPAGNE
Troyes
Seine
BURGUNDY
Chartres
Orléans
Blois
Romorantin
Tours
Rouen
Verneuil
Breteuil
Conches
Pont Audemer
Caen
1356
Argentan
NORMANDY
MAINE
ANJOU
Angers
Saint-Lô
Torigny
Carentan
Cherbourg
Rennes
Malestroit
Vannes
la Roche-Derrien
BRITTANY
Morlaix
Brest
Hennebont

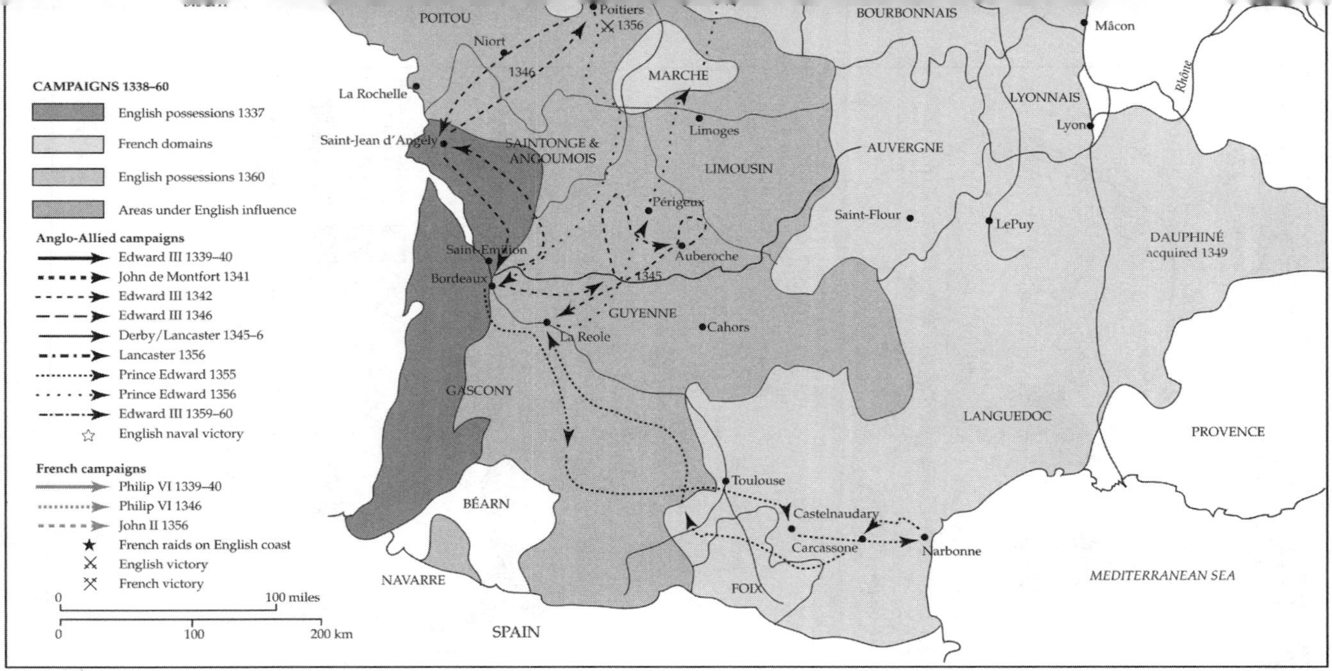

Map 4 The Hundred Years War: campaigns to 1360.

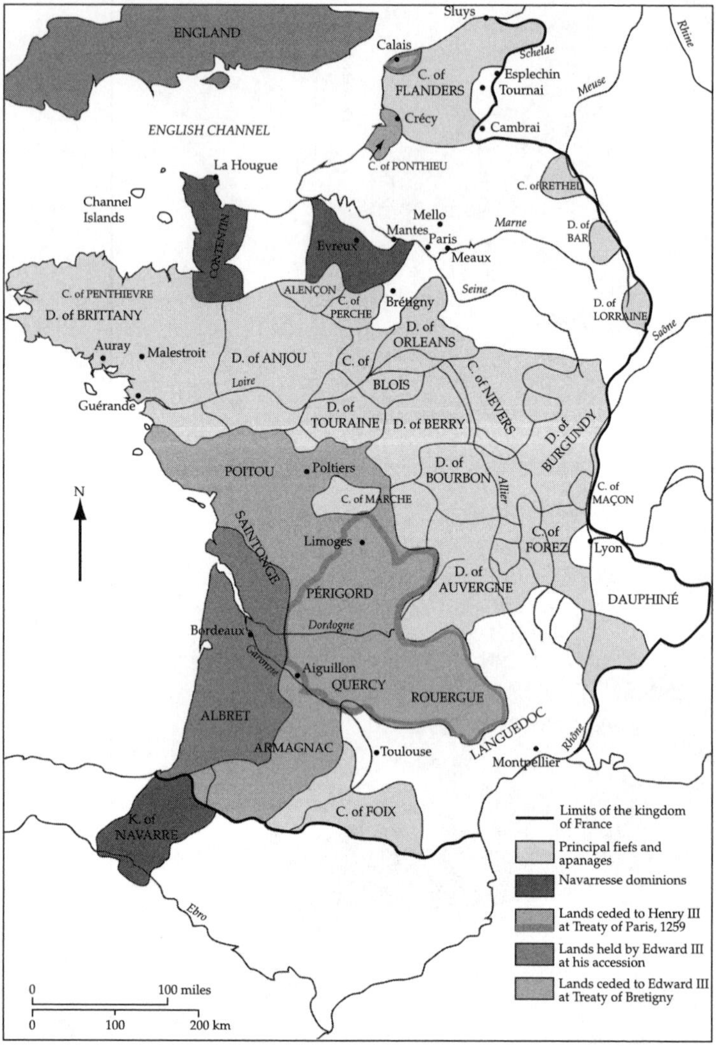

Map 5 France at the Peace of Bretigny, 1360.

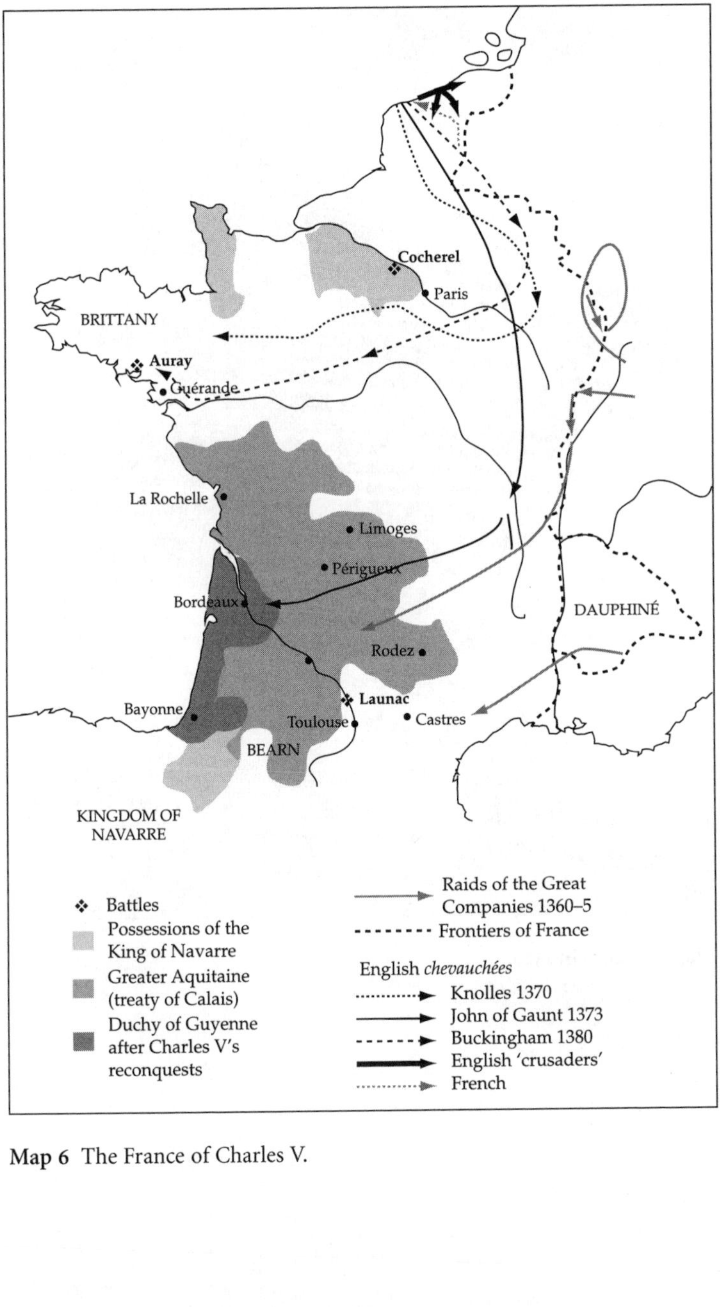

Map 6 The France of Charles V.

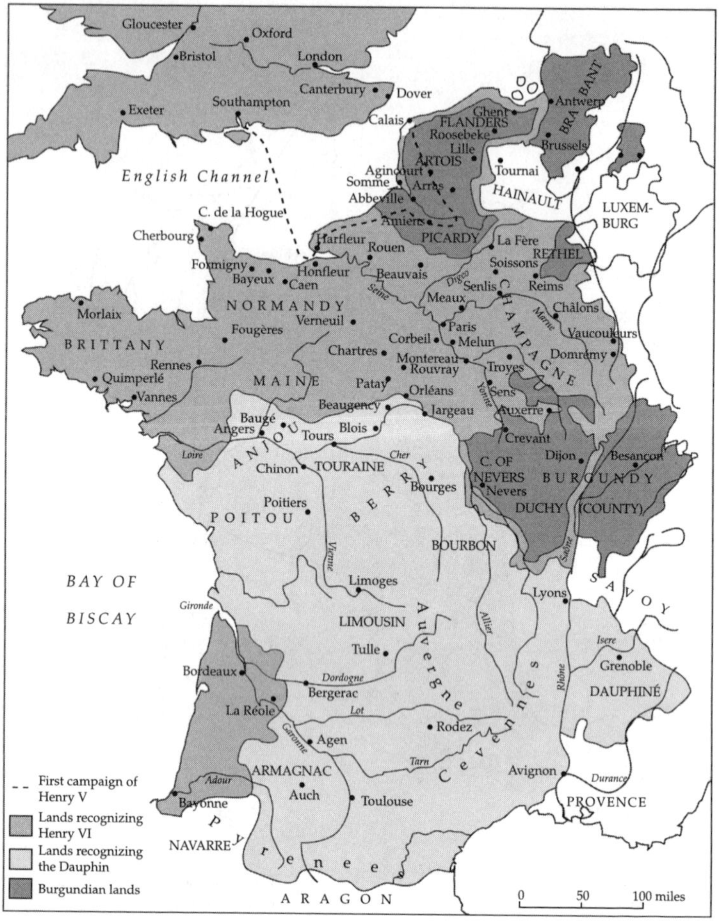

Map 7 France in 1429.

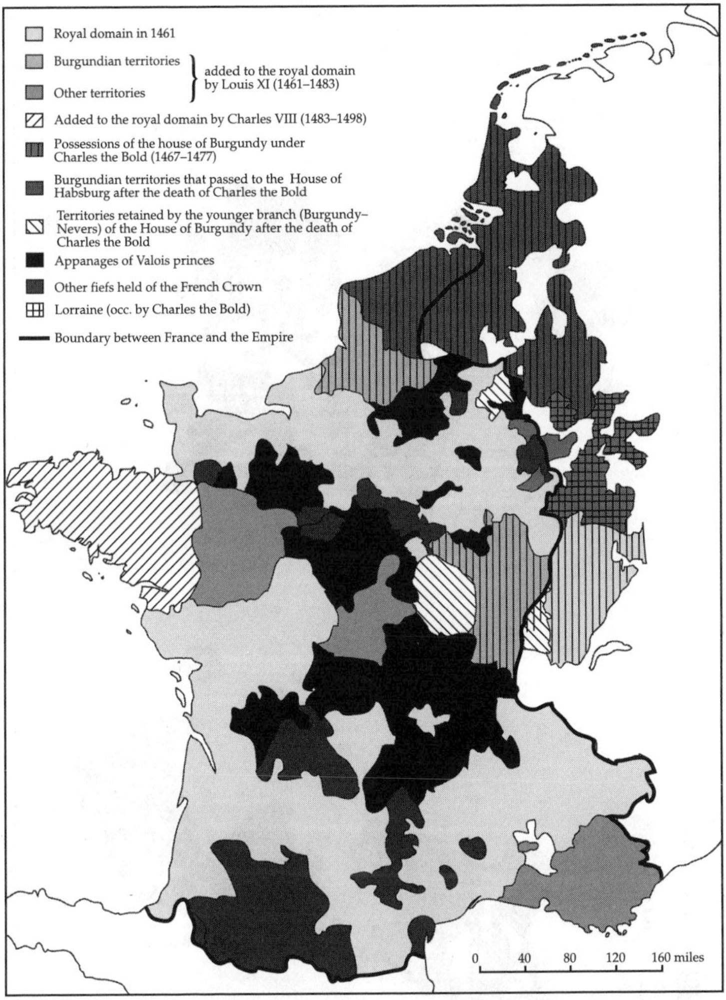

Map 8 France 1461–94.

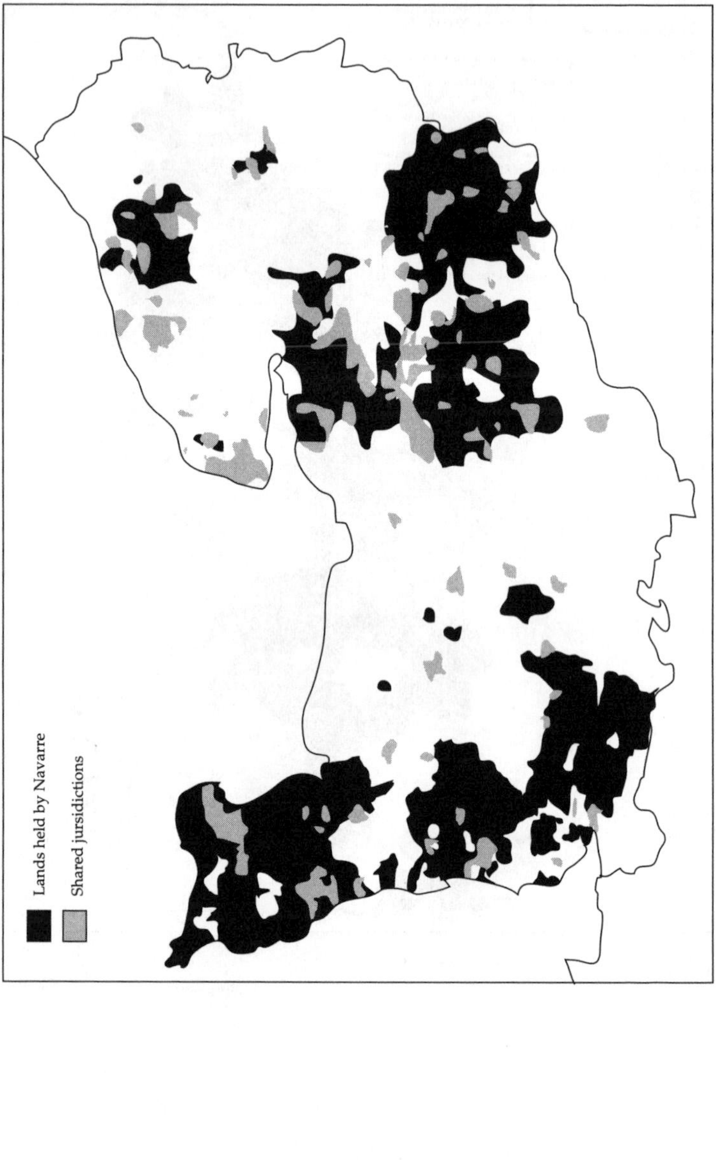

Map 9 The possessions in Normandy of Charles II king of Navarre (1332–87)

Index